Optimize Your Creative Mindset

By Dr. Sofie Nubani

2020 © Dr. Sofie Nubani

ISBN: 978-1-7350553-3-6

Copyrights & Disclaimer

Table of contents

Optimize Your Creative Mindset

Endorsements

"Dr. Sofie Nubani's new book, Optimize Your Creative Mindset, gives us a unique look into thought and creativity. In doing so, we learn that we can dramatically affect our ability to unite thought and creativity to produce unprecedented and unimaginable results. Some people will use this novel thinking to simply enrich their own lives, while others will use it to revolutionize technology, politics, or any other grand scale thinking that changes the way the world sees itself and the future."
— Dr. Nelson Bulmash Owner/Doctor/Host at Health Matters.

"The author, Dr. Sofie Nubani depicts the reality of how having a limitless mindset opens a plethora of opportunities where you can achieve all that you desire. Through specific tools which she discusses in this first part series of her book "Optimize Your Creative Mindset" you will learn to create your true reality to achieve the life you always wanted and how to master your manifestation power through your creativity. Dr. Nubani meticulously incorporates her knowledge, teachings and expertise through this first book. For those who would like to take a further step in mindset expansion, this book is definitely for you."
— Dr. Bindu Babu I-MD, PHD, Forbes Business Council Member.

"Dr. Sofie Nubani has authored the book on creativity for the 21st century. Optimize your creative mindset is sure to help readers install and instill creativity into their whole being. This multifaceted volume brings forth creative thinking to a new level with much of the knowledge is not known to the creative arena as well as to the business arena. I love how Dr. Sofie brought out the focus on the styles of thinking and intelligence that can help enhance a creative mindset. This includes multicultural intelligence and metacognition."
— Dr. Bob Choat, America's #1 Mind-Body Transformation Expert, N.L.P. Master Trainer, and Strategic-Transformational Coach

"Dr. Sofie Nubani has written a must-read primer for anyone considering taking their creativity to the next level... Read this book - and learn from one of the best."
— Dr. Lori Shemek Ph.D. 4x Best Selling Author, Speaker, Fox News, C.B.S. Doctors T.V., Huffpost Top Expert

"Optimize your creative mindset is a thought-provoking collection of engaging stories, ideas, and few new concepts that are sure to uplift, inspire, and push you to continue to evolve, create, and grow. With its focus on innovation and creativity, this book will help those who wish to adapt in this ever-changing world."
— Tim Ray Founder of UIMedia Network, Host of the Good Intention Show, Awaken Atlanta and the Wake-Up Hour, Speaker

"Optimize Your Creative Mindset Series is a powerful read! Dr. Sofie Nubani's techniques, wisdom, and experience is revealed in perfect timing for a pivoting world. Valuable reading."
— Madeline Faiella, host of Onstage-Online™, Success Profiles Magazine contributor, Speaker, Co-Author, Certified Civility Advocate, artist, former professional singer and Entrepreneurial Mindset Coach

Dedications

To my late Mother, Siham Noubani, whose presence has never left me. Thank You for being my beacon of light in all forms of your existence.

To my Father Salah Noubani, you made it hard for any man to win my heart like you do. So grateful for the kindness and wisdom you are, I am so happy to know you have such a loving wife in Badera by your side. You deserve the best always and more.

To, Rawy Rayan, my Champion, and heartbeat. My son, you are my heavenly gift and treasure. Keep shining, bright son. You always make mama so proud.

To my precious siblings Suhair, Waleed, and Mo Noubani. No matter how far or near our global distance is, you are never far from my heart.

Foreword

Dr. Sofie Nubani and I met on Facebook after both of us along with some other amazing ladies received the 2020 "She Inspires Me" award from Fashion Lifestyle and Entertainment Expert, Ada Gartenmann in London, England. Since we are both educators in our fields, published authors, and life coaches and possess a never-ending passion to help and serve others, our bond was instantaneous. I admire her zest for life and her "heart of gold". I treasure our new friendship. We believe God has connected us "on purpose" and has plans for us to work together for a better world.

I felt honored that she wanted to share her incredible book, "Optimize Your Creative Mindset" with me before its publication. As I opened the first page and delved into the inspiring collection of thought-provoking stories, interviews with successful entrepreneurs and highly creative people, her in-depth ideas, and new, ground-breaking concepts which were all beautifully written throughout her book, I could not stop reading until I had finished the entire book. This book teaches the in-depth process of creativity: its many forms—both large and small, the different types of thinking and how they relate and interact with creativity, and the growth mindset versus the fixed mindset.

It also discusses numerous & beneficial physical things and techniques the reader can use to enhance creativity through better overall health, the implementation of a more effective creative environment, the elimination of the destructive behaviors that often interfere with the creative mind, and stress management in today's world. To engage the readers, challenging questions are presented for them to ponder in their creative thinking process and to begin their transformation to a higher level of creativity. Her Yin and Yang Vision-Action-Dream Board, her acronym C.O.U.R.A.G.E., and "The Circle of Creative Masters" are powerful tools to enable the readers to become their best creative self with the perfect mindset.

Being inspired and highly enthralled by the teachings I discovered in my brilliant friend's book, I did not hesitate when she asked me to write the foreword for her book. This book is a "Must Read" for anyone wishing to learn to be more innovative through creativity whether it is for their business life or personal one. Even the most creatively successful person can benefit from the insightful content and "gifts" that Dr. Sofie Nubani has shared with the reader.

She motivates her reader to "take the venture and unleash the power of your metacognition, supercharge your imagination, and ignite your innovation to "OPTIMIZE YOUR CREATIVE MINDSET". What an incredibly perfect blueprint to live one's life!

-Randi D. Ward

Author of Because I Believed in Me (My Egyptian Fantasy Came True)

Educator, Editor of Morocco Pens, is an English teacher, Author of Because I Believed in Me (My Egyptian Fantasy Came True). Harmony Life and Holistic Emotional Intelligence Coach, a multi-award recipient, including IAOTP's 2019 Female Visionary and 2020 Educator of the Decade, 2020 She Inspires Me Award, honorary president (World Peace Forest (Africa), and USA Regional Director (Africa Nomads Conservation).

Introduction

Developing a Creative Mindset Can Be Fulfilling

"Creative geniuses redefine the desired solution. They don't just push the envelope; they create a whole new courier system." -
Puneet Bhatnagar

Do you want to bring better and more innovative ideas to your work or project?

Are you ready to bring back your innate creative self, that's been hidden away?

As the world shifts during challenging times, the need for creative thinking will be required more than ever. Here is the challenge, especially for those who believe themselves to be non-creative: "How can I come up with new and innovative ideas that make a difference?" or "Can I really become creative?" You see, the truth is every one of us is creative.

The reasoning behind this is we are taught to become non-creative due to a system of education and fixed mindsets. You'll discover in this book how the research of George Land and his work with NASA showed that creativity is chiseled off throughout the academic phase and by the time we reach our teen years, it gets completely unlearned. The fact is you were born creative and possessed a creative mindset.

I recall playing and being curious as a child. I think my curiosity would sometimes get me into trouble. The adults around me tried to squash that fiery curiosity. Yet, it stuck with me. Nowadays, it's about learning new things; this book helped me to discover new things as well as to rediscover my personal story of that curious child.

I learned from my father, Salah Noubani, one of the creative mindsets which I share in this book. His primary vocation is that of a lawyer; he was top in his field in Jordan. His passion is poetry in which he has won awards and published internationally. While he had to think deeply as a lawyer, his poetry showed that

1

creative side and where he really excelled. To say that I'm proud of his work would be an understatement.

What I want this book to accomplish is helping each reader to shine as a creative person. This is especially true of senior leaders and entrepreneurs, where both arenas need more creativity for today's world and also for the future. Too many ideas are being rehashed, and they are simply "stuck-in-the-mud" thinking. We see this even in many Hollywood movies. If they can't create, let's try to use old formulas and remake old movies and TV shows. This is non-creative thinking. Maybe it's the fear of trying to create something that might fail that steers them away from being innovative.

Throughout this book, you will discover people who possess a creative mindset. They are 14 contributors who share their inspiring stories. You can find more about each of their biographies in the back section of the book. learn more about these amazing creatrixs /creatives to connect further with them.

Meta-Thinking For Creative Success

When you understand the value of thinking for creativity, you will learn that your ability to be creative is limited only by your thinking. Thinking about thinking will help you identify those thoughts that keep you stuck and ones you can use to replace to help you to optimize your creative mindset.

In the very first chapter, you will discover a higher-level thinking that will help you in every area of your life. Just as Edward De Bono stated regarding thinking hats for creativity, so shall you. This chapter will have the tools you will need to get started.

Throughout this chapter, you will be introduced to a multitude of thinking styles. This will include thinking styles that are best suited for a creative mindset. You will learn how combining different thinking styles leads to more powerful creative thinking.

In chapter two, you will learn how a growth mindset is extremely important for creativity. In fact, a growth mindset is a positive factor in many realms. As I said earlier, most people who have stopped their creativity or tried to stop others have a fixed mindset. The growth mindset is the opposite of that, and you will learn why.

My passion for learning new things as well as trying them is based upon having a growth mindset. One of my goals is for you to also start developing the same mindset if you have not already. This mindset is typically possessed by people who want to learn new things.

Creative Storytelling

You have already been exposed to a few individual stories who use creativity. Stories are a powerful tool for being creative. Each of us has a story to tell, and once we understand ours, we can use that personal story for success as a creator, innovator, and leader. In chapter three, you will discover the power of creative storytelling.

Knowing your own narrative will help you to understand who you are at a level you probably never thought about. Being creative in storytelling will help you create a better version of yourself and of the professional endeavors in which you engage. I personally understand this regarding creative storytelling. Even now, I can create the narrative I want for myself and for what I create.

Everyone goes through challenges, and many times it can lead to despair for many. What chapter four shares with you is how you can use the challenges you face as a powerful tool that will help you become even more creative.

True growth is not handed to you on "a silver platter." On the contrary, it is through each challenging step that we take and what we learn from them where transformation happens. As a creative thinker, you will learn to embrace what life throws at you. This includes understanding of the failure simply as a feedback to teach you what does not work at that moment in time.

You'll get insights into what you can do to overcome any challenge you face towards and within your creative work. Know that you can stand tall when dealing with any creative challenge and come out stronger. I would even suggest you take the learning and exploit the heck out of the challenge in order to create something new. The great innovators have done the same thing.

The Crisis the World is Facing in Creativity

The world is facing many challenges that are inherent in a modern, highly technological time. Many industries are collapsing and new ones are springing up. As I currently write this introduction, the world is in a crisis. We are facing a pandemic, a global economic collapse, and protests around the world. These are among the most challenging times the great majority of the world's people have ever faced.

What is needed are new ways of thinking, and that thinking must be creative in nature. As the world is going through the current crisis, it is also facing a crisis in creativity. We need innovators as never before. Among those are entrepreneurs, who can create new industries. We need leaders across the spectrum that possess a creative mindset. These leaders will stand out as they are able to look at dealing with challenges and to offer creative solutions. Many of the leaders will work in teams that include a diverse group of people. Diversity is needed both in utilizing creativity and bringing a successful outcome to any challenge.

Ultimately, my ideal vision with this book is to witness a level of creativity brought about where a crisis no longer exists. Perhaps, educational systems will take a look at the content of this book and use it to build a better system. This will take courage to do so.

Maybe it's time to breathe and laugh? I would surmise that to do this you will enhance your whole being to become more creative. In chapter six, you will discover why you should do both, breathing and laughing. As a Laughter Yoga Instructor and co-founder of The Laughter Mindset Experience, I taught that the power of laughter (and breathing) is important for overall health, better leadership and enhanced focus.

On top of that, when working in a team setting, the use of laughter helps to create better bonding among team members. You will learn the science behind laughter and breathing as well as the power for business success. This includes supporting a creative mindset.

Your Brain on Creativity

In Chapter Seven, you are going to get an understanding of the workings of your creative brain and the myths as well. Many people still believe in the split-brain theory; in this chapter, you will discover why it is a false belief due to the latest understanding in neuroscience.

You will also learn what parts of the brain are used for creativity and why it is usually the whole brain. I learned we do not use 5% or 25% of our brain power. This is another myth that is still being perpetuated. We use our whole brain, including when we are engaged in creative thinking. It may be true that we do not use our whole potential though. This has nothing to do with our brain.

When we are engaged in thinking, our brains are energy hogs. While it is only about 5% of the mass of our body, it uses 20% of the energy. That is a reason why we tend to be depleted towards the end of the day, or why we feel sleepy after hard studying or intense mental focus.

I mentioned earlier that it is going to take courage to help make changes regarding creativity. In the four sections of Chapter Eight, you are going to discover just that. I created the acronym **C.O.U.R.A.G.E.** to help deliver key points in each letter that leads one to become a courageous creator.

As you read through each letter, find within yourself methods to apply those letters to help you become a creative thinker with COURAGE.

In Chapter Nine, you will discover inspiring stories of entrepreneurs and leaders who use their creative mindset for success in their work. These include people who are known experts in their field.

In Chapters 10 and 11, I created the **Yin and Yang Vision-Action-Dream Board**. This system and process will enhance how you can take a typical vision board and make it truly work for you at a higher level, especially in getting creative. Whatever you can truly see in your mind's eye and feel in your body, you can create. The whole system is like a vision board on rocket fuel yet bringing in a balanced energy approach. Just like what you will discover in whole brain creativity, the Yin and Yang Vision-Action-Dream Board helps leverage a whole world view with combined action steps.

Introduction

Finally, in Chapter 12, you will learn about a new concept I created and founded, called **The Circle of Creative Masters™**. This brings together a diverse group of people that help multiply creativity and take it to another level. Imagine working on a common goal and have **The Circle of Creative Masters™** using each of their unique abilities leading to innovation. The synergy will be amazing as each participant in the COCM will bring his or her skills, talents, and experiences towards fulfilling the goals set forth by the group.

The COCM is well-positioned to help those that join as well as the contribution towards the greater good of all.

In this chapter, you will learn about this and what qualifies as COCM. This includes the qualifications of each facilitator and the standards set by the Circle of Creative Masters Institute.

I am pleased you have decided to take this journey into reading this book. As you discover a new concept or idea, see how you can apply it to your life. When you do this, you will learn at a higher level.

I want to congratulate you in advance for taking your creative growth, leading to innovation seriously. Happy reading and THANK YOU for being part of this marvelous and exciting journey with me. Together, we can do better. Together, we can accomplish more. Together, we can go further. Creativity is the cure, and now you have access to use and prescribe it to those that you lead.

Dr. Sofie Nubani, DSD, DD

Chapter 1:
Thinking Styles That Lend To Higher Creativity

In this chapter, you'll discover…

- The 4 C Model of Creativity

- The Different Types of Thinking and Their Influence on Creativity (Creative Synthesizing and its role in connecting Divergent and Convergent Thinking).

- The Transformational Grandmaster and learn how creativity played a major role in his life.

The Challenges of Those That Create and Why Study Higher Thinking Creativity

- Have you ever experienced a specific challenge in your life, and then talked about it with family members, co-workers, or strangers? They all seemed to have a myriad of ideas proposed and delivered. However, when it came to them to implement those same ideas into their own life, they have failed to apply them. Right?

- Did you ever have a meeting with higher management in your existing corporation or at any point in your life? Perhaps a time when your company was faced with big challenges and there were plenty of great, novel ideas shared in meetings, masterminds, Zoom and more. Yet a few months later the company still had to down-size and even some had to liquidate altogether? Big recognized icons that once dominated their market with their unique brand expression and high customer satisfaction levels (Sears, Kmart, Blockbuster Videos, Radio Shack, Staples, Borders, The Gap, etc...) all have gone bankrupt or left with only a handful of stores in some cases. DID YOU EVER WONDER WHY?

- Have you ever been WOWED by a "Big C Creative" figure enough to have read about their history and biography? Furthermore, have you attempted to study and learn more about their brain, thinking styles, habits, and personality? It could be someone like Nicolas Tesla,

Leonardo da Vinci, Steve Jobs, or even a Small C creative cousin who's an artist. Perhaps, his songs, writing, and music are so inviting and magical to your soul. Did you ever say to yourself I wish I was just as creative?

Well, rest assured you're not the only one. YOU do have creative abilities within you, perhaps just on a different level. You may just not even recognize it.

In this chapter, you will learn about different thinking styles and how applying them in various situations may bridge your dormant creative resources. Depending on your interest, intentions, and goals, you will be able to utilize them for better functionality and value in both your personal and professional endeavors.

Regarding the first question above, surely, a lot of us can relate to at one point or another in their life. That is where many seem to be an expert in the area of your challenge. Those self-aggrandizing "experts" go on, suggesting, recommending, and giving you great ideas. Yet, when it came time for them to take action, most failed to show up or even apply them to their own life when faced with the same challenges. Why? Even though we may have floods of great ideas, we face big droughts when it comes to implementation and innovation.

That is the same reason why a lot of big, recognized brands, who had success, don't adapt to changes in the marketplace. When faced with a technological revolution, they never adapted to the new ways. They eventually lost their customer base and loyalty because they did not provide enough value for their customers' needs and demands.

For example, *Borders Books* did not prepare for the evolution of e-books. *Blockbuster Video* Stores did not prepare for or anticipate the evolution of the streaming service created by *Netflix*. *Blockbuster* filed for bankruptcy, with almost $1 billion in debt. This was because it failed to keep up with competitors offering more convenient home services.

We could go on and on with a similar analysis. They all had one common denominator leading to their downfall. It was a lack of creative solutions toward innovation. This resulted in losses of billions of dollars, causing them to go bankrupt and close down their once recognized and very successful businesses.

What about the area of fascination with the big or small C creatives? With the full recognition of abilities, talents, and cognition that some may possess (even different than others), the understanding of a creative mindset has been so unclear to many. Thus, they continue to compare their creative abilities to others. That decreases their chance to create at optimal levels. They end up feeling handicapped even before exploring and discovering how they can spark, stimulate, or inspire their creativity.

You see, we are creating on many levels daily. Because we have been programmed by association and connection with what creative people do and how they look and/or perform, we tend not to recognize creativity, even on mini C levels.

If you can't sing, paint, or impressively juggle, you may not be considered to be someone with a creative spark. How about a meal that you have prepared and added a few new spices to it? Then, you just could not have enough of its so-called, "YUMMINESS." Now that is being creative!

How about a poem you wrote to your first love? You did not know how your words would rhyme; yet it turned out beautiful and poetic. What about the brilliant idea that you came up with? That helped your nephew's project, and he won first place?

It's important to understand the life cycle of creativity. This way, you can spark more creative states. This will help you to unchain limiting beliefs. These are the kind that may hinder your creative process and development.

I like the work of James Kaufman and Ronald Beghetto (2009). They provided us with a neat framework they call: ***The Four C Model of Creativity.***

It fills the gap between the original concept of the Big C and Small C creatives. It is for those who are not familiar with the Big and Small C creatives. According to Chuck Frey's blog @ *Innovation Management*, they are defined as follows:

Small C:

"Small C" creativity describes the small ideas and "a-ha's" that enhance and enrich our lives. These would include creating a new recipe, teaching your dog a new trick, or coming up with a new way to format a report for your company. However, such creativity rarely brings us fame or fortune. Many people don't even consider these accomplishments as a form of creative thinking.

Big C:

"Big C" creativity is defined here as the breakthrough kind of thinking that most people are familiar with, but it's relatively rare.

Big C is more like an elite definition. For example, they include Albert Einstein, Benjamin Franklin, and Sir Isaac Newton. These were creative geniuses with legendary work.

With that concept of a Big and Small C, we are identified as an everyday creative or a rare inventive.

That might be a good base to understand both kinds of C creatives, but what about the C that is more creative than a small C, but not yet at the Big C level?

In Book One, the goal is to shed light on the different types of creativity. Furthermore, it is to help you evolve from one "C" stage to another, as you become more informed and equipped with tools and strategies. These are the kind that will help you progress in your C creative levels.

The transition between each level demonstrates creative metacognition and helpful feedback. That is a good way to measure creative progress or even setbacks.

Walden University/Education for good explains James Kaufman and Ronald Beghetto's *The 4C Model of Creativity* as follows:

Mini-C (personal creativity):

Creativity is inherent in learning. Any time a person attempts a new task, there is a level of creativity involved. At the mini-c level of creativity, one creates something that might not be revolutionary, but it is new and meaningful to them.

Example: Rawy brings his first artwork from school today. It is his first attempt to be appropriate to the task. It is new and meaningful to him.

Little-C (everyday creativity):

The Little-C level of creativity is a reflection of an aspect of growth from the mini-c level. With appropriate feedback, advancements are made, and what was created might be of value to others.

Example: Rawy's parents love the new painting he brought home from school today. They place it in their living room due to its beauty. They now can get enjoyment out of looking at it. It's then on its way to becoming ART.

Pro-C (expert creativity):

This represents professional-level expertise in any creative area.

At this point, one would have had that many years of deliberate practice and training. Not everyone at the Pro-C level can make a living with their creative pursuit. However, it is generally the goal of those at this level to support themselves in doing something they love.

Example: Example: Rawy majored in photography at college, and his photographs are now hanging in galleries. His photographs are now recognized by well-known experts and critics as being creative. His photography now hangs in the homes of others, not just his friends and family, also people who do not know Rawy personally (They appreciate his work and are moved by his photography).

Big-C (genius creativity):

Those at the Big-C level will be remembered in the history books. The Big-C level includes an evaluation of one's entire career and the entire body of work. It then evaluates the entire body of work against other great contributors and then decides where one fits in.

Example: Over the years, Rawy's photographs were bought by people who have valuable collections of artworks. His photography hangs in famous galleries and is regularly discussed by experts. Decades from now, Rawy will be considered to be among the greatest photographers all time.

Learning more about creativity and understanding it better will assist in facilitating more coherency into your creative mindset growth.

Enjoy the gratitude and embrace each level of your C creativity. Know that what you are creating is good, encouraging, and inspiring enough to charge, push, and motivate you to the next level.

What level of 'creative' are you?

How can you get to the next level?

Why may you want to get to the next level?

Be compassionate and patient with yourself. This way, you can transition with more ease, clarity, and understanding into your next C creative level.

What does "being creative" mean?

The ability to create is to be able to think inside and outside the box. You will do this by generating many great, original, and novel ideas. Those would be generated either deliberately or spontaneously using both the conscious and unconscious mind, which includes applied associations, links, and connections of previous knowledge. Creative thinking also brings in inspired 'a-ha' moments or epiphanies that are functional, useful, and valuable.

It is through the bridging of all these ideas, thoughts, beliefs, possibilities (even doubts and fears) that lead to new and inspired realms of charged thoughts and connections using a whole-brain function. This is inspired by intellectual curiosity, openness, interest, intention, imagination, incubation, abstraction, adaptability, fluency, courage, risk-taking, and understanding relationships along with the right creative attitude and environment. We weave them in through contemplation, self-reflection, imagination, and/or visualization.

Processes can be channeled through inspired thoughts, images, sound, intellectual ideas, intuition, and even universal signs that speak loudly to the self-trusting soul in a present moment.

When the above is applied (along with proper positive discipline, verification, cognitive flexibility, evaluation, and supportive meta-thinking styles), it will result in implementations leading to innovation.

I presented what is my current definition of creativity. To expand further on this definition of a creative mindset, I would like to examine the different types of thinking. This way, you can understand a variety of how people process and apply information, providing various outcomes and creative solutions.

Types of Thinking can be divided into several opposing categories, as follows:

- Abstract Thinking vs. Concrete Thinking.

- Divergent Thinking vs. Convergent Thinking.

- Creative Thinking vs. Analytical Thinking.

- Holistic Thinking vs. Sequential (linear) Thinking.

- Lateral Thinking vs. Vertical Thinking.

- Blue Sky Thinking vs. Limited Thinking.

- Practical Thinking vs. Unrealistic Thinking.

Keep in mind exploring different thinking styles is very supportive to your creative journey and depending on what stage of your creative process you are in; some are more helpful than others.

Personally, I would like to highlight the types of thinking that are more open and encouraging to your imagination and creativity. That is not by all means discounting the importance of critical, analytical, or convergent thinking. Understand that applying different thinking styles at the right stage of your expanded awareness and possible solutions is essential for creativity that will lead to innovation.

Here is a good example from *The Peak Performance Center*:

Analytical thinking is about breaking information down into its parts and examining those parts of their relationship. It involves thinking in a logical, step-by-step manner in order to analyze data, solve problems, make decisions, and/or use information. Creative thinking, on the other hand, refers to conceiving new and innovative ideas by breaking from established thoughts, theories, rules, and procedures. It is not about breaking things down or taking them apart, but rather putting things together in new and imaginative ways.

Example:

An analytical thinker may look at a car to determine how it works or what is wrong with it. A creative thinker may look at the same car and think of a new way to make it faster or a new way to use it.

Both thinking styles are important, depending on what we are using them for and when…

"…economies are built upon convergent thinkers, people that execute things, get them done. But artists and designers are divergent thinkers: they expand the horizon of possibilities. Superior innovation comes from bringing divergents (artists and designers and convergents (scientists and engineers) together" ~John Maeda

Learn from the different types of thinking and explore how they can assist your creative process.

For now, let's learn more about the following:

1-Creative Thinking

2-Divergent Thinking

3-Lateral Thinking

4-Blue Sky Thinking

5-Design Thinking

6-Holistic thinking

Let's take a step into each area:

1. Creative Thinking:

It is the ability to come up with something new, original, unique solutions to problems or ideas. It is a way to develop unorthodox solutions. These are the kind that doesn't depend wholly on past or current solutions.

2. Divergent Thinking:

Solving problems with many possible solutions.

It is creative and open-ended thinking aimed to generate fresh views and novel solutions.

3. Lateral Thinking:

It is the solving of problems by an indirect and creative approach, typically through viewing the problem in a new and unusual light. It is not just concerned with generating alternatives but also with changing patterns with switching to new and better patterns. Lateral thinking is a tool for creativity, which then leads to innovation.

4. Blue-Sky Thinking:

It refers to Brainstorming with zero limits. With this approach to idea generation, ideas don't need to be grounded in reality. This includes letting one's imagination run free with no boundaries or barriers. In essence, "The Sky's the limit!"

It is the activity of finding completely new ideas with free and open thinking.

5. Design Thinking:

Design thinking is an approach to practical and creative problem-solving. It starts with empathy. It's about understanding what the end-user wants, their constraints, and desires. This is because design thinking focuses on humans and understanding people's needs, and then coming up with effective solutions to meet them, it can be applied to nearly any field.

The design thinking process consists of five stages:

1-Empathise – with your users

2-Define – your users' needs, their problems, and your insights

3-Ideate – by challenging assumptions and creating ideas for innovative solutions

4-Prototype – to start creating solutions

5-Test – solutions

This is the final phase of the model. This is where designers/evaluators precisely test the complete product using the best solutions identified in the Prototype phase. Designers can then choose to return to previous stages in the process to make further adjustments, modifications, or alterations.

Design Thinking is a marriage of both creativity and critical-thinking skills. It requires designers to generate lots of ideas and prototype them, so they can become comfortable with failure.

This thinking style forces you to keep your mind open and to try out many ideas early on, so you don't get too invested in just one of them.

The process harnesses creativity through inquiry. At its core, it's a structured and systematic way of solving problems.

6. Holistic Thinking

This would be defined as the inquiry of a complex whole. It takes account of its purpose, values function in its environment, process & structure. Holistic thinking is the Thinking that combines cutting edge neuroscience & psychology. It is an ancient practice for self-awareness and mindfulness to form a comprehensive foundation for greater creativity and innovation.

Let us not leave out "Abstract thinking." This, at the origin, is from a Latin word (abstractus), meaning "pulled away, detached." It is something that is detached from physical or concrete reality. You may have seen abstract art, such as those done by the legendary Pablo Picasso. His work doesn't represent reality. Instead of that, his art (Cubism) is based on his perception of reality.

This is a level of thinking about things that are removed from facts during the present moment. This includes specific examples, theories, or concepts known to us or being thought about.

For example, a concrete thinker can think about a specific tree. However, a more abstract thinker can think about trees in general. It's like seeing a Blue Spruce (specific) versus seeing a forest (holistic).

Be mindful. This is because we are using our imagination and coming up with the many great ideas of possible creative solutions during the creative process. That is why it is equally important to have good skills using Convergent, Critical, and Analytical Thinking styles for a better and more coherent approach during the creative process.

"In truth we need both modes of thinking. They are different components of the same process. Rather than switching between modes in an unplanned way, which can stifle innovation, we suggest a more coherent approach. When developing divergent stages followed by a convergent phase. A creative perestroika."

~Gill Thackray

As you may have concluded, there is a connecting thread between all types of thinking that evoke creativity from different perspectives. That includes brainstorming, having original, unique ideas, connecting concepts, being a visionary, applying integrated thinking, system thinking, or simply being an out of the box thinker.

You can DEVELOP better decision making and clarity. This can be achieved by being more conscious and aware through the practice of MINDFULNESS in both stages of divergent as well as convergent thinking. Such practice will silence your inner critic and breed better divergent ideas. It can increase more epiphanies, revelations, and eureka moments as and when they do happen. Therefore, during the verification stage of your creative thinking, you will shift the activity in the right prefrontal cortex to the left side. The left side of the brain supports better decision making and clarity of thought during your creative process.

"Creativity leading to innovation will require both, the fluency and diversity of divergent thinking and the detective retrieval, and analytical/rational approach of convergent thinking."- Dr. Sofie Nubani

Let us ponder these questions…

- **Were you familiar with all the thinking styles shared above?**

- Do you have a creative project that you can start practicing different thinking styles on? If not, maybe it's time to have some fun, be present and create.

- Which of the thinking styles intrigued your curiosity most, and why?

- What thinking style do you require more practice to stimulate and increase your creative abilities?

"Every human has four endowments — self-awareness, conscience, independent will, and creative imagination. These give us the ultimate human freedom... The power to choose, to respond, to change." -Stephen Covey

Striking a balance

Let me suggest that you should start from the foundation of divergent and convergent thinking. This is very helpful. It could also be a good marker of differentiation between the functionality, value, and quality of the finished creative products.

The balance between the two, therefore, is important.

"Scientists and engineers must diverge before they can converge, and artists must converge after diverging to make their idea real"-Miller Klein

Most people at a young age are taught to be convergent thinkers from the earliest ages, including in school. The lack of a divergent thinking practice hinders creativity and innovation. Realize that both are equally important.

In later chapters, I will mention a few of my favorite school/educational systems and why.

Meanwhile, I invite you to diversify/expand your interests. Then explore, experience, and apply different thinking systems. I am suggesting the kind that will connect you with higher functions of imagination and intellect.

A good way to practice is by looking into different thinking styles individually. Consider exploring a new city or country that you may have thought about visiting. I suggest that you enter with an open mind, knowing your end goal. Discover as much as you can about the culture from the perspectives of dining, entertainment, and history.

Ask what you like most and least about this particular city/country, and why?

In comparison to other similar cities/countries you have visited, what makes this city more unique to you, and how?

Just as you would ask different questions to find and explore more about a city/country, learn and explore different thinking styles.

You would want to learn more than what is traditional and familiar to you. Depending on your need at the time, you can apply the most supportive styles of thinking.

While you are going through the process, apply **CREATIVE SYNTHESIS** as you are understanding and applying at a higher level. Synthesis involves combining ideas and allowing an evolving understanding of the text (Fries-Gaither, 2010).

SYNTHESIZING is more synonymous with understanding and applying rather than creating. I believe that it is a great tool to help optimize your creative mindset, along with the different thinking styles.

Divergent + Convergent thinking = Creative Thinking

One should know that by using both divergent and convergent thinking during the creative process, we are developing, sustaining, and refining solutions that lead to innovation as opposed to simply generating an abundance of great ideas that may never lead to creating anything.

Divergent + Convergent + Holistic Thinking = Optimal Creative Thinking

Optimize Your Creative Mindset

For a planned or unplanned creative project, either for personal implication or for serving the masses, the practice of adding holistic thinking during the evaluation process is wise. Looking at the bigger picture and understanding that our personal reality is interconnected with the bigger parts of reality provides a multidimensional perspective in our assessment stage.

Furthermore, holistic thinking will take into account the business or individuals' purpose and values during the evaluation process. It will generate better insights and informed decisions. As a result, the combination of divergent thinking gathering of original ideas and organizing them during the selection process of coming up with the best solution applying convergent thinking, adding holistic thinking during the evaluation, and implementation process will offer a bigger impact on the overall success of the whole. When all three thinking styles are used for individual or professional purposes, it makes room for a healthier work or home environment as well as a better culture.

Combining or synthesizing existing ideas, images, or expertise in original ways, along with applying different thinking styles (You can include responding, reacting, and working with your creative imagination, divergent, convergent, and holistic thinking, intellectual openness, curiosity, and calculated risk-taking) will stimulate your mind, supercharge your imagination and ignite your innovation.

Keep in mind that the more experiences and knowledge you have, the more associations and connections you will make, and the better you will become at connecting the dots and understanding their relationships.

Improve Your creative thinking by applying, combining and experimenting with different thinking styles.

On that note, I would like to share with you a conversation that will have you stretch your imagination as you learn and discover more about some incredible creative minds.

The creative mind of a Transformational Grandmaster

The Crow and The Pitcher

A thirsty Crow comes across a pitcher, which had been full of water. But when it puts beak into the mouth of the pitcher, he cannot reach the water. He keeps trying but then gives up. At last he comes up with an idea. He keeps dropping pebbles into the pitcher, soon the water rises up to the top and is able to quench his thirst. (Aesop's Fables)

There's always a way of overcoming any challenge. Many times, you have to use a different way of thinking to get creative for the right solution.

Let me introduce you to Dr. Bob Choat who is known as "The Transformational Grandmaster." He has lived a multifaceted life, full of challenges and growth. He has authored and published several books, a subscription newsletter, and hosted a radio show in Hollywood, CA. He is currently the host of "The School of Transformation" Podcast and founder of the online school, "Mind Hack Academy."

Dr. Bob is a lifelong martial artist, grappler, boxer, and a master instructor in close quarter combat. He has competed in multiple sports, does parkour (in his 60's), has been a stage hypnotist and is an NLP Master Trainer.

I started my interview of Dr. Bob Choat with this question...

"How was Creativity an Instrumental Part in his Life?"

Dr. Bob: "Being a Martial Artist has been my foundation. My mother was my first teacher. Later, I studied Goju Ryu Karate as a child living in Okinawa for about three years. I would have many teachers in various martial arts to this day.

It was hard to find instructors during my childhood years in the United States (unlike today). Since then, I was able to earn multiple black belts and rankings in multiple styles. Also, I reached senior instructor levels in other systems. I also boxed and wrestled."

Me: "Interesting, as we know exercise has been shown as evidence for better health on multiple occasions. It must be the increased amount of oxygen in our blood. It is that which plays a part in providing us with more mental energy needed to come up with new creative concepts."

Dr. Bob: "Absolutely, the production of new cells in the hippocampus (a part in the brain responsible for future thinking, imagination, and memory recall) can be increased during certain physical workouts. This is according to a Harvard study that was originally done on animals. It concluded that researchers suggest humans might gain the same benefits as well. In other areas, including martial arts, boxing, and even aerobics, all can increase the production of neurotrophins (chemicals that promote the growth of new nerve endings).

Having to focus on every technique and tapping into your memory recall, and using it as needed makes you live in the present moment more. That results in marking more space for some great ideas to be generated."

"Love it, that is pretty cool and insightful, please tell me more," I responded.

Dr. Bob: "My story has been diverse and continues to this day....

I recently stumbled upon an old children's short story with drawings by my mother, Fumie Yukinori. It was written in Japanese. I remember them from my childhood. She would tell me this story when I was quite little. While I've forgotten most of the story, her actions had an impact on my life. That's including me getting into art.

My mother was also a martial artist, having learned from her older brothers. What she did learn in kendo, she taught to me. Interestingly, my love of drawing and painting, as well as martial arts, came from her. I would later learn that my Uncle Keiji Yukinori, my mom's brother, was also both a martial artist and an artist. He was a leading commercial advertising artist in Japan. He did that as his primary career until he retired from that field. After leaving, he started writing books and lecturing throughout Japan. He also practices the martial arts into his 100's."

Me: "Wow!!! What great early mentors your mother, Fumie, and uncle Keiji were! You were very fortunate to have such a positive influence at such an early age.

Creativity itself flourishes in ways that go beyond different thinking styles. Emotional states such as being in a good mood and feeling good help lower one's stress level. That creates a better environment for a flow state. How was your father's influence on you?"

What kind of influence did your father have in your life?"

Dr. Bob: "Growing up, I dealt with violence from my father as well as my stuttering. I was also diagnosed as being mentally retarded. My father thought I was. My mother thought just the opposite. She kept encouraging me. That was even after my father was beating and/or whipping me until I was black, blue, and bleeding. I suffered from what we call today, Post-Traumatic Stress Disorder (PTSD). I remember being terrified of him. I would shake all over when he came home. Many times, I would hide from him, even hiding under the sink at times."

"So sorry to hear this about your father, it was nothing close to a peaceful relationship. Instead, it seems it was a very abusive one. It must have been hard on your mother, especially since she had a positive impact in your childhood," I added.

Dr. Bob: "Being Japanese, my mother had to stay in this marriage, so she kept quiet as to what was going on. Had she not, she could have been deported. I would then be forced to stay with my father. Mind you, this wasn't long after World War II, and she was Japanese. My father was a career soldier in the U.S. Army and later an aerospace engineer. He even graduated from the University of Alabama with a BSEE and Stanford with an MSEE. While he was good at his job, he was terrible as a father. It didn't know of the reason until after he passed away in 1983. That is another story."

Me: "Your father had important roles in society. He seemed very educated. To do well in his career, he must have had good focus, ability, and dedication. I guess that had nothing to do with his role as a father. It will be interesting to find out what caused such behavior towards his child, that means you. Since you mentioned that is another story, I will keep that in mind in the future. So how did you manage to handle your childhood abuse from your father?" I asked.

Dr. Bob: "My escape in life was through martial arts and drawing. I excelled in both as well as sports. I, therefore, got creative in those areas. Much of those days are not that clear to me anymore. I can, however, say that without my passion in what I did, I don't know if I would have survived (as I thought about killing myself many times)."

Me: "Oh, NO! That is horrific!

How did you overcome such thoughts and survive?"

Dr. Bob: "I stayed focused on what I did best. My best wasn't in school either. Though, I did win art contests in school. I also loved to read books.

During my childhood, I lived in several parts of the world. That includes Okinawa and Germany, as well as in many states across the United States. Boy, it was interesting for me to learn about different cultures, including even across the country.

Yes, Americans seem to have a different way of Thinking in different areas. I did my best to make friends despite my stuttering problem. I kept quiet most of the time due to that."

Me: "That is great in that you had this early exposure to different cultures. I'm sure you enjoyed that, and despite your stuttering, you still managed to make new friends. Many kids could feel very challenged since they have to learn more about their new environment and culture. This is after they are settled in and made new friends, then it is time for them to move again.

So, is there a time in school during your childhood that was more challenging to you, and how?"

Dr. Bob: "One of the places I lived in twice was Huntsville, AL. During my first time there, I was 9 years old. I recall the prejudice I felt due to being half-Japanese. It wasn't until I started playing football when I felt accepted. I remember how mindset became an early part of my life outside of the martial arts. That was when I played football. In one game, when I was waiting to go in, several of my teammates showed fear, including my best friend. This was our first game, and the coach sent me in. I knew I would get hit. Therefore, I was able to shift my thinking akin to a warrior's and dealt with the hits. I was also the smallest person on the team.

The school was a challenge, and it wasn't until the sixth grade I started doing better. In the seventh grade, I started to excel, especially in math and science. It was like something clicked and then…. BOOM!!! I took off. From there, I think I was unstoppable."

Me: "Oh, how interesting it is to see how shifting to thinking like a warrior made you go through the process with better adaptability skills. So, how do you think you became UNSTOPPABLE?"

Dr. Bob: "It was a mindset shift. While I still stuttered, I noticed I didn't do it while singing. It was in the ninth grade when I entered the school talent show with my two best friends, and we won. We did a singing and dancing number.

Also, during my Junior High years, I found a book on hypnosis. I started reading it and was enthused by what I discovered. I then applied some of what I read into my life. Learning about how the subconscious mind worked was eye-opening to me. By the way, I still have that copy."

Me: "How amusing. I do remember researching to find out about how a person who stutters can sing without doing it. It was while listening to one of your interviews at U.I. Media with founder Tim Ray. I remember going on Google after the show to research more info on that topic. I learned that when we sing, we use our internal operation from vocal cords, tongue, and lips differently than when we talk."

Dr. Bob: "That's correct, Dr. Sofie! There is now evidence that the brain functions differently for singing as compared to talking."

Barry Guitar, Ph.D., of the University of Vermont, author of several Stuttering Foundation publications, talked and wrote a lot on this subject.

"There is no time pressure in singing, nor is there any communicative pressure.

When we sing, we generally know the words of the song by heart. Word retrieval or searching for the words may play a role in stuttering."

"I totally agree. I can understand, according to his theory. I also understood later through my studies further on this subject why I did not stutter when I sang."

"How funny as Barry Guitar, Ph.D. is where I remember reading on this topic too. You had mentioned learning about 'Hypnosis.' That is a very interesting subject to me as I have utilized it myself as well. I went through Chris Howard's Training on it. I think it's fascinating, HOW did it help your creativity and progress?"

Dr. Bob: "I figured if I could take control of my subconscious mind, I could accomplish anything. It was fun. While in high school, I delved deeper into this. You see with hypnosis, and in a deeply relaxed state, you can send messages to your brain, and ideas and images can be suggested and put to use. I learned how I can replace negative self-talk and think in more creative terms."

"Love it!" I responded, "And how did that help you in your senior high school years?" I asked Dr. Bob.

Dr. Bob: "In my senior year, I was elected president of our school's Junior Achievement Club. Junior Achievement is when teens create their own business with the help of outside mentors. I learned a lot. It was also my second year of doing this. I started believing in myself. Even while I stuttered, others didn't notice."

"Alluring! That sure takes some courage to deal with all that you have gone through, including stuttering, and you continue to have steady progress," I responded.

Dr. Bob: "I don't know if anything I did in my life would be termed as courageous. I would like to think I did what I had to do to grow.'

"So, what did you do after your high school senior year?" I asked.

Dr. Bob: "After high school, I enlisted in the Marines. I later joined the LAPD. I wanted to challenge myself at the highest levels."

Me: "Challenging yourself to go higher and, at the same time, being able to embrace things that are different than what you're familiar with is only where true growth happens," I responded. "So, could you share an experience from your Marine days that you felt challenged? It could be through an experience that helped you build resilience and that you felt you grew from?"

Dr. Bob: "I recall an early incident during training in the Marine Corps. It was where my hands were tied behind my back as well as my legs. I jumped into the deep end of the water and had to stay there for one hour. Unlike the ocean water, the pool smelled of chlorine. The splashing of my fellow Marines vibrated. This was part of my indoctrination into Recon.

Those that panicked and wanted out failed the test. I remember one Marine who had freaked out bad. He had been superb in the physical skills on land. In the water, he was completely out of his element. He ended up dropping out of the test."

Me: "Wow!!! That sounds like a tough test to pass, is no joke indoctrination into Recon.

I could see how many couldn't pass it and while being able to make it through is a big accomplishment and is much respected. So, how did you do?"

Dr Bob: "As for me, I was able to float down to the bottom of the pool as the dolphin kicked myself back to the surface (when I would take another breath before descending back down). I simply maintained that rhythm until the completion of the test.

Also, it was all about the strength of my mind that enabled me to make it through this. Though, the water was easy for me due to being a competitive swimmer and a lifeguard.

I had to go through many tests in the Marines, where I had to bring out my best. It was a mental test more than a physical one. Sure, in order to reach such a point, each Marine had to qualify as 1st Class in the Marine Corps Physical Fitness Test (PFT). The maximum points you could get was 300. I did that each year."

Me: "I take my hat off to you. It is an amazing and challenging accomplishment. You must have a great ability to focus and control over your body. What other areas during your service did you apply your increased focus ability?"

Dr. Bob: "I also qualified as an Expert in shooting both a rifle and pistol. That took a lot of focused concentration.

I had the same experience with shooting while I was with the Los Angeles Police Department. Back then, we were assigned a Colt revolver, which was different from the M1911 .45 pistol I used in the Marines. I had to adjust to the feel of the .38 caliber revolver.

Again, it was more about my mind versus the actual weapon fired. It was about following a few simple rules.

Why do we do what we do became my focus."

Me: "Your mindset, I can totally relate to that. Based on what you shared, I see how it has played a major role in your continued progress and growth, including your achievements.

You mentioned that you had an interest in learning about 'why we do the things the way we do' so what did you find out most concerning about this topic?"

Dr. Bob: "I had a chance to study Neurolinguistics Programming (NLP) during those years. It was not as known back then as it is today. I had a profound curiosity as to how the mind worked, and I still do.

NLP seems like another piece of the puzzle for me. The more I learned, the more I was able to creatively put the pieces together. Since much of the NLP came from hypnosis, I felt comfortable learning and applying it. Though, I knew that there was much more to learn in these areas."

Me: "Now that I know the backstory of your HYPNOSIS & NLP story, it is pretty interesting, and the fact you excelled in both is just incredible," "I know you have an online school named Mind Hack Academy and you also conduct NLP Basic Practitioner, Master Practitioner and Trainer Certification Trainings as a Master Trainer. It seems like you always wanted to reach your best self in areas that you have challenged yourself. How inspiring and diverse are your interests? Can you explain to me how, and did you incorporate a few of your skills in new areas that optimized your creative mindset?"

Dr. Bob: "Later in life, I would continue my studies in hypnosis and the martial arts, even being inducted into three martial arts halls of fame. In both areas, I learned how to get creative. I recall Bruce Lee's take from his experiences in multiple fighting arts and bringing them together into his "Jeet Kune Do." He once stated, "Absorb what is useful, discard what is useless and add what is your own." That was the basis of what he created, a style of no style. He did not believe in styles in martial arts. Each of us can create what works and does not work for us.

For me, studying various martial arts and fighting styles taught me to become more creative.

I learned to adapt, which was the same in the Marines. Adapt, improvise, and overcome. And it is the improv where being creative is important. We take what we have and improvise in the situation at hand. When one is too confined to a structure, and the situation changes, the structure breaks down.

It is true of fighting and true of anything in life. It helps to have many experiences and learnings. You will be able to adapt to multiple areas and be able to see similarities where you can take from one and use it in another.

So, I went on a course of study in many different areas as well as various experiences. Each experience allowed me to draw off of them."

Me: "That is just fascinating, and the more experiences we invite to our life and the challenges we face, the better we understand the relationships between different experiences. This includes similarities as well as differences that may help us relate and create better."

"With such a desire to learn, grow, and challenge yourself, I am curious to know what areas did you expand your education in."

Dr. Bob: "My studies included going to law school, studying physics, psychology (all the way to getting my Ph.D.), a postdoc in neuroscience, MBA, studying computer programming, Neuro-linguistic Programming (becoming a Master Trainer), hypnotherapy, Flow State Practitioner, EEG Neurofeedback and much more.

Me: "Omg, that is all? Hahaha! That is marvelous, and may I ask what got you interested in studying in such different areas?"

Dr. Bob: "I had a reason for studying in different areas. I believe in a breadth of knowledge, in addition to depth is a key to true success. This is what is referred to as a polymath way of being. Leonardo Da Vinci is one example of a polymath and so was Benjamin Franklin.

Through various learnings, I discovered how to think better from many disciplines. This includes what Edward De Bono created lateral thinking. Typically, most people are taught to think in a linear or vertical manner. True creatives will draw from their senses, experiences, other people's experiences, and nature.

In this sense, thinking outside the box. Polymaths do this too. Instead of "being stuck in a box," thinking in multiple structures helps to create something new. And even what may not be obvious at first, becomes obvious."

Me: "Lovely! Could you give me an example of how you applied creative thinking in the past, including time in your childhood, possibly?"

Dr. Bob: "Back when I was in Jr. High School, I created an abstract sculpture using simple materials. This includes some balloons and a milk carton. I looked at nature and noticed the present flow. From there, I was able to use the balloons to help bring about the shapes I wanted along with the sculpture. Later, I used other tools to help chip away that did not belong to expose what was there. I had to go outside myself to find the facets of art through the environment."

Me: "How interesting is it that at such a young age to have such awareness and ability to connect the dots as you did. I see you have used a combination of thinking styles here, including lateral thinking. You did not follow the traditional step-by-step logic to arrive at a solution, and instead, going outside of yourself and finding art through the environment, as you did in your abstract sculpture project, where you combined balloons and a milk carton. Very good, and thank you for sharing. So how did that help you later in life?"

Dr. Bob: "Later in life, I would use the same way of multiple thinking styles to help me in other areas of my life.

As I studied and applied what I was learning in personal training and human biomechanics, I noticed how my actions affected how I felt. I used what I learned to help in coaching and psychology with my clients.

Instead of the basic step-by-step processes that were normally taught to help people, this newfound method combined with psychological methods worked much better."

"What helped your creativity the most?" I asked.

Dr. Bob: "I believe that it was through the multitude of various educational programs that I went through in my life has enabled me to think this way. It's more holistic, too, just the way Mother Nature had intended."

Me: "Excellent, my friend. It is time for leaders of our time to truly embrace holistic thinking for the betterment of us all. This includes thinking of the big picture, and its connection to community and the natural world can only reap good outcomes.

Dr. Bob what the secret about his passion for learning so much is?"

31

Dr. Bob: "I love to learn because I believe that growth comes from learning, and when what is learned is applied. Learning has a purpose and function to it. It's not about the gaining of knowledge that is important to me. It's able to take what I learn and see how it fits into what I do to assist others to grow (as well as myself)."

"That is wonderful. I love your bigger WHY behind learning." I responded.

Dr. Bob: "I believe that simply going to school to gain knowledge is never enough. This includes going after certain advanced degrees. Another aspect of learning is in learning how to learn. In a way, it's thinking about thinking (meta-cognition)."

"Please can you explain more about that?" I added.

"Sure," he replied:

"Too many people I have noticed don't know how to think. Because of this, they get stuck in an ineffective mindset, thinking they think when they're not.

I think we all can digress in this way regarding ineffective thinking. I know I have, and it is also a reason why I keep challenging myself, especially my beliefs."

Me: "I totally agree and see how many people truly do not know HOW to think. In fact, it was why the first chapter of this book started with different thinking styles, especially ones related to creativity." I added. "You mentioned that you keep challenging yourself, especially your beliefs, could you give me an example on that?"

Dr. Bob: "One of the things I had realized was that I had been stuck in my Marine Corps and warrior mindset without giving thought to the other areas as well. I've learned to embrace the nerd side of me."

I see it is a great combination and good outcomes in your life." I responded.

Dr. Bob: "While I have learned much from my past, I have a lot to learn in the present where I can grow from. I still know very little about many areas, including the areas of my supposed expertise."

Me: "You are as humble just as much as you are an outstanding mentor and coach to many. It is this which differentiates successful people from others, their lifelong passion, and effort to learning. It is what keeps them always moving forward and continuing learning in new areas that they never explored before.

I know you are a fan of Dr. Seuss, so I will share a quote by him on this topic: 'The more that you read, the more things you shall know. The more that you learn, the more places you will go.'

I can confirm that this quote describes your learning journey and results along the way. How were you able to transform your life after experiencing such a traumatic and abusive childhood due to your father's abuse? You mentioned bleeding and bruising and whipping by him; to a degree, it caused you to stutter. How can someone who is facing such conditions learn from you?"

Dr. Bob took a deep breath on this one, then replied: "By thinking I can create. By thinking, I can write a new story. By thinking, I can transform. And when I do, I will also learn to think better as well.

The most profound aspect of my life is that I learned that I had the ability to shift my story as well as my mindset.

Nothing is set in stone as was once thought. I changed my story and how I looked at my past. I was not to change anything, even what my father did to that younger version of myself. I have changed myself by moving towards a higher version. It's not so much about peak potential as much as it is about transcending.

I realize now that what happened in the past is in the past. I own my present, and I can create my future. It is why I coach and train others to do it. Also, to be the best leader that they can be."

Me: "Very nice. I like the part that you said, 'I learned that I have the ability to shift my story and my mindset.' As I know you are big on storytelling, especially the one, we live within our own heads and constantly repeat to ourselves.

Can people transform into better versions of themselves?"

Dr. Bob: "I believe that most anyone can transform into a much better version of themselves. Heck, I believe that even I can get better too."

"Can you expand some more on that?" I asked.

Dr. Bob: "Let me leave you with this; the dynamics of life are constantly evolving, and so should you. It happens through a belief in your ability, and you possess the resources necessary, a life purpose, and a personal mission. Align your actions with those three, and you'll go far.

Educate yourself beyond the traditional educational systems. Challenge past beliefs that restricted your potential. And then go forward, onward and upward."

Me: "Bravo! What great feedback and good advice to follow. Thank You, Dr. Bob, for your inspiring and enlightening story. I am so grateful for you and your teachings."

Dr. Bob: "You are more than welcome, and it was an honor and pleasure to share with you Dr. Sofie "The Queen of Laughter and Wisdom" and the *Optimize Creative Mindset* readers a glimpse of how creativity and improvising played a part in my story. I hope it will help anyone going through possible abuse, self-sabotaging thoughts, low self-esteem, and more to transcend their situation. Doing so, they will apply and learn new ways of thinking and achieve a mindset that will empower them to move forward with more comfort, knowing that they have the ability to change their story TODAY."

"To that, I say, Amen!"

Insightful lessons to learn from The Transformational Grandmaster, Dr. Bob Choat:

1. How "Your temporary situation is not your final destination."

2. Stay Focused on getting through your challenges, and remain curious in life.

3. Develop resilience and toughness as it will help you overcome any difficulty. When faced with anything out of the ordinary, learn to adapt, improvise, and overcome. Many times, it will take having a creative mindset.

The good news is that you can practice to improvise and gradually get better.

Train your brain to think creatively by looking for ways to improvise in your daily life.

Tap into your deepest passion. It can be drawing, singing, dancing, gardening, martial arts, or any activity you enjoy. It is that of many great inventors, philosophers, legends that have applied combinatorial creativity, including the greatest genius of his time, Albert Einstein.

Einstein was known to play the violin whenever he found himself stuck on a tough problem and often spoke of how music had influenced the way he thought about math and science. His sister, Maja, said that sometimes after playing the piano, he'd get up and say, "There, now I have got it."

One of the things that creative people who are able to improvise, using different areas of expertise, are also known as polymaths. Leonardo Da Vinci was one of them. He was an inventor, engineer, artist, and more.

You might have heard the quote, "A jack of all Trades is a master of none," many took it seriously by becoming experts only in one specific area, leaving them totally ignorant in many areas.

The demand for Polymaths in the 21st century is high and back up again.

Though many people may have what is called multi-potentiality, this refers to a person who has many different interests and creative pursuits in life but has no "one true calling" the way certain specialists do.

This was a topic Emilie Wapnick passionately talked about in her TedTalk. Today we need more of such people back. People can pursue different fields and be able to master some.

Answer these questions:

What is your current passion?

What skills could you add to your current reality that may be exciting and functional?

What areas can you challenge yourself to excel in (cooking, sports, writing), even more than what you are currently able to do?

Are you good at improvising? And if so, how can you improve your skill?

What did YOU LEARN from Dr. Bob Choat's story, mindset, and thinking styles that can be useful to your life?

Are you able to apply more lateral thinking in your life? How would you do that? Think of an area that you can practice applying just lateral thinking to, then, evaluate the outcome?

"Everyone has the right to doubt everything as often as he pleases and the duty to do it at least once. No way of looking at things is too sacred to be reconsidered. No way of doing things is beyond improvement." -Edward de Bono

To achieve the best results, practice often, and develop a habit of using different styles of thinking while you synthesize your personal knowledge, beliefs, and experiences. Use this to help you create better, and in due time you will feel more confident and at ease going through your creative process as you are getting better and more PREPARED.

The keyword here is "Prepared!"

It is just like how a CPR class and up-to-date certifications are mandatory requirements if you are a doctor, nurse, healthcare provider, law enforcement officer, firefighter, rescue personnel, and other emergency responders.

It is just as important to learn, master, and apply different types of thinking and Creative Synthesizing when it comes to necessary tools in your creative CPR kit. When you have access and know-how to use your creative CPR tools, when needed, you will ensure that creative projects are kept from experiencing possible setbacks as well as unnecessary losses.

You may be thinking, "Well, I am a banker, and I don't need to learn a lot of those or other ways of thinking for my work or my personal life." If that Is YOU or in similar positions or a different field, I still believe that learning those different ways of thinking may be helpful. In fact, this type of meta-thinking can be considered a plus to your life, allowing you to be better prepared in times when others are not.

If you are not in any career field that requires you to be certified in CPR, just like most people, you will not attempt to take that Class and get certified.

Did you know: The American Heart Association reports that around 70% of Americans feel helpless to act in the event of a cardiac emergency because either they do not know how to effectively administer CPR or their training has lapsed. According to an online resource for emergency medical services personnel, EMS1 notes that "Although evidence indicates that bystander CPR and AED use could significantly improve survival and outcomes from a cardiac arrest, each year less than 3% of the U.S. population receives CPR training, leaving many bystanders unprepared to respond to a cardiac arrest!

With the many natural disasters, accidents, and unexpected emergencies, we all possibly witnessed or heard how it is wise that more people learn CPR.

No one is immune to such emergencies happening to them, and the life being saved may be that of a dear loved one!

It is estimated that four out of five cardiac arrests occur at home, yet many will underestimate the urgency of knowing how to perform a CPR and the necessity of such teaching in times of need; by then, it may just be too late while waiting for the right help to arrive.

I share this example with you with a sense of deep sorrow as I revisited a sad memory, one where I had to perform CPR. It was a little too late for a life that could have easily been saved. I wish I would have known how to perform CPR. At that time, I just followed instructions without any training, which kept me wondering about, A. "Did I arrive too late?" or B. "Did I not perform it accurately?" In either case, it was eye-opening and shed awareness on the importance of learning CPR. No one knows when and who they may need to use it.

Being equipped with the tools and the confidence of knowing how to perform CPR will transform your role from a bystander in life emergencies to an immediate LIFESAVER!

Just like how saving a life and learning CPR CAN be taught to individuals outside jobs that require such training. It's even recommended as a necessary skill to learn. In my opinion, a very positive one, as it serves a noble human service.

So, could CREATIVITY SKILLS be learned?

You do not learn creative skills from sitting at a lecture. You learn them by applying creative thinking processes as well as synthesizing your experiences as you connect them to new ideas.

For example, when faced with a certain challenge, learning how to apply analytical and creative thinking to decide which solution fits the best in solving that particular problem best is a plus. It can speed up the process of finding creative solutions.

Using your meta-thinking skills will help you develop more powerful creative skills. This will help you go through the process much better as you feel more engaged, starting at the base with the new knowledge learned, memory recall of your experiences, then, understanding and applying them. Incorporating positive discipline while you are practicing will help you master new ways of thinking.

Now that you are aware that you are able to train your mind

and learn creative skills, at the same time, just like how "You

can kill someone if you perform CPR incorrectly. Learning

partial skills can kill your creative fluency, flow, and process."

~Dr. Sofie Nubani

For example, you are a surgeon that learned "Blue-Sky" thinking and trying to apply it on a patient during surgery or a mechanic and trying to apply divergent thinking assisting helping someone with a flat tire on a highway. Okay, it does not have to be that dramatic, but you get the point, right?

So, if creativity could be taught, then developing a Creative Mindset is achievable.

In the upcoming section of this chapter, you will learn more about different mindsets, with more emphasis on the **CREATIVE MINDSET**, this way you may see and evaluate better what mindset you are operating on and functioning from, how it is serving you and what other mindsets might you adopt or replace.

At this moment, if you need to take a little potty break, stretch, breathe, or have a nap, please do so now.

This way, when you are to come back, you will be more refreshed, energized, and focused. You will pay better attention and gain a better memory recall on what you are reading and needing to learn.

I could repeat this same advice at the end of each section or chapter, but I won't. Just remember to apply it whenever needed.

"Unleash the power of METACOGNITION to supercharge

your IMAGINATION and Ignite your INNOVATION." --

Dr. Sofie Nubani

Chapter 2:
The Potentiality of a Creative Mindset

In this chapter, you'll discover...

The Power of Mindset in Creativity

- Traverse your understanding of Different MINDSETS.

- Learn more advanced details about the CREATIVE MINDSET.

- Meet some interesting individuals like the Creative Genius Dr. David Friedman, Innovative Genius Steve Jobs, and Record-Setting Creative Author Chitra Lele.

What is a MINDSET to begin with?

In both the decision theories (4 basic elements: acts, events, outcomes, and payoffs) and the general systems theory (An interconnected set of elements that work together in a cohesive manner that achieves some sort of outcome or purpose.), a mindset is a set of assumptions, methods, or notions held by one or more people or groups of people. Mindset can be seen as part of a person's worldview or philosophy about life.

Mindset.com defines Mindset as a collection of different beliefs and thoughts: "Mindsets are the collections of beliefs and thoughts that make up the mental attitude, inclination, habit or disposition that pre-determines a person's interpretations and responses to certain events, circumstances, and situations."

Mindset as a noun is described as: "The established set of attitudes held by an individual." In other words, it is a collection of your thoughts, opinions, and beliefs that shapes up your attitude towards a particular thing or a person.

Attitude can be faked, especially when it's based on conformity and expectations. But a mindset sets out who you actually are and how you make sense of yourself and the world. Our mindset determines the way we assess, and our attitude determines the way we behave. By our mindset, we make decisions that lead to the habits we develop.

There are different types of mindsets, and based on the type of mindset we adapt to, it will reflect the outcomes and results we experience.

This includes joy, success, wealth, inner peace, or the opposite in areas such as negative self-esteem, low self-worth, or blaming others. Mindset also plays a part in self-confidence.

"Do you know great minds enjoy excellence, average minds love mediocrity, and small minds adore comfort zones?" --Onyi Anyado

In order to optimize your mind for success, it is necessary to understand the different mindsets and their influence on your attitude, habits, and behaviors.

Furthermore, your mindset will influence your relationship with yourself as well as with others. This includes areas such as parenting, leadership skills, and management skills.

Below you will see a list of some of the most popular mindsets that people possess. This is according to an article by the Leadership and Executive Coach Lolly Daskal and in addition to a few thoughtful leaders in this topic such as Steven K. Cload of Mind-Sets.com, founder of Wealthy Gorilla-Dan Western, Founder of Mentality® Chris Zook and Jim Taylor, Ph.D. (who specializes in the psychology of sports and parenting).

One mindset that I will like to add to the mix is one of the *Laughter Mindset*. This is after the Laughter Mindset Program that Dr. Bob Choat and I had co-founded. A necessary mindset to have when it comes to overall wellness in mind, body, and spirit. In addition, it is also important for a business's success.

Your mindset plays a big role in how you can cope with life challenges, handle adversity, and embrace a change. It affects your daily self-dialogue and can reinforce or weaken your most intimate beliefs, attitude, and feelings about yourself, the world, and others.

Go through the list below so you could further relate, reflect, and understand the different types of mindsets that most people fall into. This will also give you a better feel, expansion, and awareness of what mindset or mindsets you possess.

1-The Creative Mindset.

2-The Laughter Mindset.

3-The Growth Mindset.

4-The Business Mindset.

5-The Owner Mindset.

6-The Entrepreneurs Mindset.

7-The Goal-Setting Mindset.

8-The Success Mindset.

9-The Focused Mindset.

10-The Innovative Mindset.

11-The Courageous Mindset.

12-The Champions Mindset.

13-The Goal Setting Mindset.

14-The Winners Mindset.

15-The Fixed Mindset.

16-The Fear Mindset.

17-The Angry Mindset.

19-The Envy Mindset.

20-The Negative Mindset.

21-The Follower Mindset.

22-The Short-Term Mindset.

23-The Limited Mindset.

24-The Experimental Mindset.

25-The Competitive Mindset.

26-The Aggressive Mindset.

27-The Dreamers Mindset.

28-The Self-Trusting Mindset.

29-The Self-Esteem Mindset.

30-The Self-Image Mindset.

31-The Patient Mindset.

32-The Calm Mindset.

33-The Happy Mindset.

All the above mindsets can be broken down into two categories as a foundation to start from.

Growth Mindset vs. Fixed Mindset

The two main mindsets explained in the seminal work of Carol Dweck and her "must-read" book, ***Mindset: The New Psychology of Success.***

Let me invite you to create a column from the list of mindsets above that separates both the fixed and the growth mindset. Distinguish and categorize each of the mindsets based on your personal understanding and awareness that describes either a fixed or a growth mindset.

From there, evaluate, assess, replace, and adopt a mindset that will contribute to you and/or your company's highest and best good. Realize that the difference between the two mindsets will minimize and expand your life experience, success, growth, inner peace, and prosperity.

For example:

A Creative Mindset, A Laughter Mindset, A Gratitude Mindset, A Learning Mindset, A Winners Mindset, and/or a Self-Trusting Mindset typically fall under the **Growth Mindset.**

An Angry Mindset, A Fear Mindset, A Negative Mindset, and/or An Envy Mindset tend to fall under the **Fixed Mindset.**

The Glossary of Education Reform explains:

A mindset, according to Dweck, is a self-perception or a "self-theory" that people hold about themselves. Believing that you are either "intelligent" or "unintelligent" is a simple example of a certain mindset. People may also have a mindset relating to their personal or professional lives— "I'm a good teacher" or "I'm a bad parent," for instance. People can be aware or unaware of their mindsets, according to Dweck. Still, they can have a profound effect on learning achievement, skill acquisition, personal relationships, professional success, and many other dimensions of life.

Let me share with you the definition of both mindsets for further insight on how they work: A Growth Mindset is "the understanding that ability and understanding can both be developed." Those who possess a growth mindset believe that they could get smarter, more intelligent, and more talented through putting time and effort.

"Finally, it means creating a growth-mindset environment under which people can thrive. This involves: • Presenting skills as learnable • Conveying that the organization values learning and perseverance, not just ready-made genius or talent • Giving feedback in a way that promotes learning and future success • Presenting managers as resources for learning without a belief in human development, many corporate training programs become exercises of limited value."-Carol S. Dweck

A Fixed Mindset, on the other side, assumes that abilities and understandings are relatively fixed. Those with a fixed mindset believe that their personal qualities (such as intelligence and/or other personality traits) are "set in stone." You either have it or you don't. It is just how God created you when it comes to abilities and talents.

"Becoming is better than being." The fixed mindset does not allow people the luxury of becoming. They have to be already."-
Carol S. Dweck

They don't believe that one's traits can be practiced or developed. This includes talents. Even talents can be grown and are not fixed.

Daniel Coyle, in his book, *The Talent Code*, described how so-called talented people are actually made, not born. Through practice, both skills and talents can be improved and greatly enhanced. It all starts with the right mindset.

Direct your attention, energy, and effort wisely.

Develop a healthy process to access and apply an effective way of evolved thinking, one that would fuel your creativity and keep you grounded and level-headed.

As you observe your emotions, actions, interactions, behavior, and responses onto others, as well as yourself, you might need to make some adjustments based on your new learnings. Make sure as you do this, it supports your overall well-being and keeps you in the right mindset.

Take some time to connect and learn about the different types of mindsets out there. Learn how each can help you understand, transition, and apply an appealing, supportive, and more empowered mindset.

What is a Creative Mindset?

First and foremost, a Creative Mindset starts with the habit of having a Creative Attitude towards life and to know how to teach yourself to think creatively on your own. In your heart, you know that you are the first to think of a certain original thought, discover the idea, or create that invention (Though someone else might have thought or invented the same prior to you, you weren't aware of that, to you it was your own original thought and idea). Or a creative mindset can be inspired and motivated through collaborative creativity.

You belong to a circle of *creative masters* (similar to the mastermind meeting in other domains). You will be able to expand your imagination and access a collection of generating ideas through the trusted creative masters. Everyone will maximize and diversify their creative efforts, skills, and talents towards a common purpose or goal.

Having a Creative Mindset means you have positive habits and higher than normal will-power. YOU are a smart risk-taker and are not afraid of setbacks. You courageously step into better ways of asking questions and thinking.

A Creative Mindset is one that doesn't follow the mainstream and can generate explanations and offer certain effective plans. In fact, you are thought of as a so-called "outcast" when you go against the grain.

You are open to broader life experiences and have the ability to connect dots from past elements and experiences and then combine them to create something new. You have the motivation to identify and develop a creative idea (that, in essence, depends mainly on your ability to see and understand relationships).

Having a mindset for creativity or living in a state of creativity opens you up to opportunities and possibilities. You can live in a way that allows you to think, feel, and act with deep personal soul liberation, engaged in the sense of purpose and meaningful values.

Being creative allows you to embody enthusiasm and originality to your goals and objectives in life. In other words, having a creative mindset is like genuinely feeling alive, allowing yourself to participate in the process of co-creating your day, with what you choose to create and how you choose to do it.

Along with utilizing different Thinking Styles and owning the right Mindset, an area of importance to be aware of is that of *Creative Metacognition* (especially in creative areas of strategy).

Creative Metacognition

"Creative work may involve more than cognition, but specific

cognitive processes may be necessary for virtually all creativity."

-*Warren W. Tryon*

To have a creative potential, one must remember, learn, and think (Divergent, Convergent, Lateral, Holistic, and Associative thinking use different thinking styles that are supportive to the creative project at hand or simply have the ability to organize and reorganize a particular type of information).

A creative process involves the attainment of knowledge and skill that could be transformed to design, style, structure, or form that can later result in a shareable product.

Applying all the above during the creative process requires the use of one's cognition. The best COGNITIVE MODEL to learn and apply, especially when it comes to cultivating creative skills and developing a creative potential, would, without a doubt, be **CREATIVE METACOGNITION**.

Before continuing forward, I would like to share with you the definition of METACOGNITION: *It is the awareness and understanding of one's thought processes.* Metacognition is simply "cognition about cognition," "thinking about thinking," "knowing about knowing," becoming "aware of one's awareness," and higher-order thinking skills. This plays a significant regulatory role in various cognitive processes, such as learning, memory, decision-making skills, and other high-level cognition.

According to *"Frontiers in Psychology,"* Metacognition may take many forms:

1. Metacognitive knowledge. When and how to use certain strategies for learning or problem-solving.

2. Metacognitive experience. Not a cognitive operation but an individual's subjective perception of the ease or difficulty of particular cognitive operations (Rummer et al., 2016).

3. Metacognitive monitoring and control. Is one worth mentioning that metacognition could be divided into the "knowledge of cognition" and the "regulation of cognition" by the use of a dichotomy (Brown, 1978). The regulation of the cognition component includes an individual's planning, examining, monitoring, testing, and evaluating of cognitive activities, which corresponds to "metacognitive monitoring and control." Hence, we now comprehensively introduce the relationship between "metacognitive monitoring and control" and the "regulation of cognition" and creativity.

For example, when it comes to metacognitive knowledge, a person has to make behavioral decisions based on the available metacognitive knowledge, for better or worse. In this sense, it is the awareness that one has regarding one's thinking and being able to apply the correct strategies needed in order to learn a given topic.

"Introspective Observation is what we have to rely on first and foremost and always." -William James

However, when it comes to metacognitive monitoring and control, it's connected with one's comprehension and awareness of their thought process and applying the discovery to help change the behavior, both during learning and remembering. As you do this, you are engaged in a system of evaluating the progress to the completion of a given task.

For example, I learned that the best way of learning and remembering via metacognitive knowledge was by reading aloud, active listening, and then, summarizing through notes. Then by using metacognitive monitoring and control, I self-assessed, using my best judgment through my awareness and memory recall, for the progress of my ability of comprehension.

I recall during my NLP certification program, we had longer days while attending classes. My classmates and I practiced and applied what we had learned as a group and as part of an evaluation of the complete certification program. By applying my active listening skills during class, then later, in the evening, revising the material and the content in addition to my summarizing through my notes helped me in both understandings and remembering what I was taught.

The next day, in class, I applied my cognitive knowledge, answered the questions, participated, and engaged in the given exercises. This added more ease to my cognitive experience and allowed my cognitive monitoring and control to be of valuable assistance, by measuring and evaluating my progress as I was developing my skills in NLP at a personal (and a professional) level.

"The more we invite new experiences in our lives, the more associations we have. The more associations we have, the better we understand disciplines and relationships. The better we understand disciplines and relationships, the better our creative metacognition becomes, and the sharper our meta-awareness is enforced and utilized."-Dr. Sofie Nubani

Creative and metacognitive skills, when taught and learned, will definitely stimulate the creative potential of future professionals. I invite you to learn more about your creative metacognition by understanding the method in which you learn, process, and understand information. Answering the following two questions will help:

What type of environment supports your metacognitive knowledge? Visit an experience where you had to apply metacognitive monitoring and control.

How did the environment influence your outcome? By becoming more aware, you'll be able to connect the dots faster and easier as well as tap further into your best creative potential and abilities.

Another factor that is important in enhancing your creative skills and talents is *The model of Self-Concept* by Carl Rogers which states, (to truly dive into your best creative potential you must understand your self-concept, personality, mindset, thinking, beliefs and psychology).

"We behave as we do because of the way we perceive our

situation. No one else can know how we perceive; we are the best

experts on ourselves." -Carl Rogers

Creative Self-Concept

An idea of the self-constructed from the beliefs that one holds about oneself and the responses of others.

According to Carl Rogers, self-concept has three components:

1-Self-Image
(The idea that one has of his or her abilities, appearance, and personality)

2-Self-Esteem
(Confidence in your self-worth/ abilities, self-respect)

3-Ideal Self

What one aspires and wishes to be in life, an ideal self is an idealized version of yourself created out of what you've learned from your life experiences, the demands of the society, and what you admire in your role models.

Haworth et al. (2010) suggest that numerous factors can affect your self-concept, such as age, education, media, appearance, culture, abuses, relationships, gender, and income. These factors are also known as socio-economic factors.

It is of great benefit to comprehend the theory of self-concept and components.

You will understand much better how you think of yourself and how you SHOULD think instead. This includes as you lead, serve, behave, and act out your different roles in life, which will result in optimal creative success and help you achieve the highest level of 'human-beingness.'

For example, if your self-image and self-esteem are not congruent with your ideal-self, then most likely, you will have a self-concept that is experiencing a disharmony, an inner conflict on a subconscious level, and a not satisfied whole self. When the real-self is at odds with the ideal-self, sadness is increased, and happiness is decreased. All are affecting you negatively, stopping you from reaching your highest levels of creativity.

Along with understanding one's self-concept, it is necessary to have a belief in one's ability to create. Hence, this is where the significance of measuring creative self-efficacy plays an important role during the creative process.

Measuring Creative Self-Efficacy

"The belief one has the ability to produce creative outcomes."

(Tierney & Farmer, 2002)

According to an article in Science Direct, Measuring Creative Self-Efficacy is highly dynamic in that it is influenced by a variety of internal and external (including contextual and sociocultural) factors.

Creative self-efficacy and creative personal identity are positively related to rated creativity and originality/fluency.

Creative performance is guided by a sense of self as creative and by a person's sense of the significance of creativity in their identity. Creative self-efficacy shows good metacognition in regards to the actual creative performance.

According to a study by Ewa Wisniewska, "revealed positive

links of creative self-efficacy and creative personal identity with self-reported originality and test for Creative Thinking (TCT-DP), and weaker, yet expected connections with intelligence, as well as positive relations with self-esteem, emotional intelligence and intrinsic motivations."

Just as having high self-efficacy relates to the belief that one can achieve the desired outcome, so does being able to have the right creative mindset. Years ago, a well-known children's story, *The Little Engine That Could*, told the tale of a little train engine that believed it could pull a train over the steep hill where other engines didn't want to attempt it. Its mantra was, "I think I can; I think I can." That story emphasized high self-efficacy and is also essential for a good creative mindset.

"Whatever you can do, or dream you can, begin it. Boldness has genius, power and magic in it." -Johann Wolfgang von Goethe, Author

Developing a creative mindset requires a dosage of:

COURAGE when facing rejection.

DETERMINATION when facing mental exhaustion.

FOCUS when facing distractions.

PERSEVERANCE when facing discouragement.

PATIENCE when facing desperation.

SURRENDER when facing resistance.

TRUST when facing obstacles.

FAITH when facing doubt.

As you take this journey, go after your creative goals and grow while you do.

It has been said you will be the same person you are today five years from now but for the books you read and the people you meet. We can learn a lot from our own lessons, experiences, setbacks, and mistakes, just as we can avoid a lot of that by learning from other people's setbacks and victories.

"One can choose to go back toward safety or forward toward growth. Growth must be chosen, again, and again, fear must be overcome again and again." -Abraham Maslow

Finding Gold Among Those Who You Associate With And Beyond

Being a co-host of two shows, a Professional Coach, Admin of five Facebook groups and active on many social media platforms, I was able to connect and meet with many amazing and inspiring people.

Through participation and interaction, and depending on the field of contribution, I was surrounded by high achievers and higher-level thinkers.

"Walk with the dreamers, the believers, the courageous, the cheerful, the planners, the doers, the successful people with their heads in the clouds and their feet on the ground." -Wilfred Peterson

I remember one evening (while I was writing my book and just about finished with a chapter. I took a little break time and read Dr. David Friedman's book, *Food Sanity*) telling myself what a fantastic depth of knowledge combined with humor that the content of Dr. David's book had (I remember listening to one of his live shows earlier that week on how his book had won best health book at the *Author Academy Awards*) offered. After hearing the story about how many times his book was rejected by many publishing companies, I decided to discover more about the mindset he had adopted that enabled him to reach VICTORY. Something I was interested in knowing for myself, and I thought it would be inspiring for others.

I loved this mindset of holding the intention that many could stand into their own power when they believe in the WHY behind their aspiration, and never give up on their dreams.

I decided to message Dr. David and share how I would love to have his contribution in my book.

(I believed that his process of creative thinking, decision making and taking action towards his goals/dreams in his journey would be a great addition in my upcoming book.)

He responded: "I would be honored to contribute."

I remember smiling as I was reading his response and said to myself, how generous and kind of him, but again I was not surprised knowing the quality of his genuine soul and loyal friendship.

Learn the Mindset Strategies of the Creative Genius, Dr. David Friedman

How he used his REJECTION to REDIRECTION by applying his thinking skills obtaining creative solutions to what some may consider as a roadblock and dead-end, to him it was a reconstruction that resulted in creating new road paths through his:

1-Creative Thinking.

2-Divergent Thinking.

3-Lateral Thinking.

4. Analytical Thinking.

Many lessons could be learned from Dr. David's story. I will highlight a few and leave you to your conclusions and additional takeaways you may observe yourself after reading, THE POWER OF "NO" by Dr. David Friedman that you can:

Understand how personal values and material evolution differ from one person to another.

While money might be an inspiration to Ramzy, Act of Service may be to his brother Ibrahim, Status to Samantha, Experience to Sam, and Growth to Vishen.

VALUE SYSTEMS influence our thoughts and behaviors, resulting in inaction, reaction, and action, so be mindful of it.

Know your own value system and let it inspire your creativity and the creativity of your loved ones, clients, or friends if you are involved in creative projects together.

Understand why NEGATIVE AFFIRMATIONS are as meaningful as positive ones on a subconscious level and how you could use them to fuel your drive and inspire your actions, ensuring the defeat of birth or growth of a negative reality and assurance of achieving a positive one.

Discover how THINKING OUT OF THE BOX (besides the traditional educational system) and exploring alternatives of certain unconventional ideas such as CREATIVE WRITING can open unexpected doors of opportunities.

Why do medical labels not define who you are and how FAILURE IS ONLY FEEDBACK to a determined soul?

To quote Roger Schank from his book, **The Creative Attitude**, "The process of failing and then recovering from that failure can be the source of the creative spark. Failure builds a creative character because the more failures one recovers from, the better-equipped one is to fail again. No creative idea can ever be dreamed up if its dreamer is afraid to take the risk of being called a fool. Risk-taking and creativity go hand in hand."

Let me share a story with you that has inspired many I know. One to remember, anytime you NEED a dose of ENCOURAGEMENT to charge yourself and push you forward towards your creative goals.

The Power of "NO!" Dr. David Friedman's Story

"As an overachiever (I have five doctorate degrees) syndicated television health expert, international award-winning, and #1 best-selling author, people often think success just runs in my genes.

As a child, I suffered from A.D.D (Attention Deficit Disorder.) I could not focus and follow through with many tasks. Because of this, I ended up always tardy, in detention, and flunking most of my classes.

While many parents offered money to their kids when they got an "A," my mom gave me $20 for every "D" I received.

I earned an incentive to work harder and not get an "F."

Unfortunately, money did not motivate me. I skipped school, failed out of many classes, and ended up not attending my own graduation. Instead, I had to go to summer school in my senior year to get my high school diploma.

Even though my SAT scores were pretty high, no college would consider me because "I never applied myself in school."

It was the words said to me by my high school principal that would forever alter my path; 'David, be glad a college won't accept you because you would end up failing. You are just not smart enough!' Those stabbing words resonated into my spirit.

One gift that I did possess was writing. Using this talent, I submitted a creative essay on why I should be accepted to college even though I did not have good grades.

I sent this out to several colleges, and, to my total disbelief, two of them had sent me back an acceptance letter.

On the first day of college, I put a sticky note on my dorm room mirror that stated, "David, you are not smart enough for college!" Those words from my high school principal would fuel my motivation not to fail.

It had far more power than the twenty-dollar incentive my mother offered me. I ended up getting straight A's in college and graduated as valedictorian of my class. I was featured on the National Dean's List, which was a prestigious recognition for academic excellence.

I was then accepted to Chiropractic College.

On the first day of neuroanatomy class, the teacher was bragging, "My class is considered the most difficult in this college! In fact, I have the highest failure rate, and no one has ever earned an A."

I felt like he spoke directly to me! I went on to earn the first A in neuroanatomy. This led to me eventually teaching his class, and I went on to author a college textbook on neurology. All this happened because I was told that I could not make an A.

I became a Doctor of Naturopathy, with an emphasis on diet and nutrition. While in practice, I witnessed first-hand the power that food had on our health. I wrote a book called **Food Sanity,** which was rejected by 50 leading publishers. I was told, "Your book is not good enough to publish," "Nothing new here to pursue," and "It is not worth the cost of the paper we'd print it on." Ouch! This was like a dagger being stuck into my chest! But I turned this REJECTION into REDIRECTION, and I stayed the course. When I hear "NO," I shout out a four-letter word: "NEXT!"

Food Sanity went on to become an International award-winning, #1 national best-seller. My book earned the prestigious honor of getting first place at the Author Academy Awards.

During my acceptance speech, I thanked all the people that had told me "no"! As I held up my award, I said, "In the words of Julia Roberts from Pretty Woman...BIG MISTAKE!"

Do not let the naysayers derail your dreams. Instead, use their words as a wonderful opportunity to roll up your sleeves and prove them wrong."

"WOW," I thought to myself after reading **The Power of NO** by Dr. David as he mentioned a few things I never knew or read about him before, which made his story and leadership even more exciting and inspiring.

For those around the globe, meeting Dr. Friedman for the first time and after reading his story, not only is Dr. David Friedman an International award-winning, #1 national best-selling author of *Food Sanity: How to Eat in a World of Fads and Fiction.* His book had achieved the honor of winning first place at the International Book Awards and best health book at the Author Academy Awards. Dr. Friedman is also a Doctor of Naturopathy, Clinical Nutritionist, and a Chiropractic Neurologist.

He is a former teacher of neurology and author of the college textbook, ***"Understanding the Nervous System."***

Also, Dr. Friedman is a contributing writer for a plethora of leading news, health and fitness magazines, including *U.S News & World Report*, *Newsweek*, *Reader's Digest*, *Better Nutrition*, *AARP Magazine*, and *Woman's World*, to name a few. Dr. Friedman has been featured on ABC, CBS, NBC, Discovery Health, FOX, FitTV, The Food Network, Discovery Channel, and many more.

His bestselling CD, **America's Unbalanced Diet**, has sold over a million copies, helping to raise awareness about the unhealthy foods people are consuming.

Dr. Friedman is currently working on a documentary with Netflix." I am looking forward to checking it out. "

I mentioned all of this in detail with you that you will forever remember the power of "NO" and how it gave birth to a CREATIVE GENIUS who had mastered what he needs to do NEXT to arrive at his desired destination.

Next time you hear a NO or have dream stealers and naysayers corrupt your personal flow, say NEXT and tap to your creative thinking skills as you continue moving forward.

When NO means NEXT, it feels better and easier to CREATE.

On that note, I would like to share a quote with you by the GENIUS VISIONARY Steve Jobs (a man whose vision of technology changed the world for the better) that the power of NO was an important reminder for us to use:

"People think focus means saying yes to the thing you have got to focus on. But that is not what it means at all. It means saying NO to the hundred other good ideas that there are. You have to pick carefully. I am actually as proud of the things we have not done as the things I have done. Innovation is saying 'NO' to 1,000 things."

So, Dr. David heard No about fifty times from publishers who rejected his book, and every No had him saying to himself, "No. I am not taking this for an answer, NEXT". It is the same when you're presented with many friendship requests, offers or invitations, staying on course and focused requires a lot of NO's for an answer.

When receiving help, advice, opportunities, favor, knowledge, YES is supportive of your growth, success, and overall well-being. However, when you're living the everyday life, working towards your goals, accomplishing your dreams and completing your projects, saying NO is what would make space and time for the right YES'S to be accomplished successfully, celebrated and appreciated in your life.

Another thing the business magnate Steve Job had advised, is to stay away from critics as they will usually find a problem in every solution you offer. Never discounting their essential role in some areas of life, as he had them as part of his operational team, yet there were set boundaries to ensure the success of all teams.

The key to driving corporate creativity is to make sure the process flows through teams in the following order: creatives, problem solvers, critics, with firm boundaries at each step. His warning was, do not bring in the critics too early; they are nice people, but they can be idea killers.

"Gather ten smart people into a room, and one or two will be creative, two are great at solving problems, and the rest are critics. Keep the creatives away from the critics."

Great advice from GENIUS INVENTOR Steve Jobs on Critics as "Idea Killers" and CREATIVE GENIUS DR. David Friedman on Naysayers as "Dream-Stealers."

Let NO be your anchor to remember, and tell yourself "next" when faced with rejection and let "NO" be your focused anchor when you are faced with distractions.

NO is powerful when used with positive intentions, which serves a bigger WHY.

NO is your most durable ARMOR against weak desires, distractions, and disempowering beliefs, and NEXT is your ARROW aiming towards your next goal, your next victory, your next YES!!!!

"If you're going to make connections which are innovative ...

you have not to have the same bag of experiences as everyone else

does." ~Steve Jobs

You will never create unique experiences following the crowd, copying trends, and allowing distractions and rejections to shape those experiences.

Make choices that will invite better and more valuable and meaningful experiences in your life.

Experiences create the knowledge and hold a stronger vibration with SELF than just the knowledge learned, with both being valuable, yet there is something about personal experiences that can SHIFT, CHANGE, and TRANSFORM LIVES!

"Life does not always give you what you want, but if you look

closely, you will see that it gives you what you need for your

growth." -Leon Brown

Let me share an interesting story about a bright young lady I am connected with on LinkedIn (a business social media platform), and with interactions through our posts, I learned a few interesting things about her. I admired her integrated style of creativity and a unique approach to problem-solving.

Let me introduce you to the BRILLIANT Strategic Synergist Chitra Lele, a young software engineer, a solution architect, record-setting author, a keynote speaker, a peace ambassador, a world record holder, and an award-winning poet.

Her publications include poetry anthologies, scholarly articles, research papers, academic and reference books.

Apart from consulting corporate houses in the field of software project management and team management, she also devotes her time towards building a seamless web of peace ambassadors as well as change creators.

Since she has been doing a lot of research in multiple domains, she also wears the hat of an academic researcher.

Chitra Lele's Story

Reading a few of Brilliant Chitra's blogs and posts, I was inquisitive to learn about her thinking style, and how it helped her to be more creative, so I asked her:

Question: "How does your mindset + divergent/critical thinking, help you to be more creative and accomplish what you have?"

Answer: "Apart from progressing in my computer science and software engineering field, I want to contribute to society. I wanted to make many more beginnings, set, and achieve many more milestones in the fields of literature, education, and peace-making.

In order to encourage youngsters of my age to join the bandwagon of peace-making and social transformation is one of my most significant aims. I began my work in this field through my on-the-field efforts, books, seminars as well as my association with peace organizations like the Peace Writers Organization (USA) and the World Peace Organization (USA). I am only in the first step of my journey, and I still have a long way to go!

These are some things I do regularly to bring about 'seamless cohesion' in all aspects of my life to enhance my divergent mindset, critical thinking, and creativity: Share my originality with others and let others share their uniqueness with me. Focusing on this sharing, not as a way of putting down each other but rather a unique learning experience; At times learning and studying the deeper dynamics about specific systems or practices helps to change my perspective and rigid attitude, and overcome the impulse of rejecting behavior or people whom I cannot understand or relate to.

For example, if I hold a preconceived notion about a certain person and tend to dismiss everything that the person says, then only and only I am losing out. The reason is simple: I am not letting myself be open to receive new inputs. There is a huge chance that this person has something new to share, which may give my thoughts a new direction, or his/her inputs may even help me to find a solution. I try and not limit my thought patterns by shutting out external inputs.

I began writing short stories and poems from the age of eight. Slowly and steadily, as I developed a deep reading habit, I became exposed to a wide variety of genres. And this, in turn, gave me the confidence to write on a wide variety of subjects. Initially, I contributed articles to my college and university magazines. As I received appreciation from my peers and elders, I gained the confidence to try my hand in various other mediums—online blogs, print magazines, radio poetry reading sessions, international journals, and anthologies.

With all these contributions, I began to develop an innate desire to become an author.

I started my corporate journey and inner spiritual quest at a very young age, five years ago due to a deeply spiritual and personal crisis...all thanks to the Higher Essence for showing me this path at a young age. I will share my philosophy behind my profession and passion and how these two are connected. How they help me to hone my divergent mindset and to come up with novel software solutions, interesting academic books, and path-breaking research work.

Basically, at any given point in time, I am either a software engineer or a student churning out new ideas for my next book or a research paper or an author or researcher trying to figure out how my new approaches could apply to my software field or any other particular domain.

So, this aspect kind of fuses my profession and passion in a rather seamless manner due to which the time factor becomes more manageable. Observation of and interaction with people, situations, etc. help me to hone my critical thinking and creativity. All these aspects helped me to develop solutions, theories, and approaches for filling the knowledge gaps in the workflow of any aspect of my life (personal, professional, spiritual, etc.).

Bringing about a transformation and change in others, and that too through a young person's take on life, is something that makes my audience is always interested in my works, be it a software project, a book, or a peace campaign. The

Higher Essence, blessings from my parents, and well wishes from my friends like you keep me going day in and day out. Thank you, my friend, for your love and many blessings."

Aww, our brilliant Chitra "love and many blessings to you," I say, my awesome friend.

I love seeing thriving young adults on focused missions serving with vibrant light and committed to deep values that create an impact in our world.

Chitra received 70+ Commendation Letters from many World Leaders, right from the Hon. From President of India to Her Excellency Queen Elizabeth II. She holds 10 World Records in the Fields of Peace, Culture, Literature, and Education.

Chitra has been conferred with the title of "A Versatile Writer" by the Indian Book of Records. She set this record by penning the maximum number of books in a short span of eighteen months in various genres. Her books have set records, have received positive reviews, and have been praised by world leaders, best-selling authors, management gurus, and many business experts.

In this story, you have learned how the "BRILLIANT, Savvy, Synergist" Chitra used her divergent mindset to come up with novel software solutions, interesting academic books, and path-breaking research works. As well as her Observation of and interaction with people, situations, and so on. That helped her to hone her critical thinking and creativity.

Chitra's interests in two separate domains and disciplines opposite from another does not decrease her innate creative ability; this includes when applying different thinking skills to each of them. She wore different hats, depending on the nature of the task in hand, strengthened her creative skills and diversified her creative talents and skills, all of which serves her to help others on a greater scale.

She learned and studied the deeper dynamics of particular systems or practices that helped change her perspective and rigid attitude.

With that being said, let me share some of Chitra's poetic fragrance through a short poem that was dedicated to the readers of **Optimize Your Creative Mindset** on the topic of "Creativity."

Potentiality of A Creative Mindset

Creativity

There is one such place

Where reality and dreams meet

Where in times of turmoil I retreat.

That space which I cannot trespass

That space which I cannot efface-

Is what I call the Creative Monument.

-Chitra Lele

Well, all I can say: (It is brilliant. Chitra have definitely mastered staying in flow and arriving at her Creative Monument.)

Reading a few of Chitra's books, one cannot miss her heartfelt gratitude in the acknowledgment of her parents, as she has shared earlier. For example, her acknowledgment of them in the book: *"English Language" The Gateway Way to Global Growth:*

> *"What I have learned over the past years comes as a result of*
>
> *being the daughter of wonderful parents—Mrs. Asha Lele and*
>
> *Mr. G.G. Lele. They've been the motivation that has helped me*
>
> *to maintain a laser-sharp focus on my goals. Thanks to them*
>
> *for their on-going support, helpful positive criticism, and*
>
> *valuable suggestions."*

All I can say is that I have much respect for her parents, and I would personally would like to congratulate them on being a part of their daughter's growth and journey. Being engaged, supportive, and cheering her continued success and dedicated universal human service deserves a round of applause for such a beautiful upbringing.

I personally thank them for raising such an exceptionally talented woman, who in many ways, touched my heart and the world's.

On a personal note, I would like to share with you the heart of this young multi-talented lady regarding her response to an image I had created with her quote on it:

I cannot thank you enough, so I am dedicating a verse, too, as my heartfelt appreciation here it is, for you!

The sacred sphere

With its unfaltering glow,

Splashes wisdom across your frontier.

You become your own Masterpiece of Indigo!

You descend from the saffron heaven,

On the clouds of white axis,

To spread the divine dust all around,

From your cosmic canvas.

--Chitra Lele (dedicated to you.)

Well, all I can say is that her words have touched my soul, and I see why she is such an exceptional young, thoughtful leader, constantly winning awards of achievements and is recognized on a global level.

Potentiality of A Creative Mindset

She is a wise old soul in the body of a young servant leader.

May many youthful and adult leaders be influenced by her footsteps and get inspired by her actions.

To this date, the brilliant Chitra has published (30) books in various genres, from software engineering to business management. She started at the age of 18 to her current age of 27, in a span of just nine years!!!

How does she do it? How can she wear this many hats and be so successful in everything she touches?

May it be her focused attention to her priorities, and the many NO's she says to her distractions?

I will let you ponder on that one. However, I want you to think a bit on:

What could be done in areas in your life that may need you to apply some divergent, critical, and creative thinking for optimal success?

The intention of all the stories shared in this chapter is for you to reflect upon and have some introspection that might inspire your creativity in areas of assertiveness, perseverance, positive discipline, and integrated creativity.

It's so interesting to learn from other people's creative journey and how each story individually and collectively could inspire action, even change our life. In addition, learning about what type of thinking skills they used going through their process and how we could learn from such thinking systems.

Some fields will require critical thinking, but is it in all areas or partial? Do you need to combine both? When and if so, how?

Keep in mind while you are on the thinking stages between different thinking systems to not start converging during the divergent thinking stage.

One is about creating choices; another is about making them.

Creative thinking attempts to create something new, while critical thinking seeks to assess the worth or validity of something that already exists. It requires knowledge, comprehension, application, analysis, problem-solving, and proper evaluation.

Optimize Your Creative Mindset

Creative thinking is divergent, while critical thinking is rather convergent.

Creative thinking is focused on possibilities, while critical thinking focuses on probability.

Do you recall the time when your creative ideas were listened to and acted upon? If so, what type of mindset did you have at the time?

Did you ever share your story of transformation with others or write about it?

According to *The Health Foundation*, storytelling may contribute to inclusion and connection, build confidence, and bring about a change.

Just thought that I should share with you as everyone has stories to tell, you will be surprised how your own personal story of transformation can inspire others and boost their creativity.

In the next chapter, you will learn more about the power of storytelling and its influence on your personal creativity. As you learn from people just like you, who did not think that they had an interesting enough story to share, or they might not have recognized how inspiring their story is to others.

Storytelling is the most powerful way to put ideas into the world."– Robert McKee

If you read straight through, please stretch your neck, shoulders take a 5-minute walk or a little break, come back and continue reading.

If you are not up to moving or applying any of the above suggestions, then please at least take a few deep, conscious breaths to invite deep thinking to your mind, heighten your awareness, and help you rejuvenate.

"Deep breathing brings deep thinking, and shallow breathing brings shallow thinking." -Elsie Lincoln Benedict

Let's get started on taking 3 Deep Breaths:

One for your mind,

One for your body,

One for your soul,

Breathe out a BIG SIGH... AHHHHHH!!!

"When the breath is unsteady, all is unsteady; when the breath is still; all is still. Control the breath carefully. Inhalation gives strength and a controlled body; retention gives steadiness of mind and longevity; exhalation purifies body and spirit." – Goraksasathakam

Chapter 3:
Creative Storytelling That Influences Success

In this chapter, you'll discover...

- The Power of Storytelling and its Influence on Creativity.

- Creative storytelling between facts and myths.

- The Neurochemicals of Effective Storytelling.

- Discover the most-watched surgeon in human history, Dr. Ahmad Shafi, and his best use of creative storytelling.

The Power of Storytelling and its Influence on Creativity

Storytelling is our obligation to the next generation. If all we are doing is marketing, we are doing a disservice, and not only to our profession, but to our children and their children. Give something of meaning to your audience by inspiring, engaging, and educating them with the story. Stop marketing. Start storytelling." ~Laura Holloway, Founder & Chief of the Storyteller Agency.

A great quote and advice by Laura Holloway. We have become a more highly engaged society when it comes to social media. With a lot of options to choose from, the variable that helps one's message to stand out is that of compelling storytelling. Using the many tools and options, telling the story of a business, or even the personal side of it will help amplify it.

We must not be farsighted from the value and power of our message and its immediate or continued influence for generations to come.

Let's be mindful of using our stories with Holistic Thinking in mind. It's a thinking style that truly can leave a beautiful legacy behind. (Meaning: set an intent, have a purpose and vision of why you are sharing your story with the intent of fostering social and individual wellbeing to readers/listeners.) With no judgment, any real story is purposeful as it could help others learn from or avoid those certain mistakes others have shared. The way we deliver, describe, teach, or promote it makes the biggest difference and has the most influence as a result. That's the power of stories.

In business and on a professional level

It's noticeable that many try to consistently promote their business and themselves through their story, without sharing a process, personal experiences, or insights that are advantageous to their consumers or potential customers.

In regards to the style of delivery and communication, when it comes to storytelling, I love the approach of a thought leader/top influencer best-selling author Bob Burg (also known as the King of Referrals).

Learn about the Five Laws of Stratospheric Success

You might have seen or read the books (The "Go-Giver" series) by Bob Burg and John Mann, which are definitely an excellent read. They use the power of great storytelling which teaches many valuable lessons, known as *The Five Laws of Stratospheric Success*:

The Law of Value; your true worth is determined by how much more you give in value than take in payment.

The Law of Compensation; your income is determined by how many people you serve and how well you serve them.

The Law of Influence; your influence is determined by how abundantly you place other people's interests first.

The Law of Authenticity; the most valuable gift you have to offer is yourself.

The Law of Receptivity; the key to effective giving is staying open to receiving.

The foundation that Go-Givers operate on is: Make giving rather than getting your first priority in business and life—and success will follow.

All stories within each book of the series have valuable lessons and "Golden Nuggets" for the reader to use and apply to their life.

Life's Challenges That Enhance Creative Growth

Within his book series, Bob Burg brings forth of "*The Essence of Influence.*" He teaches on the necessity of having genuine influence and defines how a genuine influencer behaves and leads by pulling people towards versus pushing. He defined pushing as trying to lead or influence others via compliance, which he explains is the opposite of commitment.

I remember laughing one day when I was listening to the YouTube series - *The Essence of Influence* when thought leader Bob Burg said: "You don't hear people saying 'She is Influential, and she has a lot of PUSH with people Right? She sure is PUSHY we will just follow her everywhere.'"

I sure had a good belly laugh on that one, HA HA HA!

He talked about the power of PULL and the successful sustainable results that "pull" had vs. "push" in building genuine influence in relationships, be it business or personal.

He emphasized on the importance of having a convincing and elegant style of pulling when you are in a sales-like situation or telling a story. He shared: It's definitely more attractive when you show your genuine interest in the people first before starting to promote your product or service.

"Successful and Genuine Influencers Attract "Pull" People

FIRST to themselves and THEN to their ideas." ~Bob Burg

I had the privilege and pleasure to meet Bob Burg when he was interviewed as a special guest on Meet the Author Show, which I happen to be a Co-Host of, and later in-person through a weekend event he had hosted in Orlando, Florida. All I can say is: what a humble and genuine soul; a true Go Giver that practices servant leadership, who is a blessing to many.

When we share stories that are authentic and purposeful, with the intention to encourage and empower as well as teach others to step towards their own greatness, people could feel the strength of our words in their whole being.

When they meet us virtually and in-person, they feel that we are that same person they respected and appreciated his or her teachings and contributions.

That was my feeling when I connected and met in person with the AWESOME Bob Burg.

Seek in your life, an adventure, one that sparks your soul, expands your imagination and excites your motivation. Then lead with your charged-up spirit of adventure and leave a positive impact, one that is pure, genuine, and serving to others.

As you are sharing stories both about your personal life or promoting a business, seek the bigger picture. Have a broader vision and be mindful of the importance, change, and influence you may impact generations to come.

Learn the art of pulling and its positive imprint in the areas of communication and relationships. Build stronger foundations and relationships that may be genuinely influenced by the value of service you provide and the care you express.

Apply a PULLING style in your storytelling!

I remember speaking to a friend who had needed a few contributors for a project he was assigned to. This was where other expert insights, a personal experience shared and collaboration was of great support.

The few people he asked to contribute had a very good response to his request. They all had thirty days to submit their contribution in the form of a story.

Six people had contributed. He was very happy to have had the help in making the task easier and more engaging.

However, one thing that he did not expect was that two out of the four people heavily promoted their business in a few paragraphs, taking away from the original mission of the project and their part of the contribution. I found out later he replaced them with more considerate participants.

"To add value to others, one must first value others." --John Maxwell

Always be mindful when you're offering to support, help, or contribute, do so with a clear understanding of what has been originally asked from you (unless there was a previous agreement that it was okay to promote your ideas, business or services). It is best that you stay considerate and courteous. Share your support with a genuine sense of service and with no strings attached.

Bring in with you the attitude of a Go-Giver!!!

Importance of Storytelling

According to *The Health Foundation*, storytelling may contribute to inclusion and connection, build confidence, and bring about a change.

Storytelling is one of the most important traditions that humans possess. Business commonwealths are built, and illusions are born through storytelling.

Stories influence our perception and understanding as many can be real, and others may be myths. Just like passed on belief systems that have never been questioned or challenged.

Did you know that MECHANICAL GENIUS, Antonio Meucci (who is of Italian origin), is the one who had originally invented the telephone, not Alexander Graham Bell?

Bell was not the inventor of the telephone like we were all taught—he was the first to patent it. He took out a patent 16 years later. It turns out that Bell was one of the several men who were working on the telephone idea at the same time, but he got to the patent office before them.

The majority of people have not heard of the great Antonio Meucci. But, to this day, many people give credit to Alexander Graham Bell for his invention of the telephone. I give him credit for taking action over a few others, who also had the same idea but did not head to the patent office as fast as Alexander Graham Bell did.

Next time you come with a creative idea or invention, have it patented as soon as you are able to do so. The universe admires speed. *If you can imagine it, it's because it exists, it is all about YOU, taking action from that point and BEING TRULY READY!*

Was there an idea or invention that you had, but never pursued, maybe getting sidetracked and possibly even forgot about?

Is there an idea that you think may help the planet or humanity, but you just did not know how it could be supported or how you can just start?

Did you ever think that there are companies and people that might have an interest in what you propose, and some may even offer to fund your whole proposed idea, invention, or project fully?

Today, we hear about the many great inventors that were credited for their contribution and efforts, years after they passed away.

It would have been pleasant and rewarding for them to know that their inventions have been put to good use as a service to humanity, leaving behind a defining legacy.

The Guardian reported, "Historians and Italian-Americans had won their battle to persuade Washington to recognize a little-known mechanical genius, named Antonio Meucci, as a father of the modern communications, 113 years after his death."

The resolution declared Meucci's "teletrofono," which was demonstrated in New York in 1860, made him the inventor of the telephone in place of Bell, even though it was Bell who took out a patent sixteen years later.

"The House of Representatives senses that the life and achievements of Antonio Meucci should be recognized, and his work in regards to the invention of the telephone should be acknowledged," the resolution stated.

Well, that is just one example of many other stories that were passed on to us that "clouded" the facts.

How about another story, "Cleopatra," for example; who many believe that she was an Egyptian, the fact is: she was not.

The misconception about her nationality may have risen from the way she represented herself in public — as if the reincarnation of Isis, an Egyptian goddess.

Cleopatra, which means "glory of the father," belonged to the Ptolemaic dynasty, a family of the Greek origin that ruled Egypt after Alexander the Great. Her family actually refused to speak the language Egyptian, and she was the first to learn the language.

So, even though she was the queen of Egypt, she wasn't Egyptian. She built up the Egyptian economy, establishing trade with many Arab nations. She was a famous ruler amongst the people of Egypt.

There must have been much creative storytelling throughout history that was embedded into our minds and passed down through the generations, WITHOUT QUESTIONING the source.

Who knows how the story had come about? It may have started by a father, an aunt, a teacher, a ruler, or a priest that continued the false honored legacy.

Let us do our best to pass TRUE FACTS THAT ARE CONFIRMED, as we become creative in our storytelling unless you're writing novels or other pieces of fiction, not based on facts. Then we OWE IT to our future generations.

Above, I shared two of the many myths and stories passed down through history, that many believed and were much different from the facts.

On the other hand, below I share with you real stories, but in this example, the story had been lost to time:

House of Wisdom

Lost to time

The *House of Wisdom* was a library and a translation institute in Abbasid-era Baghdad, Iraq. It was a key institution in the Translation Movement and considered to have been a major intellectual center of the Islamic Golden Age. The house was an unrivaled center for the study of humanities and Islamic science, including Islamic mathematics, Islamic astronomy, Islamic medicine, Islamic alchemy and chemistry, zoology, and Islamic geography.

The House of Wisdom was a library where the leading Muslim scholars translated text from languages such as Chinese, Greek, Persian, Indian and Sanskrit into Arabic- Including those of Pythagoras, Plato, Aristotle, Hippocrates, Euclid, Plotinus, Galen, Sushruta, Charaka, Aryabhata, and Brahmagupta—the scholars accumulated a vast collection of world knowledge, and built it through their own discoveries.

The pursuit of knowledge became a dominant feature of the Abbasid society, attracting many scholars and scientists from all over Europe and the Middle East to take part in this cultural birthing, including many Persians and Christians. Scholarly work, especially translation, became a hugely lucrative career. Some scholars such as Hunayn ibn Ishaq were said to earn the weight in gold of each manuscript they completed. Renowned 9th-century Arab mathematician Al Khwarizmi studied in the House of Wisdom. It is his famous Book of Restoring and Balancing of the Arabic Kitab al-Jabr wa'l-muqabala, which gives us today our term 'algebra.'

Caliph al-Mamun was also himself adept in the branches of knowledge taught at the House of Wisdom, including medicine, philosophy, and astrology, and had often visited the scholars there to discuss their research. At this time, astrology was held in the highest esteem as science in Arab society.

The stars and planets were perceived to influence events on earth, and astrology was thus carried out with the greatest attention to detail.

Unfortunately, along with the other libraries in Baghdad, the House of Wisdom was destroyed during the Mongol invasion in 1258.

It is said that the waters of the Tigris ran black for six months with ink from the enormous quantities of books that were flung into the river.

Could you imagine the number of book collections lost, causing the water in the rivers to run black and lasting many months? Yet, many never even heard about this tragedy to a big intellectual center.

I wonder if such a piece of knowledge and teaching had remained, would it have influenced more understanding between different types of mindsets, cultures, and religions?

It's said that the amount of knowledge lost that year is indescribable. It is even more surprising that while most people are quite familiar with the destruction of the *Library of Alexandria*, few know about the huge loss of the *House of Wisdom*.

"Take your time to find, know and understand what you don't

know, and in the end, you shall know that it is not all the things you know that show you something you don't know, but

something you don't know." ~Ernest Agyemang Yeboah

How sad is it, the loss of such an intellectual institution, one that attracted many scholars who were legends of their time? But how nice is to have still that legacy shared, and history visited and acknowledged by those who cared to preserve and share the story of such a significant Golden era and great intellectual centers such as the House of Wisdom.

May the rebirth of the centers of wisdom and connections of amazing philosophers, mathematicians, polymaths, engineers be of focus again, bridging ancient knowledge with greater technology and shifting our societies to such interest, growth, and riches of cultures shall return.

May the *House of Wisdom* be found within our souls and never be lost in time ever again.

May its story be shared to help ignite the fire within us, influencing many to rewrite more empowering stories about themselves and project that through their actions and attitude towards life.

There is something magical when we embrace diversity, remain open to life, and are accepting of others who may have different views or beliefs than us. Let unity and education connect us with our best self-versions and may our openness charge, increase, and optimize our creativity.

The Taj Mahal

On a romantic side, many of you may have heard or even visited the spectacular Taj Mahal, one of the *World's Seven Wonders*, but did you ever find out the actual story behind the Taj Mahal?

On March 27, 1612, Prince Khurram and his beloved, to whom he had given the name Mumtaz Mahal ("chosen one of the palaces"), were married. Mumtaz Mahal was known to be smart and tender-hearted.

Mumtaz Mahal was also renowned for her beauty and her grace and was the source of inspiration for many poets and writers who had written about her beauty and charm.

"The public was enamored with her, and not in small parts because she cared for the people. She diligently made lists of the widows and orphans to ensure that they were sufficed with food and money. The couple had 14 children together, but only seven lived past infancy. It was the birth of the 14th child early in the morning on June 17, one day after the birth of their daughter, Mumtaz Mahal died in her husband's arms.

Shah Jahan vowed to his wife that he would build for her the most magnificent mausoleum as her tomb.

She was buried right away according to the Islamic tradition near the encampment at Burhanpur. Her body would not stay there for much longer.

Reports say that in Shah Jahan's anguish, he went to his tent and cried for eight days without ceasing. He was inconsolable and ordered the country into two years of mourning, and he went into solitude. When he emerged, he was said to have aged considerably, sporting white hair, and his face was worn."

Their love story inspired one of the most magnificent structures in the world. After that, Shah Jahan spent more than twenty years building the Taj Mahal in memory of his beloved wife.

Though most pictures of the Taj Mahal show only a large white building, which looked beautiful, it still doesn't do the real structure justice. These photos leave out intricacies, and it is these details that make the Taj Mahal astoundingly feminine and opulent.

On the mosque, the guest house, and the large main gate at the southern end of the complex appear passages from the Quran, which is the holy book of Islam, written in calligraphy.

Masterfully done, the finished verses from the Quran have been inlaid with black marble. They are stately yet soft features of the building. Although made of stone, the curves mimic real handwriting.

Almost more impressive than the calligraphy is the delicate inlaid flowers found throughout the Taj Mahal complex. In a process known as Parchin Kari, highly-skilled stone cutters have carved intricate floral designs into the white marble and then inlaid them with precious and semi-precious stones to form interwoven vines and flowers.

There are forty-three different kinds of precious and semi-precious stones used for these flowers, and they came from around the world. These include lapis lazuli from Sri Lanka, jade from China, malachite from Russia, and turquoise from Tibet.

One of the allures of the Taj Mahal is its continually changing hue. From dawn to dusk, the sun transforms the whole mausoleum. It may seem pearly gray and pale pink at sunrise, dazzling white at high noon, and an orange-bronze when the sunsets. In the evenings, the Taj can appear translucent blue. Special tickets are even sold for the full moon and eclipse viewings.

At his death, Shah Jahan built the Taj Mahal to serve as a tomb.

And now is an everlasting tribute of the emperor to his beloved wife– but more than that, it's a shining monument of one of the greatest love stories in history.

"Not a piece of architecture, as other buildings are, but the

proud passions of an emperor's love wrought in living stones."

~Sir Edwin Arnold

Effective Storytelling

By the way, did you ever notice while you were reading how you got engaged emotionally with a few of the stories shared, a bit of tension, a bit of connection even care to depend on what part of the story you were connecting or relating with most at that time?

Perhaps, you felt sad about Mumtaz dying in her husband's arm right after giving birth to her 14th daughter? Or upset about the myth of who the original inventor of the telephone was after finding out it was Not Alexander Graham Bell as many believed.

Or maybe you felt happy for Antonio Meucci for being recognized for his invention since he was the first to invent such a technology? Or felt disappointed about the loss of a lot of the intellectual materials found in history from the House of Wisdom.

All those emotions are normal and precisely what happens to our brain when we are engaged in listening to stories that engage our senses and pull us in.

It is also the same exact reason why we come into the world into storytelling from the time we are conceived, is it going to be a girl or a boy? I want a boy so he can be a successful businessman like me. I will teach him everything I learned and leave my business to him when I pass away. Neighbors, friends, and families celebrate the arrival of this possible boy, and then a few years later, kid graduates and the same boy's interest turns out to be in mechanical engineering with no interest whatsoever in taking over the family business. Now the parents are upset that they have to change the story they have put in their heads all these years and will have to live a different story and reality.

"You're never going to kill storytelling, because it's built-in the human plan. We come with it." ~ Margaret Atwood, author of

The Handmaid's Tale

Whether stories are real or not, they influence our emotions and connections to what is being shared. There's a reason for that. Do you know what happens in your brain when you're listening or reading a story?

I was curious and found out that few active brain chemicals are firing during storytelling to the reader that may influence their behavior and have them take action towards somewhat of a promotion or about their own lives, habits, or perception.

Our brains record information not logically, but as patterns of experiences or stories, and we explain ourselves and connect to others through stories. After reading a few articles on how storytelling influences our brain's chemistry on Medium, Forbes, and some others. I noticed there was ONE common conclusion: That being: The presences of three main neurochemicals that activate in our brain during storytelling:

1-Cortisol, when released by the brain, induces feelings of distress. It is produced when something warrants of our attention and therefore makes the audience occupied and more engaged in the story.

2-Dopamine produced to aid in an elaborate learning system that rewards us (with pleasure).

3-Oxytocin has been identified as a chemical that promotes prosocial, empathic behavior. Establish a point of emotional resonance with characters. Oxytocin leads readers to care and to take a certain action.

I also found out that: It's estimated that as much as 65 percent of all human interactions take the form of social storytelling (i.e., gossip, complaining, and empowerment). Where there are stories, there is greater potential for empathy and discovery, inspiration, and imagination.

Storytelling is about the exchange of your ideas, sharing experiences, it is about growth, and that is learning. You learn about new worlds that did not exist in your reality, creating magic and making us more understanding of other cultures, traditions, beliefs, and philosophies, creating less gap between us and their world.

We become more empathetic and feel more connected to one another. Stories teach us lessons. They expand our consciousness and our perception, making room for us to be creative, loving, wise, and more forgiving. Every storyteller has a mission and a purpose with a message they want to share. So, what is YOUR story, and how could it inspire and teach others?

Do you find it hard to share your story?

Do you feel like you might not even have a story to tell? Or perhaps you feel your story is not worth sharing?

If so, please do not feel bad. Most people feel and think that way. I did not think I had a story. From the very start of the "WHAT IS YOUR STORY" buzzword, I kept hearing; what's your story? What is the story you tell yourself? Back from 2011 Super Soul Sundays on Oprah's show and more. I still did not think I had a story; to me, my life seemed quite ordinary. After all, we all face challenges, adversity, so what makes my story better than others or perhaps more interesting? I always thought to myself.

It was not until one day as I was talking to a business partner, and him asking me a few questions about my background, as I was explaining a little more in-depth about my journey and continued to talk about my experience, he told me. "That is such an interesting background, much growth and diversity came out as a result of all that you experienced." I, for the first time, was pretty clear about my personal story, but still did not think it was a big deal to talk about or share. It was later as I was coaching more clients that I had realized how my past experiences shared with them through advice, tips, and recommendations had actually empowered and inspired them, that I started gaining more confidence in my personal story.

Today I feel elevated and see my story as a gift I share with those who might need to be encouraged from it, (knowing they are not alone, they matter, they are worth it and they too, have a story to share and a purpose to pass forward the lessons, teachings, and blessings that they have experienced; so others may heal, transform and move forward more courageously in their life.)

Understanding better that their current reality is temporary and that their story can change at any time they are ready, all it is, a decision away.

I share this with you to inspire you. In your lifetime, you might have shared enough stories of others, though it is great and wonderful and will continue to be. However, at this moment, I want you to go in your mind's eyes and start being clear of your own story. Begin writing your own STORY. It is just as important. Not the story you just tell others about yourself, but the story you tell yourself.

"Think about the word destroy. Do you know what it is? The-

Story. Destroy. Destroy. You see. And restore. That's re-story.

Life's Challenges That Enhance Creative Growth

Do you know that only two things have been proven to help

survivors of the Holocaust? Massage is one. Telling their story

is another. Being touched and touching. Telling your story is

touching. It sets you free." ~ Francesca Lia Block, author

Everyone has their stories to tell. You will be surprised how your personal story of transformation can inspire, enrich other individuals, and boost their creative thinking, creative writing, and problem-solving skills.

We all learn from each other. YOU are either teaching or learning to some degree. It's up to us to decide what we want to learn and what we want to pass forward.

"Why was Solomon recognized as the wisest man in the world?

Because he knew more stories than anyone else." ~Alan Kay,

vice president, Walt Disney Co.

In this chapter, I would also like to add the power of the story you often tell yourself and how you can become more creative in this regard using different techniques depending on which resonates best with you.

Keeping in mind, I am all about originality and uniqueness of your flavor and soul expression; this will not take away from that. However, it will help speed the process of your creative thinking.

Dr. Pillay, a tech entrepreneur and an assistant professor at Harvard University, points to a 2016 study demonstrating the impact of certain stereotypes on one's behavior and influence on creative thinking.

He explained that the conscious action of "wearing" another self—is an exercise that, according to psychiatrist Srini Pillay, MD, is an essential tool for being creative.

So, if you do not like your current story or having a hard time creating a more empowering new story of yourself, then imagine a person that you respect, admire, and is very inspiring to you. See that you are that person's confidence, charisma, and wittiness. Feel and be as if you are that archetype. You are that Poet, Doctor, Scientist, Ballerina, or Motivational Speaker.

This reminds of a program Dr. Choat offered through his online school, Mind Hack Academy, titled "Rewrite Your Life's Movie Script." This is after working along with his students and clients through a process that has transformed them. At the end of his program, they all had special instructions to do a video and produce their movie based on the new life script they wrote.

Engaging and participating in the process of your own storytelling in the form of a movie script makes it fun and allows you to tap into your creative abilities as you discover more ways of understanding, delivering and sharing your personal story.

Let me ask you:

-Are you ready to hold a pen and start writing YOUR life's movie script?

-What steps can YOU take to be in CHARGE of your life today?

-How can YOU connect with your best self-image, self-esteem, and ideal-self today and create the life you wish you have?

-Are you seeking the right sort of help (books, coaches, mentors, classes, programs) for the development of your own self-awareness and growth?

Take action, one step at a time, and continue investing in yourself. It's the best gift you can offer yourself and to the world.

Remember,

"There is no greater agony than bearing an untold story inside

you." ~ Maya Angelou

I couldn't agree more and so love that quote!

Now that you are aware of this power, relevance, and importance of storytelling and its ability to accelerate your success and expand your influence. It's wise to learn more about creative storytelling and the value it may add to the marketplace or social network, depending on what it is used for.

Do keep in mind those skilled at creative storytelling provide an edge over those who aren't. On that note, let's discover more about creative storytelling.

Creative Storytelling

With exposure to a lot of different mediums and access to too many apps and tools, CREATIVE STORYTELLING would have a more effective and compelling influence on your market or target audiences than non-creative storytelling.

So why is it important to consider creative storytelling?

When you combine storytelling with the right volume of creativity, you have the power to set your message, product, or service apart from its competition and create content that your audience will become more emotionally invested and interested in.

Get Creative in how you want to share your story. Whether you are writing, using photos, infographics or video or ALL of them, continue to explore, test your market, and take note of the feedback you receive. This will help you improve and avoid repeated and related delays.

Discover the most-watched surgeon in human history and creative storytelling

I was reading an article by Ross Thomson, Chief Creative Officer, *Greater Than One* regarding; Ahmad Shafi Ph.D., one of the world's most-watched surgeons, teacher, futurist, innovator, and entrepreneur, who employed technology as a way to teach students around the globe and performing surgery in the form of a story.

Ross Thomson shared:

Doctors themselves are employing technology as a way to tell their story: Dr. Shafi Ahmed, "the most-watched surgeon in human history," performed the first live operation using Snapchat when the technology was a bit more than a gimmick. Where once a handful of students were hunched over a surgical team, tens of thousands of student doctors are now simultaneously able to study more intricate techniques first hand. AI, AR, VR, and other technologies are giving doctors a more intimate story of their patient's health.

Dr. Ahmad Shafi was creative in his storytelling and used different tools, gadgets, and applications to deliver his teachings. He applied a non-traditional method of teaching by using divergent and design-thinking to attract his audience to him first, then his performance and service.

In another article titled: Here is the world's first surgery broadcasted on Snapchat Spectacles by, Deniz Ergürel shared:

The world's first surgery to be broadcasted via Snapchat Spectacles had happened in London.

Dr. Shafi Ahmed, an experienced cancer surgeon at the Royal London Hospital, used social media's hottest gadget to share his inguinal hernia repair operation.

The operation was recorded into ten-second-long clips with Spectacles and pushed out to Dr. Ahmed's medical students for targeted training, and his curious Snapchat followers.

(Snapchat Spectacles are a pair of sunglasses that can shoot first-person videos with a 115-degree-angle lens and upload them to Snapchat. The glasses cost $130.)

Dr. Shafi is recognized as the planet's most-watched surgeon, with more than 2 million views and 50 million Twitter posts as the numbers keep increasing.

Those who do dare to stand out, open to new experiences, explore different tools, and are utilizing technology to assist them in reaching more people and arrive faster to their desired outcomes and destinations, will be ahead than the most, who are not as curious, Interested or do not want to put the time and effort to do the work.

What equipment will you need or tools must you acquire or apps may you add to diversify your reach and maximize on your choice of delivery to share your story more effectively and creatively?

How can you personalize your business or personal brand story in a more CREATIVE manner?

Life's Challenges That Enhance Creative Growth

When is the last time you explored new possibilities to re-brand your business so it can fit better with today's technology and market?

"It's easy to come up with new ideas; the hard part is letting go

of what worked for you two years ago, but will soon be out of

date." ~Roger von Oech

Do you recall of a time when your creative ideas were listened to and acted upon?

Did you ever use creative storytelling, and if so, how did it help you?

Did you share your personal or your business story of transformation with others or write about it?

How can you practice more creative storytelling TODAY?

"Good stories surprise us. They make us think and feel. They

stick in our minds and help us remember ideas and concepts in

a way that a PowerPoint crammed with bar graphs never can."

~Joe Lazauskas and Shane Snow, the Storytelling Edge

Our brains are wired to connect with emotions and their related triggers. Storytelling with persuasion surpasses and trumps any given statistics. Improve your conversation by optimizing your creative mindset, SUPERCHARGE your content and delivery by using Creative Storytelling. There's no right or wrong way to creative storytelling; each culture has its way of telling stories. We all tell stories. It's important to tell stories in the present form as if you are there. When you get creative and connect the emotional and sensory aspects of the story, you'll draw your audience into it at a higher level. In a sense, it is the transferring of an image from you to who you're relating the story to regarding all the five senses and related emotions.

Optimize Your Creative Mindset

"We think in story. It's hardwired in our brain. Its how we make strategic sense of the otherwise overwhelming world around us." ~Lisa Cron, Wired for Story

Chapter 4:
Life's Challenges That Enhance Creative Growth

In this chapter, you'll discover...

Get to know some exciting and very creative people like:

- Ms. Patricia Rogers and learned how networking helped her transition from retirement to entrepreneurship.

- Golf Psychology Coach/Expert/Pro Davey E Whiliems and learn how embracing a simple concept and a complex one helped him discover his creative skills and invited clarity as well as success to his life.

- America's Super Mom Lachelle Adkins on how she overcame 13 years of depression to earn her title as *America's Super Mom,* which is recognized nationally.

Patricia Rogers: From Retired Corrections Lieutenant to Entrepreneur

As we go through life, we will gain many experiences and growth through each challenge. We can also learn from others who have faced significant challenges in their life and conquered with a creative mindset.

During my life, I had the privilege of meeting many beautiful people who were able to get through the many difficulties they experienced. In this chapter, you'll meet some of those people.

Meet Spirited, Ambitious, and Determined Expert, Ms. Patricia Rogers: a shaker, maker, and doer.

I met and connected with the high-spirited expert Patricia Rogers on Facebook. We were both supportive and present in each other's journey.

I must say: SPIRITED Pat has a way to draw you in with her consistent delivery and participation not to discount her video shares about her organized event facilitation, which has made her master her craft of networking both in person and currently online as well.

"I remember one time going through my feeds, and here she pops, but this time from a hospital bed just hours after surgery, she was giving her audience updates and encouragement even during such a moment. What was so incredible is that you can feel the strength at her core on a soul level while she was speaking, her unwavering faith, and her bright light was enveloping her whole presence. I have much respect for her persistence and ability to CONQUER WHAT SHE CHASED, as my friend Noel Walsh and a fantastic sales trainer/speaker would say."

91

Life's Challenges That Enhance Creative Growth

One day, I believe it was a Sunday afternoon, a post popped my newsfeed for high spirited Pat, and she was having a book title poll of her upcoming book. Today titled "Hosting Rocking Events On & Offline" which has excellent and valuable insights about event hosting directly from an expert who has mastered her craft and is passing great information for those who are new to the field or others who may be seasoned and like to explore creative avenues in career networking/event hosting and are interested in achieving further success in their industries.

I recall sending her a voice message on her Facebook messenger right after I participated in her book title poll to congratulate her.

(It's so awesome to see people excited about reaching an end goal and achieving it, it makes my heart or shall I say my soul SMILE.)

"Productivity is never an accident. It is always the result of a

commitment to excellence, intelligent planning, and focused

effort." ~ Paul J. Meyer

A few days later, I decided to pick the vitalized Pat's brain and asked her about her personal story as I wanted to learn how her creative mindset and thinking were applied to her current success. After finding out, I was happy that I had inquired.

Let me share with you how our communication went:

"I am a retired correctional lieutenant, after working 29 years

of service in law enforcement. Before retiring a few years ago, I

began to connect with other successful entrepreneurs so that I

could learn what it takes to be in control of my destiny. I

connected with influencers and joined organizations that

inspired me to use the creative parts of my mind."

She added:

"We are all unique and were born with gifts and talents

designed to give us a life full of passion and purpose."

"I couldn't agree anymore," I thought to myself.

Ms. Pat Rogers Continued:

"It would help if you discovered your gifts and decide how you want to use them to impact the lives of others.

Keyword she touched here:

"First, discover your gifts, then you can impact the lives of others.

Today many struggles with identifying their life purpose and when I had that discussion with confused clients or perhaps friends, I always suggested:

'If you can discover your passion, you will eventually discover

your gifts, which ultimately will lead you to your purpose. And

that will just make you serve the mission of your purpose as you

share your gifts passionately and much more joyously at ease.'

Patricia Believes: "'*Motivation'* comes from within, but inspiration is passed on by the ones who have reached the pinnacle of success by sharing their experience for others to model."

She continued adding:

"Using a creative mindset is how I have made my life more meaningful. I value my creativity, embrace it, believe in it, and I honor it. Napoleon Hill in *Think and Grow Rich*, chapter 6, said it best; *"the imagination is the workshop wherein all basic or new ideas are handed over to man."* You may have heard it said that man could create anything that he can imagine.

Once I discovered my gifts and my talents, I learned that I could decide on how I wanted to use them so that I could become the entrepreneur that I envisioned myself to be.

The creative part of my mind that had been lying dormant came alive when I TOOK CONTROL of my destiny."

"Great realization Patricia!" I thought to myself and wondered how we are one decision away from creating the life we desire and truly deserve by taking control and responsibility of our journey and becoming more active in the Co-Creative process!

"So, how did you use your gifts to become the woman you are today I asked?"

An Aware Pat answered:

"My zone of genius is creating an environment that will allow everyone involved to take their personal and professional life to a new level, getting the exposure they desire to market their brand.

I have been using my gifts to connect people by hosting workshops, annual conferences, conducting live videos, group coaching, online training, and any other means that will allow me to be of service to others.

While *BELIEVING in the VISION* that I have imagined for my life, my creative mind has allowed me to be:

· Curious

· Positive

· Audacious

· Persistent

· Original

· Self-believing

Your skills are invaluable. Whether you monetize your gifts or share your talents for free, it all starts with the creative part of your mind. Genuine people skills and connections are vital to the success of every individual.

Creativity is what we were born to do, and no matter who may have done something similar, remember, you are unique, and no one will do it like you."

"I couldn't agree more," I said, "and YES, Patricia, each of us is unique in our skills and abilities, and by continuing to create and serve, WE GROW!"

"So, how do you develop a 'Creative Mindset?" I asked.

Her Answer:

"By submerging yourself around like-minded individuals, some of which are more knowledgeable than yourself.

The business of networking is one of the most powerful resources that will give you a more fulfilling life, along with the support that will allow you to walk in your purpose.

People are our best resources. Service is the key to real success, and when you connect with those who have what you want, you are sure to succeed in your endeavors. 'People Need People!'"

Her message to the readers is:

"Check my website in the Reference Section and connect with me on all my social media platforms."

Patricia is undoubtedly a "Social Butterfly" who participates in a vast amount of networking arenas.

Takeaways from Pat Rogers:

1-Live your dream by discovering your internal gifts and then decide how you want to use them to impact the lives of others around you.

2-Take charge of your life and prepare for your success by surrounding yourself with people who are successful in what you are interested in and learn from them, ask questions, read, evaluate, observe, then take courageous action towards your desired goals.

3- Use the power of collaboration through business and online social networks to increase the audience, effect, speed, impact, and power of your message

Apply a creative mindset by using your imagination, be open to opportunity, embrace risk-taking, generate ideas, stay curious and hungry towards life, grow, and serve.

A confident Patricia was self-believing, used her effectiveness, and pushed herself upwards and outwards; she had a very positive mindset. She was very dedicated to accomplishing her goals and serving her mission. She still does to this day.

"The price of success is hard work, dedication to the job at hand, and the determination that whether we win or lose, we have applied the best of ourselves to the task at hand." ~Vince Lombardi

Have you ever experienced a life-changing event and felt insecure, scared, and fearful of going through it?

How did you apply your thinking skills? What was driving you? FEAR of what? HOPE of what?

What could you have done differently back then to achieve better results? Did you use your imagination and your visualization powers to create a better future vision?

What story were you telling yourself?

If you have a good outcome, what was its leading force, did you apply any creative skills?

What was your thinking and action process?

Sometimes it's good to revisit areas that we felt challenged to learn the skill and techniques of problem-solving we used in areas of each challenge. Do this at the time to understand them better and feel more at ease in the future if/when faced with similar or different challenges.

Take notes and record your progress!

Growth is a Continuing Progression

In life, we continue to grow, change, and understand things much differently based on our life experience and our current knowledge. When we do this, both our perception and consciousness get expanded.

Has this ever happened to you? You read a book, two years later you revisit it, and all of a sudden something in it resonates more than it had before. You see it more clearly and understand it better (What it was teaching is making more sense and appears more evident).

On the other hand, you may have believed in many truths, concepts, and traditions that felt real to you, then suddenly, they started not to make much sense or have logic to their existence!

Did you ever hear a story from a friend, felt touched, engaged and believed it, you even took sides with your friend against the other party then after few weeks, months or years later realized that after hearing the story from the other party that they too have a point and felt compassion towards them as well with time and experience you understood their point of you better as well?

I share this with you, so you always are reminded to stay open to possibilities and flexibility with change as viewing matters from multiple perspectives is healthy as one same thing might have two different meanings, realities, and ways of operation depending on with what angle you are looking at it.

This leads me to the next story that I will be sharing with you, but just before we move forward, I want to encourage you to those certain evaluate areas in your life that can be improved using some of the learning from each story and shared experiences.

Life's Challenges That Enhance Creative Growth

"Fools say that they learn by experience. I prefer to profit from

others experience." ~Otto von Bismarck

I believe personal experience is essential for growth; however, we can avoid any unnecessary pain and the repetition of mistakes, learning from others that share some clever life hacks that will help us arrive safer and faster to our desired outcomes.

Achieving creative growth through struggles is not only rewarding to the individual going through it but is rather inspirational to those witnessing it as well. At that point in time, it may seem very challenging, risky, uncomfortable, overwhelming even possibly devastating, but it is through that process that one can genuinely achieve valuable creative growth.

It is almost like when someone challenges you to jump into a pool that is filled with ice-cold water. You know how to swim, but you also are not a fan of cold showers, winter months, snow, and for sure do not feel excited about jumping in a cold freezing pool.

Then all of a sudden, just when you were about to answer and refuse to accept the challenge, your friend pushes you in. You were probably mad, angry, even frustrated. Still, immediately you started swimming more into the water as you adjust with your body's temperature and started to enjoy the thrill of the feeling you're in, or you started swimming back to the edge of the pool ready to get out.

You could have felt the thrill, shock, impact, or disturbance of your experience at that moment.

However, maybe in the future, when you reflect, you will be reminded of your resilience, will power, ability to adjust and adapt when put in uncomfortable situations. Or you may have enjoyed the challenge, appreciated the experience, felt rejuvenated, and wanted to do some more of it.

"No man ever steps in the same river twice, for it's not the same

river and he's not the same man." ~Heraclitus

Davey E. Williams: The Journey of a Golf Pro, Coach, and Teacher

This leads me to Golf Psychology Coach/Expert Davey E. Williams who is also the Creator of *The CSure Lifestyle, CSure Golf & the PARTEE Method,* and how his view and perception shifted about ideas that once were complex and in a state of surrender. Even golf, which once seemed complicated, became a favorite sport, and he is now coaching in that arena.

Davey E Williams was a guest on *Meet the Author Show,* and throughout our social media interactions, we maintained a respectful connection that developed to loyal friendship, and now he considers me a soul sister to him, which in return makes him a soul brother of mine.

Reading Introspective Davey's book, *"The CSure Lifestyle,"* I came to realize the gift he possesses in simplifying things. It was interesting to read his own lifetime partner/wife share his very unique thinking out of the box style school of thought, which she mentions in the foreword of his book, and that there was not a box, in reality, to begin with, was fascinating to her.

Well, all I can tell beautiful Breanne Williams you're not alone on that conclusion sweetheart, as you mentioned many are as well.

I so love to see life partners acknowledging, empowering, and appreciating each other—something both Davey and beautiful Breann both express and share.

I see how Introspective Davey has truly dove into two interesting life concepts in his coaching career. Many can gain useful insights, more clarity, and better direction from.

That is life at the Seashore and in the game of golf. You will learn more about each as Davey shares his insights on how he had tapped into his creative mindset and how he was aware and connected to his inner self as his creative juices taste different as he transitions the seasons of his life.

Davey is focused on teaching the importance of embracing simplicity with one's process rather than chasing results; he emphasizes on the importance of EMPOWERING the process for better, sustainable results.

Life's Challenges That Enhance Creative Growth

I asked Davey what his thoughts on creativity are when it comes to mindset especially that is an area in Golf Coaching you focused on?

His Answer:

"We all have a creative side. Some of us use it artistically, while others channel it through singing, instruments, and so on. My creativity was something I always had, but I always lacked an understanding of my gifts.

When we think about being creative, there needs to be a foundation as to what inspires that fire and stimulates those juices.

As a boy and young man, I was always fascinated by two things more than anything else. The simplicity of the beach and the complications of mastering the game of golf.

As my life and career began to take shape in my early twenties, I focused more on the beach, which became the foundation of my platform, The *CSure Lifestyle*. I still followed golf, but my energy and path directed me towards personal development & motivational speaking.

At thirty-nine years of age, my creative juices began tasting differently than my successful years as an entrepreneur. I could not place it. Then, something magical happened. I went to play a round of golf for the first time in fifteen years.

All of a sudden, the juices started tasting better. The flavors became clearer. My path was paved already, and I had simply taken a detour, or may I say I was meant to experience what I needed to be better prepared in and understand what the game of golf meant on many levels in my life and mindset.

As 2019 continued, so did my clarity. The beach was designed to be my foundation, my mentality.

The misunderstanding of how to channel my creativity was in my methodology. Though I was achieving success, something was still off. Something was missing, but what was so becoming, is the fact that missing thing found ME! It was the game of golf, there all along.

You see, in my prior decisions within my process, I embraced my new mantra of "adopting a mentality and adopting a methodology, creating the results needed," but it still seemed to be forced.

It was when a few months back, I allowed the universe to find me more than me finding it. Now, at 40 years of age, after 15 years of taking time off, my creativity has teed itself off, and the entire ocean became vividly bright, and that creative juice was amazing in taste.

I was able to bridge my prior knowledge and experience with its success results from my *CSure* concept and created *CSure golf* as a path for others to find their alignment off and on the course.

The simplicity of *The CSure Lifestyle* brings empowerment to building your mental equipment first as a golfer and building a bag around that foundation.

Today I feel content and fulfilled. I am serving my purpose, but also living my passion.

What I learned along the rough, the bunkers and hazards of my path granted me the power to see my fairway as the ocean of opportunity and the holes as my waves."

"So, how did that influence your creativity?" I asked him.

He answered:

"My creativity wasn't forced. My process wasn't forced. Everything aligned because I chose to be aware of all of these things, which fueled my ability to maximize my gifts to empower others in an entertaining, unique, and exciting way!

If I can create a brand of simplicity and can align analogies and humor, I know that anyone can channel their creativity when they allow it to stem from a clear foundation and an awareness that the universe reciprocates what we deliver to it.

Currently, I am playing and coaching full time within golf & that of Golf Psychology."

"Wonderful!" I was thinking to myself as he continued talking, "I do love to hear when people are living on a purpose and feel fulfilled and enjoying serving their mission like Purpose-driven work positions is to be a victor in life, dealing with challenges better, marking room for us to be more efficient and effective like Davey was able to do."

"So, what is some advice you can leave for anyone reading your story Davey," I asked?

He responded:

"You cannot do much with a $10k set of clubs and a ten-cent mentality. You can thrive, sustainably, with a $10k mentality and ten cents set of clubs."

"Great advice Davey" I added, "As it is with a prosperous mindset that we may progress. A lacking mentality always is limiting and hindering on many levels and areas of our lives."

"So how are you combining your two concepts of the *CSure* Simplicity and the Complexity of the game of golf?"

He replied:

"I created *CSure golf* around the same principles of simplicity within The *CSure Lifestyle* platform.

Now I can help show people how simple this is! The good news is all it takes is a choice and courage to take action.

If you'd like to learn more about taking control of your entire process, on and off the course, you need to align with the right mentors and coaches.

I take much pride in my authentic delivery and

accomplishments of sustainable success, helping individuals

find their own CSure and always remember, "A Mentality plus

a Methodology Equal the Lifestyle!" ~DEW Jr.

Don't find magic. CREATE IT!"

Well, all I can say is: Learn from Davey how sometimes the process of surrender and allowing itself can CREATE MAGIC.

Davey's insights:

1-Understand the wisdom of connecting two separate concepts to create something new.

2-Simplicity is an art not many will master, but when it is, the process becomes more sustainable.

3-Coach Davey believes that there is a synergy between the game of life and that of golf. Observe, learn and apply it into your life.

I find it so interesting how we create analogies that, with their connections, we understand as different areas of our life become a lot easier.

So, why not go out there and create your own magical moments!

Being creative gives us opportunities to try out new ideas and ways of thinking. See the big picture of your life, use what you have learned from the past, create a better framework so you can be in an ethical and balanced emotional state, and become better at problem-solving.

Every science innovation, technological break-through, communication advance, were sparked by creative thinking.

So, what could it be that is standing in the way between you and your creative potential?

What parts of the puzzle are you missing to complete your beautiful artwork and creative projects or perhaps a new curriculum?

Creativity makes life more exciting, enjoyable, fun, and exciting!

Last, I will leave you to ponder on this question:

"If today were the last of your life, would you do what you were going to do today?" ~ *Steve Jobs*

Then ask yourself: Why?

Mental Health and Creativity

A View into the Mind and What You Can Do to Liberate
Yourself

Aside from a loud background noise that some might be able to shut off or distractions that they may choose to eliminate by saying NO, may that be of people, noise, and thoughts.

There is some rising concern of distractions that many may feel uneasy about shutting off, Distractions that may be invading their mental and emotional space, and make them feel stuck in unhealthy environments.

"People who have worked in the arts throughout history have

dealt with poverty, persecution, social alienation, psychological

trauma, substance abuse, high stress, and other such

environmental factors which are associated with developing and

perhaps causing mental illness." (Wikipedia)

A rising concern in the area of mental health and illness is noticeable, and we must not overlook its possible side effects on our creativity and innovation. Generating ideas and being creative is not enough to achieve successful outcomes. Having a system that makes such creative ideas harvest more innovation requires focus, positive discipline, a bright and healthy mindset.

According to the *World Mental Health Organization*, one in four people in the world is affected by mental or neurological disorders at some point in their lives. Now that is a high ratio of 1 out of 4 when we think about it.

Around 450 million people currently suffer from such a condition, placing mental disorders amongst the leading causes of ill-health and disability worldwide.

Whether it is a lack of creativity and innovation or being creative and dealing with mental illnesses such as bipolar disorder, schizophrenia, substance abuse, alcohol dependence, and other destructive factors.

These are the areas that need to be visited and clarified for optimal results when it comes to optimizing a creative mindset.

We see and know of many artists and creators who were diagnosed with such mental illnesses, all of which can be exhausting, if not addressed, treated, and managed well—leading many to dark nights of the soul.

The most typical symptoms commonly found amongst artists are substance abuse, depression, bipolar disorder, and suicide, according to Shelley Carson, a lecturer researcher at Harvard University.

"Mental illness is not a personal failure. If there is a failure, it is to be found in the way we have responded to people with mental and brain disorders," said Dr. Gro Harlem Brundtland, Director-General of WHO, on releasing the World Health Report. "I hope this report will dispel long-held doubts and dogma as well as mark the beginning of a new public health era in the field of mental health.

I share this with you in the hope that we can all be both aware and compassionate to the ones around us; we can't see the hidden scars of verbal and emotional abuse neither read the self-sabotaging thoughts people are hiding and suffering from internally or the void they are experiencing. So, we must not take things personally, help when, and with what we can.

If you are reading this and it is YOU (that may be going through some mental pressure and feeling strong emotions such as anxiety, pressure, high levels of mental stress, and lack of focus/ proper cognition) please STOP THE SUFFERING, ask for help and make an effort to seek professional help.

People judge themself thinking that dealing with such issues makes them look weak, not sane, or even crazy depending on their cultural background they grew up in, or programmed beliefs downloaded deep into their minds. They become more sensitive and suppress more of their emotions, and with time, they just cannot hold more, and their situation gets worse.

The disease of the mind creates the disease of the body. It takes more courage and self-love for us to face our inner demons than to fake our happiness.

Courage is a critical word to understand, a powerful noun. The definition of courage is the bravery and strength to do something that could be dangerous to do something quite frightening. An example of courage is the ability to stand up to a bully.

Even if your bully is a FEAR that keeps frightening you from standing up for yourself or even others, or it may perhaps be a relationship that you need to have left yesterday.

A new chapter with your new movie script that YOU choose to write can START TODAY. Why not permit yourself to feel better? Yes, you may be more comfortable living in the certainty that you have, and choosing to suffer may seem more comfortable than facing the unknown and sure to you.

Why not permit yourself to feel better?

That is normal, as it may feel safer at the moment in your head.

However, what if on the other side of fear and acceptance to your existing suffering reality was liberation and joy?

What if you re-discovered YOURSELF after a long time, what if the result was so much co-creating and participating in life?

What if you realized the caged bird that was comfortable knowing its being fed by its homeowners, has wings, and can fly not just out of the cage but above even the ceilings of their house?

What if that bird escaped out of the door and discovered his true nature landing on different trees, realizing it can, in fact, tweet, Twitter "cheep" and "chirp?"

What if drinking from different sources of water, springs, rivers, ocean tasted even better than the one it was used to by his loving owners?

What if this bird now makes friends and traveled the world freely and fearlessly discovering new places and creating fun experiences?

What if that bird was YOU?

Just know, you deserve inner peace along with mental clarity and focus (a great base to create from).

It is essential to understand your emotions and be able to describe your feelings. You do not have to go through anything alone. Remember that and never forget the power of merely ASKING for help when you need it—changing your mindset when you need it.

Take action steps when you need it!

This leads me to share a story of a woman who suffered from depression for 13 years. YES, thirteen years, and NO, she did not commit suicide but was able to step out of her comfort zone, change her mindset, and make much better and healthier choices for her life.

"It doesn't have to take over your life, it doesn't have to define

you as a person, it's just important that you ask for help. It's

not a sign of weakness." ~Demi Lovato

LaChelle Adkins: Finding Her Calling through Depression

Let me introduce you to Inspirational speaker and Coach LaChelle Adkins, also known as *"America's Super Mom."*

YOU heard it, "that is in your EYES if you're reading this... HAHAHA!"

Yes, America's Super Mom, and to be worthy of such a title, you know there is a story behind it, and there is!!!

First, I would like to share with you a bit about Super Lachelle Adkins's background as her story has inspired many across the globe.

As for Me, I met Super Lachelle through friends on the Facebook platform then later on a closer parameter via a few webinars hosted by Speaker, Coach, Artist, and Singer Madeline Faiella. I was curious to find out more about her back story, especially after I found out that she has a total of thirteen children of her own, and 2 adopted a total of fifteen.

I have noticed her engagement in the areas of growth and learning was consistent. What keeps her going, I thought to myself?

How is she managing to dedicate her time while having such a big responsibility and a big family to cater at home?

I mean, I had to raise one son and remember how occupied my schedule had become, especially after picking him up from school. Between schoolwork, picking up and dropping him off to his martial arts class, basketball, piano, and later guitar, all that was quite demanding. This was especially when I had regularly had signed for additional self-awareness classes or certifications for my personal growth.

I always looked up to my older sister, who had seven children and homeschooled them mostly till elementary. Seeing her alone made me often wonder how she was able to do that.

What I admire most about her family unit was her kids (my nieces and nephews) were smart, respectful, and very affectionate. Both she and her husband did a great job raising them.

I always looked up to my sister as she was a dedicated mother and wife at the same time in many seasons of our life, If any time I called to ask her opinion about anything, she seemed always to have a logical answer. She was a book worm growing up and won many contests, even scholarships in school and during her Master's Program at George Washington University.

It was always fascinating to me as she was the closest in the immediate family that I got to witness a family unit of seven children with such involved parents to me that was just amazing.

Years later, I got to meet a dear friend through work who today I consider as a family to me, and that is the powerful Don Crupi, who is of Italian origin and has nine children. As we developed a good friendship, he introduced me to his beautiful wife, Deborah, and later to all their beautiful children.

Today, Deb is a DIVA for grandma; she never lost her charisma, beauty, and sense of humor after all the years I have known her.

I was honored to attend several occasions of the awesome Crupi's, including their beautiful son's wedding, birthday parties, and Christmas Eve dinner celebrations, and more.

Don and Deborah Crupi have such an interesting story of how they got married, and their life journey will need another book to give it a fair share. However, they, too, had managed to maintain such a bonded family unit.

Don would cook pasta and meatballs every Sunday as part of their family tradition, and that was prepared by his own secret Italian recipe spaghetti sauce.

Yes, his SECRET recipe because I remember when someone asked him how he prepared this amazing spaghetti sauce? He responded: If I tell you, I must kill you. Okay, he was kidding, but the recipe of the sauce remains to be a secret of the Crupi's!

I continued to be amazed by these examples (my sister's family and the Crupi family) as my only genuine personal connection, direct experience, and relationships of what I considered a big family in our time and day.

Then, I met and learned about America's Super Mom LaChelle. It was a notch further in my heightened curiosity just from the bit of info I gathered through our brief media interaction and research.

I decided to give her a call and ask her some questions to understand better her back story, also to see if she would be willing to share it with all of *OPTIMIZE YOUR CREATIVE MINDSET* community and readers, after all, she managed to get many people's attention including the National Media, such as *The Rachael Ray Show*, *NBC News* and more!

My first call was smooth and delightful; Super LaChelle was very welcoming and expressed her gratitude to be able to contribute, hoping that others can be inspired and empowered by her journey.

"There's always room for a story that can transport people to another place." ~ J.K. Rowling, novelist, screenwriter and film producer

FYI, See the power of storytelling? I believe it does wonders for the one sharing the story and one learning about.

Unstoppable LaChelle expressed her passion for sharing her experiences to help empower women and to overcome life's obstacles and live a fulfilled life, hoping they could learn from her experiences and not have to go through years of depression before they can finally come out and some sadly do not.

When I asked Super LaChelle to share a little about her journey of depression to determination and now contribution.

She Responded:

"How do I condense my journey of depression and hospitalization in a conversation or to even paragraphs?

The downward spiral that was ever-present, but I just didn't see it.

Let's begin in a suitable place. I was an only child that was raised to be independent and value education, which I was told would provide the lifestyle that I desired. This mindset of being self-sufficient and the belief that I could control all the elements was a recipe for disaster that would take 13 years to break free."

"Can you explain more on that?" I asked.

She continued:

"How do I cook, clean, breastfeed, manage relationships, manage finances, help with homework, and maintain a healthy marriage?

My childhood included both of my parents working and attending School field trips and class parties was not possible.

So, while I had the ambitious goal of staying home, I had no example or formula to follow.

My only example was the mothers on soap operas, and their access to a lifestyle with no financial limits was not my reality.

I was raised to believe; I can have anything if I worked hard, so I believed this fixed convergent thinking would serve me with being a stay home mom.

The idea of applying a few solutions to all that I encountered seemed to make sense to me. I believed my children would fit nicely in a parenting box, and one form of discipline and communication would work for everyone.

I believed that analysis of their needs allowed me to compose one list of standards that would work well on all the children regardless of their age, gender, or personality.

I had no idea that this mindset would position me to be powerless. I would be the victim of other people's definitions of what working hard looked like."

"I fully agree," I said.

She continued:

"I sought validation from my husband, children, church members, and strangers. I was always led to my actions by pleasing others and working to help them often at my own expense.

My mindset was that sacrifice is reasonable, and I will have joy when I complete my mission with my children.

I continued to seek validation and approval from others, and when I didn't receive it, I added another brick to my wall of isolation. My coping strategy for protection served to isolate me from receiving real connections because I only valued connections that catered to my recognition. I craved all the accolades and worked tirelessly to receive them, yet when I achieved them, I still felt empty and unfulfilled."

"I can understand what you are saying as living in many parts of the world and being raised by a stay at home mother, and for the first few years after my only child was born being one myself, I was often surrounded by many women who felt the same way about their children and themselves," I responded.

Super LaChelle continued:

"I believed their happiness and development was the number one priority and had no idea that I could be happy simultaneously."

"And how did that mindset serve you?" I asked.

Super LaChelle answered:

"Well, that mindset led me down a dark path.

How can I receive so much attention and respect when I feel powerless with no direction or courage to be my authentic self?

There was no creative or divergent thinking - everything was one size fits all, no hope of other possibilities or solutions but one."

"That would cause a blurry vision and could be rather exhausting to our soul." I added."

Super LaChelle responded:

"Yes, it was very exhausting to my soul and provided a very blurry vision to my path that led me to confusion, emotional isolation, and later depression."

"Can you explain more to me on that?" I asked

She responded:

"I lost my identity with people-pleasing and didn't recognize myself in the mirror. I was tired of hiding behind masks and went on the journey to find that person that I lost 13 years ago.

Although to many, I looked like that mom who had it all together, I did hit a breaking point three times with hospitalization for depression—starting from 2003 to 2016.

For 13 years, I was on autopilot and numb to any emotional connections. I was in a house surrounded by children and my spouse, yet, I felt alone and isolated. I don't recall crying and showing any emotion. I was numb if my children were in pain from receiving immunizations to accidents with playtime. I had no empathy and felt like I followed a script of "the motherly" thing to say and do. I might have been comforting them, but I was emotionally disconnected."

"OH, WOW that is quite a time, so sorry to hear that," I answered. Three times and to reach a stage that you had to get hospitalized, it must have been very stressful; feeling numb and alone when you were surrounded by your family is not a good emotion to live with. Having a mental illness, in your case, in the form of a long period of "depression," does not make one a bad parent. As a parent, you did the best you can for your children at that time. But sometimes, mental illness might make it hard to be the parent you wanted to be.

Indeed, frequently turning off your emotions may lead to unhealthy behaviors like lack of empathy like you mentioned earlier, which can lead to a series of unstable shallow relationships. Including people-pleasing and losing your own voice and identity like what you faced. I responded, "So, how did you put an end to getting to such low points?" I asked?

Super LaChelle responded:

"I desired a change, so I began to analyze why this happened three times? What were the similarities? Triggers? Habits/daily routines? I viewed this experience as a public failure, and how did I know it wasn't going to happen a fourth time?

These questions sparked a desire to empower myself to ensure it didn't occur again."

I responded:

"You have asked yourself some really good questions, asking questions truly expands our minds and vision to possibilities that we otherwise might have never discovered!

So how did you ensure this never happened again as you mentioned in one the questions you asked yourself?"

Super LaChelle responded:

"I was no longer interested in a Band-Aid but a permanent lifestyle change.

How could I blend that physical reality with a new mindset?"

"Fascinating and great observation, you managed to see clearly after some deep soul searching and asking some important questions. Just as Eugene Ionesco once quoted: *'It is not the answer that enlightens, but the question.'*" I responded.

"So, what was your process and the mindset you had that helped you transition from your many long years of depression?" I asked.

She responded:

"I created a strategy, which I named fresh start. It is an acronym for a set of principles that have guided me to a more fulfilled life that consists of joy and balance."

"How wonderful is that," I responded. "I love the name you gave your strategy through your acronym FRESH START, as that is such a great foundation to build on.

I love acronyms when used right, as they make us remember faster and relate better to what we want to prioritize, implement, and apply to our life.

I must add that they are used by a conscious choice with clear intention and are defined the first time they are shared with another so they can make sense of them both in verbal and written communications."

"So, can you explain and define your strategy and your acronym Fresh Start?" I asked.

"Sure," she responded:

"The Fresh strategy consists of five pillars that are an acronym for the word fresh. F - Fear as fuel; R - reframe your story; E- envision your goals; S - support; H - healing. In each of these pillars, you have the power to choose the outcome you desire.

In my case, I was just allowing life to happen to me. I was reactive rather than proactive. I walked around wearing my victimization like it was a badge of honor.

Now I understand why I felt defeated because, in many cases, I lacked vision and clarity. As a result, I blamed others for my circumstances and rarely examined my actions and the part I played in my outcomes. It was not until I applied this strategy that I was able to have self-awareness and not be threatened by my past and my previous life choices.

I was able to stand up and realize that my real power was in being a victor instead of a victim. Besides, I realized that the only change I could ultimately control was my own."

"Love it and what a great realization and outcome you arrived at. As it is only when we take responsibility for our actions and own them can we really make necessary changes that are indeed vital for our growth." I responded. "During this process of transition and progress, did you seek any outside support from friends or get professional help?" I asked.

She replied:

"Now that was a challenge when you have 13 children at home waiting to see how long this "change" will last. Yet, it was those doubts that led me to seek help from a coach and to surround myself with likeminded people who could see where I was headed and show me how to get there.

Those alliances helped me to transform my mindset from surviving to thriving. A reality that was completely foreign to me.

This reminds me of a quote by Mariah Carey, "It was too heavy a burden to carry, and I simply couldn't do that anymore. I sought and received treatment, I put positive people around me, and I got back to doing what I love – writing songs and making music."

How beautiful! The more people I talk to, who had gone through adversities and personal challenges, share they had some sort of support either through coaching, therapy, support groups, mentors, and religious organizations.

As many times as much as we love our loved ones yet, what or how we explain or say things to them might not resonate the same as a total wise stranger may deliver the same message."

"So happy to see such a transformation in your life Super LaChelle," I responded. "How did your transformation influence your thinking and life?"

She responded:

"My experiences have led me to apply divergent thinking more to my life, which leads me to thrive daily."

I responded:

"Coming up with many solutions to one problem and asking open-ended questions, as well as adapting to, diversifying and modifying and eliminating as you did to transition from your fixed one size fit all convergent thinking to recognizing there are other possibilities and better options of thinking styles when used and applied can make such massive impact to our lives.

You mentioned thriving daily, how are you able to reach sustainable success as a result of your transformation?"

She responded:

"The core principles that I use to maintain success are authenticity, learning, and collaboration. I have successfully found my true voice: I am clear about my beliefs and convictions, and they are my moral compass. I now know who I am and have no need to seek validation from others."

"Finding YOUR voice and understanding YOUR beliefs as well as knowing yourself and living without the need to seek validation is a big discovery and accomplishment, many suffer from and end their own lives from too. That must have been very freeing to your soul." I responded.

"In the past, you needed to control outcomes you mentioned, how were you able to Real Estate such need?" I asked.

Super LaChelle responded:

Learning has helped me to evolve and have gratitude, empathy, and realize I don't know everything.

I happily embrace every day with a childlike curiosity and enthusiasm for trying new things."

Aha, I thought to myself, Bingo!

"There is such joy and excitement when we connect to our childlike curiosity, the unfolding of the unknown invites, and keeps us more on our toes and waiting to see what of the new that is waiting to enter. Trying new things invites new experiences to our soul, something we all on a deeper level crave."

"You mentioned learning helped you evolve what else contributed to your successful transformation?" I asked.

She responded:

Collaboration, collaboration has allowed me to embrace my limits and realize that I can accomplish more with a team rather than alone.

This team mindset has opened me up to opportunities I would have never dreamed of as well as some phenomenal connections."

"Very cool," I responded.

According to experts in the *National Education Association.*

The 4C's that are in demand in the 21st century are:

COMMUNICATION.

COLLABORATION.

CREATIVITY.

CRITICAL THINKING.

I would add Divergent and Holistic thinking to that. Also, I teach on the importance of understanding the power of positive collaboration and when, where, and how to apply it. That is awesome that you realized the value of collaboration, and it is now a grand alliance supporting your growth and personal mission.

So, looking at your past, if you had the power to, would you have changed anything in particular?"

Super LaChelle responded:

"In conclusion, I am shocked to admit that I have no regrets from my past.

I have grown from every disappointment, and I am genuinely passionate about helping other women come from that darkness that plagued me for forty-six years."

"That is very good to know; you reached an awareness of seeing the growth that every disappointment you lived has had to offer. Today you are taking all the lessons and wanting to help other women overcome such obstacles. That is when we know we are truly in a good place when we want and can serve others." I responded.

Life's Challenges That Enhance Creative Growth

When asked what LaChelle's typical day looks like today.

She responded:

"My typical days consist of juggling marriage, ministry, career, charity, and tending to 13 of my 15 children with a smile instead of stress.

Is everyday sunshine- no. I have just managed to understand that I can choose the life I want, and my power is in what I choose to do and how I choose to respond. So today and always - I choose to be happy."

"WOW!" I thought to myself, "What a great personal transformation thirteen children that she is attending to had suffered from depression for thirteen years and managed to overcome all the pressure she was under."

"Vulnerability is the birthplace of innovation, creativity and

change." ~Brené Brown

Points to Embrace as learned from LaChelle:

Always question and challenge your beliefs if they are not serving you in the best way possible.

Take responsibility for your actions and the blame game. This will build your inner core as well as strengthen your mental muscle when you experience emotional or physical pain. This will assist in your personal growth.

Stop being a people pleaser all the time. You should not be seeking validation from others about your decisions. You'll only end up "going down a rabbit hole" towards depression.

Give up trying to take control of outcomes. You should, instead, make space for creative thinking and better problem solving using divergent thinking. Embrace it with a child-like curiosity.

Don't go about creating the life you want alone. Find a team to assist and support you on your journey. When you do, your life will improve dramatically and faster.

"The EMOTIONAL CLIMATE we create will influence both how WE feel and make OTHERS around us feel. Living with NO REGRETS is such a liberated feeling to have." ~Dr. Sofie Nubani

Living with no regrets was something Super LaChelle was able to foster through her efforts of understanding herself better and on deeper levels.

It is unhealthy to oppress thoughts. As admitting to ourselves, true feelings are vital to reaching a present happy moment. Admitting to ourselves any regrets from our past. It is perfectly ok and healthy; it will help us understand better ourselves and our feelings.

Though it may sound negative for some anything that we don't manage well and have clarity on will haunt us down until we are ready to face it and deal with it, it will never go away.

Life can be overwhelming, and because of the high demand for our energy, sometimes that we may feel empty or drained.

In such a state, it's very hard to create. Self-care, love, and above all being aware of that are vital to your progress and transition.

"There is such Liberation to our Soul when we UNDERSTAND what the underlying emotion that is directing our behavior is. For you to understand others best, it is wise to start with Self First." -Dr. Sofie Nubani

How can understand yourself better? What patterns are you repeating that are destructive to your creativity?

What outcomes in your life are you blaming others about?

What can you create TODAY? Who may be a good collaboration to consider with both a personal/professional level and why?

Life's Challenges That Enhance Creative Growth

Don't limit yourself to only your available resources. You should instead explore and see who might be a good vibrational fit, purposely aligned, and mission/vision in agreement with your values, principles, and passion.

Don't stand in your own way. Instead, turn your struggles to sparkles! Be your best cheerleader and ***GO OUT THERE, BE PRESENT AND CREATE!***

"There is no doubt that creativity is the most important human

resource of all. Without creativity, there would be no progress,

and we would be forever repeating the same patterns." ~

Edward de Bono, Author

Chapter 5:
Crisis in Creativity?

In this chapter, you'll discover...

- Creativity Crisis

- Creative Mindset vs. Destructive Mindset

We Are Facing a Creativity Crisis

The above statement was posted, according to a study by *William & Mary's* Dr. Kyung-Hee Kim. She spent the last 25 years researching creativity in the United States as well as a *Reception of Torrance Award* from the *American Creativity Association*. In 2010, she coined the phrase "Creativity Crisis." It referred to the steady decline in scores on the *Torrance Tests of Creative Thinking* (equivalent to an IQ test in creativity) since 1990.

A research study, *"The Creativity Crisis,"* was the subject of a 2010 Newsweek cover story that captured the world's attention. Frequently sought after by the media, Dr. Kim has shared her expertise with numerous outlets. These include *the New York Times, Wall Street Journal, U.S. News & World Report*, and other publications. Her studies found that, even though America's IQ scores are on the rise, the country's scores on the Torrance Tests of Creative Thinking have been declining since 1990.

An article from Harvard Business Review: "America's Looming Creativity Crisis" by Richard Florida shared much insightful information that is summed up by this message "The real long-term predicament facing the United States and the world is the looming shortage of creative talent."

A press release by *The Toy Association's* Adrienne Appell expanded on this: *HOW CAN WE SOLVE AMERICA'S "CREATIVITY CRISIS"?* There's no denying that we are faced with a creativity crisis, with studies showing that American creativity has been on the decline since the 1990s. "Unfortunately, really young children are suffering the most," said Ken Seiter, the executive vice president of marketing communications at *The Toy Association*. "Many parents and educators see playtime as an extracurricular activity, when in fact it is crucial to helping children learn how to think outside of the box, and instrumental in ensuring a bright and prosperous future for our country.

Arthur Daemmrich, Ph.D., director of the Smithsonian's Lemelson Center for the Study of Invention and Innovation, said: "Supporting play is key to broadening the demographics of who becomes an inventor, scientist, or engineer,"

Such feedback is coming from credible organizations, research centers, and thought leaders, all addressing the same concern. This is why we can't help but notice the importance of paying attention to such a creativity crisis. There is a general decline of creativity in the world, generally, and in the United States precisely. It is not to be taken lightly, especially with the influence and role the US plays in many countries.

On the other hand, we are also noticing the increased demand for creative skills in many leading organizations. The focus on hiring employees with creative skills are in demand. The added plus is that it will give them an edge over others that do not possess these skills.

Many businesses and industries have realized that creative people are known to be better at problem-solving, more innovative, better at handling uncertainties, have a broader outlook and approach, and have better adaptability skills that help them to flow under pressure. On top of that, it has been shown how the creative process itself encourages collaboration and better team building.

We can see why in such transitioning times; one can appreciate the high-value creative skills provided to the overall success of an organization.

With a low supply and high demand for creative skills, the overall success of a company, organization, and society, in general, will come when these skills are in place for the long term.

The gap between supply and demand has to be minimized to ensure a balance between both.

Children are being raised in a way where creativity is put into second place. It is indeed a highly sought-after skill in the real world. That leads me to a question:

Who will be filling positions in domains that are requiring more and more creative skills?

Just because you see your kids, grandkids, nieces, or nephews operate electronic devices, watching their favorite cartoons with their iPad at the age of two or knowing how to use your cell phone and take pictures for you at three, does not make them smarter or more creative. All it is, just a matter of how you feel about yourself versus the younger generation.

Being older, it is possible that you may be feeling challenged operating your own devices and might view those youngsters as being geniuses.

Crisis in Creativity?

The truth is that you NEVER had access to the same tools and technology when you were at their age. At the same time, having access and being able to practice early in their life makes them look brilliant at their age.

They have a natural desire to explore and an ongoing curiosity in addition to their high-level energy and persistence. It gives them good practice while they are being entertained.

Unless you are consciously engaging them in games that are brain stimulating on their smart devices, what results is just the opposite of having them to be more creative. They just become savvier in using electronics. It is similar to just like you learned how to drive a car. With practice, you master your driving skills and get comfortable being on the road, and not much of your brain is being used in terms of thinking at that point. Many people reported that after arriving at their homes, they did not know how they got there. They were perhaps driving on autopilot mode. That is exactly how those little ones are. They become familiar and confident with operating technological devices. This is different from them being creative.

Make sure the toys and games you are engaging your kids with are both brain-stimulating and creativity boosting. Hence, they will be equipped and prepared for a better future.

"Creativity in the 21st century is crucial for societies,

businesses, and individuals who need to juggle fulfillment with

the demands of the rapid-change culture." -Shelly Carson,

Ph.D. (via HuffPost)

Research shows creative thinkers are more optimistic, more confident, and more flexible. They can cope with stress better and are healthier. Creative people tend to achieve at a higher level, are more engaged in their work, and have higher self-esteem.

A global study by *Adobe* found that businesses which invest in creativity experience:

- Increased employee productivity (78 percent)

- Have satisfied customers (80 percent), and produce a better customer experience (78 percent)

- Foster innovation (83 percent), and are financially successful (73 percent)

It's all about being aware and asking the right questions. That is very helpful when it comes to finding solutions.

Questions such as:

What are the root causes of our creativity Crisis?

Where is it stemming from?

How can we undo it?

One Forbes article titled *How America's Education Model Kills Creativity and Entrepreneurship* (Batten Institute University of Virginia Darden School of Business) answered the question of why is this happening?

"The answer is complicated. It partly relates to the psychology of social conformity that generally increases with age and enhanced social awareness. But it seems that something more is at play. Sir Ken Robinson in his now-famous Ted Talk, "How Schools Kill Creativity," argues for the need to reform existing education models (that were originally designed to support industrialization), calling on us to fundamentally "reconstitute our conception of the richness of human capacity" and adjust our education systems accordingly. Robinson argues that because the world is changing in transformational ways, "creativity now is as important in education as literacy," and should, therefore, be treated with the same status. And if our children are "not prepared to be wrong, [they] will never come up with anything original…" He further contends that as a society, "we stigmatize mistakes," and the result "is that we're educating people out of their creative capacities" and destroying children's natural willingness to take chances."

I can see how "stigmatizing mistakes" can harm not having good adaptability skills. It, therefore. Reduces a student's resilience and success when facing challenges. It will create future adults that are less curious and afraid to take risks.

Crisis in Creativity?

Well, Sir Ken Robinson sure made a great point as well as other top experts, including Roger C Schank, Ph.D. The latter is a strong critic of today's educational system, an American artificial intelligence theorist, cognitive psychologist, learning scientist, educational reformer, entrepreneur, and author.

Dr. Schank shared this, *"LEARNING OCCURS WHEN SOMEONE WANTS TO LEARN, NOT WHEN SOMEONE WANTS TO TEACH.* I was a professor for most of my life. In 2000, after 32 years of teaching (at Stanford, Yale, and Northwestern), I decided to quit."

Dr. Roger Schank stated that there are "only two things wrong with education: 1) What we teach; 2) How we teach."

Many highly educated "thought leaders" see the current educational system as preparing students for undergraduate testing. Unfortunately, it is not preparing them for life! I believe it starts with traditional educational systems. The increased focused efforts on convergent thinking for kids in schools at such a young age explains why creative thinking seems to be dying off at an alarming rate.

While 98% of children score as geniuses in divergent thinking, only 2% of adults reach this score according to multiple resources (whokilledcreativity.com and other studies, including George Land). Yet, our school systems still are trying to evaluate children's ability based on their Test Scores.

Not being able to apply divergent thinking limits our ability to create. Both Convergent and Divergent thinking are important in the creative process with more expansion in divergent thinking and other supportive thinking styles.

We must pay attention to our youth and encourage their creativity. Our youth will be the adults leading our country, including those senior/wiser, years into the future. Let's encourage a creative environment in our homes and work, starting by having a creative attitude, creative mindset, and creative thinking skills.

The journey you take does not have to be one you take alone. Know that what you see as a result of creative solutions, invention, and innovation is truly not a one-person show. It may be that one person was very focused and disciplined, and his or her commitment and dedication led to a successful result...however, even that person had a support team.

Richard and Joan Branson, a Creative-Collaborative Love Story

I recently read a Tweet by Sir Richard Branson sharing his gratitude and honor to his wife, Joan, of 30 years. He added "partner of 44 years, the mother of our two wonderful children and my constant rock. Joan has always been a steady source of wisdom and has played no small part in some of my better life decisions. In fact, I owe *Necker Island* to Joan."

He continued, "I wouldn't have been able to do all of it without Joan, and I wouldn't have it any other way."

Aside from your business partners, every duration of your creative journey will require a certain type of attention and focus, including team supporters, while you're going through the process.

I would suggest that you learn from inventors of the world how they, too, had a support team directly or indirectly involved and/or engaged in their creative journey.

When you think creating is a journey with no company, something that you have to do alone, that thought is very destructive and possibly hindering a lot of your creative progress. Positive and aligned collaboration is a great tool if you can learn in maximizing its application/influence and can assist you in reaching a state of optimal creative growth and results.

Collaboration, if used effectively, can help take away a heavy burden from your creative process. This includes the beginning, middle, and end stages.

Collaboration can ensure better productivity and can harness the best out of two or more individuals. That is especially when you and the team, organization, or the person that you are collaborating with are organized.

Having like-minded people with different combined skill sets, while working on the same project, can ease the feelings of being stuck or stagnant. They can also take the load off one person doing everything alone or having to know everything themselves. This is like what we learned from America's Super Mom LaChelle in the previous chapter.

Crisis in Creativity?

You don't have to collaborate to create, but if you choose to, you can go further, gather more ideas, have the long-lasting motivation, and discover more possibilities. This includes coming up with more creative output and having greater efficiency. All of this will help you save more time and accomplish faster delivery.

"A team member with more in-depth knowledge, previous experience with a specific task, another perspective on a situation requiring problem-solving, or even just a new shortcut in your favorite software, can teach you new information in practice, while you and others are applying it together in real-time." (Julius Dobos, 2017)

Remember, a team of creative support can consist of: Your household helpers to take some chores off your plate. It could be a trusted friend that you can get feedback from. It could also be your furry babies that help keep your company and charged with their unconditional love. They are all important during the creative process.

Communication and collaboration are great tools to use. Just make sure you access them for smoother creative processes as or when needed. Don't forget the great effect of recognizing and acknowledging your team by showing gratitude and appreciation for their efforts and contribution. That will create better harmony during the creative process.

Another area I would like to bring attention to is MASTERMINDS. It's been a common trend in organizations and with higher achievers' networks. That happens by attending masterminds to cultivate creative thinking and enhance creative skills.

While masterminds are great, they could be an enemy to your creativity.

If you don't practice gathering your ideas first, then in a group, you will not learn to tap into your higher imagination skills and confidence.

My suggestion is to mastermind with other participants but don't be reliant on them to start. It is great to be inspired by some of your team members ideas, however it is best that you would train and program your brain to practice idea generation FIRST and then participate with your mastermind group. Listen to their suggestions and ideas and then share yours.

The importance of encouraging creative ideas & engaging in more creative projects is crucial in today's world.

"Thus the man who is responsive to artistic stimuli reacts to the reality of dreams as does the philosopher to the reality of existence; he observes closely, and he enjoys his observation: for it is out of these images that he interprets life, out of these processes that he trains himself for life." ~Friedrich Nietzsche

Understanding the definition of **stimulation** will help you learn more about its importance, need, and use in creativity.

Definition: stim·u·la·tion

"Encouragement of something to make it develop or become more active. The stimulation of a revolution in intelligence affairs."

-the action of arousing interest, enthusiasm, or excitement. "The child needs plenty of stimulation as bored hands can make mischief."

-The raising of levels of physiological or nervous activity in the body or any biological system.

An article from *EMS World* explained how the brain regulates our responses to stimulation. It needs to be engaged to function well. Optimal arousal enables brains to be alert, receptive, and ready to attend and learn. For example, children are motivated by their search for optimal stimulation, rather than by what others label as important. Something that adults are suffering from.

This is creating a big concern for many educators as a decline in creative thinking is being noticed.

It is time for great leaders, influencers, teachers, and parents to apply *intellectual stimulation*. Such stimuli encourage creativity and innovation, problem-solving, critical thinking, as well as imagination. All of this **stimulates** thoughts when it comes to identifying and solving problems creatively.

When your brain is stimulated, it is easier to connect with your creativity.

Know that by being curious about *optimizing your creative mindset* and having an interest in learning more about creativity, you are attracting, connecting, and focusing your attention on inviting more creativity into your life.

The more we learn about something, the easier it becomes to understand, practice, and apply it to our life.

"What You Understand, You Can Conquer." ~Michelle

Hamel

Understanding not just listening, learning, or memorizing is important for your progress and self-development.

It's important to understand something well to fully benefit from its teachings and appreciate the value it's adding to your life.

Reading more about a given subject and asking questions will help you understand it better.

So, before you take in a new creative task make sure you understand the goal, mission, and vision to have the best RESULTS

Creative vs. Destructive Mindset: Know the Way to Success

If you are creative and happy with where you are in your creative journey while you're reading this book to expand your knowledge and awareness on how you can optimize your creativity, then you are already tuned into a creative mindset. This will be a reassurance to you that you are on the right track.

However, if you're feeling challenged and may be frustrated with yourself and possibly doubting your creative abilities, then learning more about the Creative vs. Destructive Mindset will be very helpful to you.

As you're reading, you can participate by answering the questions, digging deeper, and practice coming up with more than one solution to each question.

First and foremost, be kind and compassionate to yourself as you evaluate/understand more concepts and teachings in creativity. It is important to stay focused on your results and progress. Always acknowledge that!

"In the history of men, each act of destruction meets with a response, sooner or later, with an act of creation." ~Eduardo Galeano

QUESTIONS TO PONDER UPON

What type of behavior are you developing?

Are you creating through joy and purpose or fear and destruction?

Are you self-empowering or self-disempowering?

Are you celebrating your achievements or belittling yourself after the fact?

Are you giving your power away by not standing up for yourself (even when you know how to and what to do)? Otherwise, are you letting others control and manipulate you?

Are you on a deeper level, feeling unworthy of love, success, recognition, or appreciation? Otherwise, are you simply just even open to receiving?

Are you silently suffering and feel others should suffer in the same way?

Are you operating from a weak ego self, greed, or unauthentic intentions?

Evaluate your creative intentions on a deep core soul level. This means that the more honest you are with yourself, the better the results.

Don't try to justify and convince yourself of your intentions to what consciously is clear to you. Do not delay your progress towards freedom. START owning responsibility for your intentions as they will guide your actions and create your results.

This is the time for you to tap in your highest pure energy form and towards your creative endeavors. TAKE ACTION and SERVE your calling!!!

"The belief that life is bad, and will continue to go badly, is a

sign of a self-destructive mentality. It is based on a deep belief

that the person is not worthy of good things. At school, a student

may only see the 'down' side of situations, for example."

~Michael Quist (Study.com)

Destructive behavior is often looked at as a symptom of other underlying psychological issues. It is wise to visit areas that need attention, including healing the emotional, mental, and psychological challenges in your life.

It is of great importance to truly understand yourself, your behavior, and your identity. Identify if you are working from a constructive or destructive base. Then, choose a healthy foundation to work within the best of intentions and vibrations as you share your creative work.

Habits make life easier, but not every habit. You need to dig deep and truly understand what is causing any destructive behavior, patterns, or negative cycles.

"Although almost everyone has a hard time resisting the action

urge of powerful emotion, some people have a harder time

regulating their emotions due to their temperament and learning

history. As a result, they have more problems with impulsivity,

relationships, and a sense of self. When people with this kind of

temperament grow up in environments that don't teach them the skills they need to manage their moods and emotions, the result

is pervasive emotion dysregulation." -Cedar R. Koons

Emotional dysregulation is a phrase that is used in mental health to denote an emotional response. It is one that falls outside of the scope of what one considers as typical.

People with emotional dysregulation may either feel emotions with greater intensity or clarity. They may be either highly-sensitive or exceptionally emotional as a person.

It's not necessarily negative. These individuals may also be more creative and empathetic as compared to the average person.

They may have been raised under a hectic environment. They could have grown in very challenging or abusive circumstances. They could have some chemical imbalances. In such cases, they should be referred to and addressed by a qualified licensed mental health professional.

Emotional pain and trauma MUST BE identified, addressed, and dealt with. It should be done in a healthy coping mechanism to achieve true healing. Masking, pretending, or numbing the pain will never get rid of it or is the best solution. Unfortunately, things will only get worse and more intense over time.

Drinking your pain away or drugging yourself is only temporary relief with major negative long-term side-effects.

It is better to express yourself through painting, writing, singing, dancing, walking, or sleeping. All will help ease your pain away, in addition to building a habit towards redirecting your emotions into creative solutions.

It may require a lot of inward work, therapy, counseling, coaching, and mentoring to get to that stage, but it is worth it!

Why not give yourself a chance by permitting yourself to live with: less pain, guilt, shame, jealousy, envy, lack of confidence, insecurities, or low self-esteem?

This may be a phase you're going through and something you're experiencing. However, it doesn't have to be your permanent situation or a story you live and repeatedly tell yourself.

ASK YOURSELF THESE QUESTIONS

What if all you need is a little leap of faith?

How would you feel if you found your freedom, self-love, and peace just on the other side of your fears and doubts?

What is triggering your emotional turbulence?

Have you sought help? Or Are you afraid to ask for help?

Is your weak ego, pride, or mind playing a number in you?

Ask yourself why?

Ask yourself WHY again and again until you find out THE REAL reason you are AFRAID to ask for help.

GO DEEP AND THEN GO ASK FOR HELP IF NEEDED!!!

Start helping yourself by being kind and compassionate to yourself, but not mean and destructive.

"There will be no enjoyment of success or growth or feeling of satisfaction lived by your soul, without celebrating it with inner peace, good health, gratitude, and joy." ~Dr. Sofie Nubani

The Challenge of Asking for Help

Asking for help was hard for me. It is still a work in progress. The first time I stepped out of my comfort zone was when I was reading a GoFundMe Fundraiser post by a daughter of a dear Facebook friend. That friend is a very respected Doctor Owner of the Naturopath Wellness center. This post explained the unique case of throat cancer that her dad had as well as the burden of excessive medical bills he encountered. It was his choice and preference of going through with homeopathic and natural pathetic treatments instead of conventional chemotherapy treatments.

I and Doctor Todd (my friend that I mentioned above) have been connected for a while. We have been of support to one another through our social media interactions. I had shared a few of his posts as he always loved educating people on natural ways of living and healing.

I felt in my spirit that I wanted to do more than pray for him or aid his daughter's fundraiser. By asking others to do the same, I felt there would be a greater chance for him to get the needed help. After all, it may help in reducing his stress levels over the financial expenses he is facing, especially while dealing with the pain and healing of his own body.

Asking for help for the first time felt less of a burden on my soul. It felt a LOT easier. When I thought of how my action can support Dr. Todd's progress and healing, I felt more courageous to ASK for help. I decided to write a post and share it with all the contacts on my page.

I wrote from my heart and shared his story with the GoFundMe Fundraiser link created by his daughter. I remember feeling so satisfied after sharing the post. This was especially after a few people took action to support him. I was happy that I participated and chose to be part of the solution to someone I had much gratitude, respect, and appreciation for.

I learned from the post shares by Dr. Todd, a lot of valuable information and I was so happy to help. I felt it was the least I can do to say: "THANK YOU, Dr. TODD" for all the contributions you made that helped many and that you continue doing."

A few months later, Dr. Todd was back in action and even recently held a workshop teaching what he does best.

I was so happy when I was reading his posts that were sharing the location and time of his workshop. With the grace of God, divine mercy, and intervention, he was recovering well and transitioning gradually to his normal routine.

Never underestimate the power of prayers, donations, and community. Your effort, combined with the contribution and efforts of others, can truly make a difference. It all collectively can have a huge impact and even save lives. Be brave, ASK FOR HELP for yourself or others. Be part of fixing a problem when you can, and continue to think of CREATIVE solutions. It will liberate your soul and add more life to your years!!!

"Thousands of candles can be lighted from a single candle, and the life of the candle will not be shortened." ~Buddha

Struggles and Triumphs of a Songstress: The Story of Amy

A few months later, I connected with a talented singer. I met her through my business partner. She was to originally contribute to the 'Sound, Frequency, and Vibration" chapter of **Book 2** of the *Optimize Your Creative Mindset* series. She surprised us about what she was going through. This was noticed after she was not responding to any phone calls or messages. What happened was:

While she was waiting to submit her story, she shared that she was being evicted from her home. She reached out and asked both my business partner and me, separately, for a loan to help her through her desperate times. Both my business partner and I were sad to hear about her challenging circumstances. After listening to her story in more depth, we both knew lending her the amounts she asked for would only be a temporary bandage. At the same time, she will struggle the following month or months.

The best suggestion given was to create a crowdfunding campaign. I remember lighting a candle for her after our conversation. The intention was to pray for her fast recovery from the tough situation she was facing and for her overall wellbeing.

The cool thing that happened was that a crowdfunding campaign was created right away. I noticed it on her Facebook page. This happened in just less than two hours of her original loan request.

Again, I stepped out of my comfort zone and shared her post with a message to all my friends and social network connections. I wrote about her and what she was going through. Of course, I made my contribution as well. Mind you, many knew of her from her music CDs and live performances.

An awesome situation happened. In only six hours of the original post that she shared; Amy had raised the amount needed. What is more amazing is that, in less than 24 hours, she even raised more than the amount she had originally asked for.

I remember taking a screenshot of her page, messaging her, and sharing my excitement about her accomplishment. She finally had the necessary funds to maintain her housing arrangement. She was so grateful and even apologized to me about her not being able to share her contribution to the book series because of her current unstable conditions. She shared that even her dog was very sick and will be passing away at any time, after living with her for 19 years. "OMG!" I told her, "Are you kidding me?" I SOOOO understand.

"Having COMPASSION and not Pity when others are facing difficulties and seeking our help, will direct our energy to serve out of love and not an obligation. A significant difference in the warmth of the emotions shared." ~Dr. Sofie Nubani

I saw the results after going through the experience of asking. It was then I thought to myself, "HOW could I have overlooked this action just so I can please and be courteous to others?"

I always thought that I might be bothering people when I am asking for help. After all, most are consumed with their own concerns and issues!

I learned through the two times I asked and experienced a positive outcome. As a result, what happened was that: it was much easier to ask for help for someone else versus for myself.

I ALWAYS FELT IT WAS HARD TO ASK FOR HELP!

I learned a lot through the journey of writing this book. I had spent a multitude of nights and days writing it and dealt with writer's block along the way.

Through all of that, the journey became more challenging, interesting, inspiring, and exciting to me.

I felt very connected to the message in the book and its teachings. My soul was celebrating every little accomplishment and completion of a chapter. I was so grateful to be able to share it with all of YOU and the future generations. Until all chapters were complete, and it was sent to editing, the feedback I got was not what I wanted to hear, but needed to know.

I was advised to add more stories in some areas of the book so that you, the readers, can connect more with the understanding of each concept and message delivered.

"What do you mean?!?" I asked after writing over 600 pages. I was thinking that I was done from the original intent of writing one book. There were already a huge number of pages. I turned it to a three-book series due to the number of pages I had.

"I mean, that was a lot already," I thought to myself. All these thoughts were in and out of my head. It was until I had to breathe and feel, see, and hear what this advice and message was all about. It finally sunk in and made more sense.

Now all the stories that I already had were real stories from my personal experience, my clients, friends, and so on. Evidently, with that many chapters and pages, I needed more stories to add for better engagement and connection with the readers.

At that point, I could not think of any more stories off the top of my head. Though my expanded imagination could have created a few, "Ha Ha Ha." However, I wanted real stories from real people. Now, I was tested to ASK FOR HELP, but this time it was for MYSELF and for the first time!!

Imagine all through my *life, if You are wondering what that represents?* That is 46 years of living on this earth. I have never asked for help, including when I could have used some at one point. However, I was never comfortable doing so, luckily, I managed to survive and overcome my few challenges.

At this point, I had to get out of my comfort zone for the best of 'Optimize Your Creative Mindset' book series' vision and mission. I took the challenge upon myself this time. I contacted a few of my friends, experts, and individuals in my network that I felt their story would fit in a certain chapter. It was to highlight a concept or a thinking process that may help everyone reading this book. (Like the few stories you read in previous chapters and will read more of in book 2 & 3.)

It was only when I gave myself permission to surrender and ask for help, that the hearts and minds of the people I asked were open, receptive, and gladly willing to contribute. This was to the degree that I had tears in my eyes from the intense sense of appreciation that I felt, and this sense expanded to everyone.

The responses were beyond soul-fulfilling. I truly learned to receive and appreciate it in kind. My friend Chris Salem quoted: *"Receive with No Resistance,"* so I did that. I allowed myself to receive, appreciate it in kind, and no resistance.

For that, I thank my good intentions in writing this book and the soul and consciousness of *Optimize Your Creative Mindset* that I made a connection with.

I witnessed through this book's journey what it truly feels like when we receive. I observed the goodness and willingness of people to help, support, and contribute to others' success naturally when they are asked to help.

I felt the love and good seeds of intentions that were planted as they all echoed back ten-fold. I share this with you in faith that you do not delay ASKING for help or support. You should not hesitate when you need it or assisting someone who may be ASKING YOU to help them.

"He who wished to secure the good of others has already secured

his own." -Confucius

Sometimes, the hold on what you're meant to receive is nothing but a lesson that you had to learn by ASKING FOR HELP. You will allow blessings over the person helping you as well by YOU ASKING, the flow and cycle of giving and receiving are in balance. Your receiving may be from a total stranger as opposed to someone you helped in the past. Know that is normal and okay, be thankful, and always remember to PASS IT FORWARD!

Don't ask for help or give help with any expectations. When asking from your heart, do not worry, not about the crowd. You just train your brain to reach out and have no doubts. You do it when you're not using, abusing, or have any special agendas to carry out. The whole universe starts showing up to serve you. Believe that, keep moving forward, and prosper!

With all that has been said, I know sometimes you might be thinking, "Really, Dr. Sofie? All those examples are there just so we get the message on ASKING?" "Yes!" I say, Precious Ones. This was such a key lesson that I learned later on in life. Even then, many still have difficulties applying.

There's no need to continue living more years on this earth before YOU start getting comfortable in asking for help like I did.

The advice above applies even if you are 80+ years in age. It is such a great feeling to experience, and believe me, you don't want to live without at least trying.

THINK ABOUT THE TWO QUESTIONS MENTIONED BELOW

What areas in your life you may need help with today and can ask someone to help you with, but you have been delaying that request or feel uncomfortable ASKING?

Is there someone you know that is going through a rough time and may need you to help them by ASKING FOR HELP on their behalf? (e.g., donations, fundraisers, etc.)

Learn how to be Creative in asking, and at the same time, remaining genuine with your intentions.

"From what I've seen, it isn't so much the act of asking that paralyzes us--it's what lies beneath. That is the fear of being vulnerable, the fear of rejection, and the fear of looking needy or weak. It is the fear of being seen as a burdensome member of the community instead of a productive one. It points, fundamentally, to our separation from one another." ~Amanda Palme

There is a mindset within many people that helps to build and that of which to destroy. It's important to understand the differences between what is a creative mindset and what is a destructive mindset. As a creator, your mindset plays an important part in creating.

If you seek the path of a truly creative, then it is wise to embrace the right mindset as opposed to the way of a destructive one.

"A seed grows with no sound, but a tree falls with a huge noise. Destruction has noise, but creation is quiet. This is the power of silence. Grow Silently" ~Confucius

Know The Way: Understanding The Creative Vs. Destructive Mindset

A Creative Mindset Includes:

Energetic but Focused

Playful but Disciplined

Open-Minded

Take Smart Risks

Ask Questions

Realistic Dreamers

Curious

Self-actualizer

Problem Solvers

A Destructive Mindset:

Energetic but Destructive

Playful but Irresponsible & Undisciplined

Crisis in Creativity?

Closed-Minded

Take Unrealistic & Dangerous Risks

Afraid to Ask BIG Questions or Ask for Help

Unrealistic Dreamers

Thrill Seeking Curiosity

Self-Destructive

Illogical/Unconstructive

Identify your traits and work on boosting your creativity by having a creative attitude, adopting new habits, and establishing better environments that support your creative path.

Practice and Develop a Creative Mindset

Have a Creative Attitude

Commit yourself to develop your creativity

Experience Creativity

Improve creativity through imagination, association, & higher-level questions.

Practice Dialogue instead of Discussion

Apply Combinatory play/Use Combinational Creativity

Join a Circle of Creative Masters/ Mastermind, Use the Six Hat Techniques

Take Creative Tests and EXPLORE Morphological Analysis

"LEARN from Yesterday, CREATE today, and PLAN for tomorrow." ~Dr. Sofie Nubani

Be gentle with yourself as you are developing your creative skills, as that will generate more ease, and help you to explore/rediscover your creativity.

You WILL get back into action, as you open your creative vortex with your creator and creation. You most likely will experience gentle yet, powerful shifts at the same time. You will have a mystical union emerging between all three: The Creator, Creation, and Self, ALL CREATING.

Once United, all three will be Magically connected!!!

On the other hand, if you feel that you have been on the destructive side of your mindset, experiencing a creative block, or feel stuck in a rut (no matter what you did), you still weren't able to achieve a breakthrough. You've tried everything. You've brainstormed, focused, asked for help, tried thinking outside of the box, pumped-up music, embraced silence, etc. You simply can't get out of your head, no matter what, and how you try.

Then, understand this is quite normal, and many have been there at one time or another.

A creative block could be frustrating– especially if you are on some sort of deadline. In that case, the best suggestion I can think of (if you are struggling creatively) is to try this technique;

Mindlessness To Creative Success

Do something mindless.

For example: Pick an unrelated mindless chore and work on that instead.

According to a 2006 study from the *University of California, Davis*, embracing mindless chores gives your brain the freedom to think creatively.

When your brain is wrapped up in mindless activities such as dusting or washing dishes, it allows the creative part of your mind the freedom to ponder on its own. Don't feel limited to just cleaning, though.

Any menial and mindless task that keeps your muscle memory engaged will help accomplish the same thing.

You could try going for a walk, brushing your pet, organizing your junk drawer, or even something as simple as taking a shower.

BTW, how many times have you come up with your "next big idea" while you are washing your hair?

There is a whole Twitter hashtag dedicated to "shower thoughts." The simple truth is that it is a mindless activity during your showering process that allows your brain to think more creatively. The showering itself is not the activity.

Remember that the key here is to ensure that your muscle memory is engaged with a task you don't have to think about too hard. That way, the creative part of your brain has the freedom to do its own thing. You don't want to break out a 1000-piece puzzle to put together!!!

The next time you are struggling with coming up with a blog post idea, create your course, a social media graphic, or anything else creative – stop what you are doing and engage in a mindless task.

Tidy the clutter in your office. Take the dog for a walk. Do those dishes that are in the sink. There is a good chance that before you even finish those tasks – you will get a light bulb moment that helps you get over your creative struggles.

A state zero is required to have a fresh start, reach deep relaxation, and with no attachments. A blank slate, in that case, would be mindlessness. That is always the best for a starting point.

Connecting back to awareness and insights from a 'blank state' results in powerful outcomes, better idea generation, and creative solutions.

Learn to clear your mind and practice mindlessness if you are in a creative rut or block!

"The Mindful state of awareness limits us to our sensory

perceptions and to the present moment. The Mindless state

helps us free ourselves from time and space boundaries and body

and mind boundaries." ~Ram Ramanathan

Tame a Negative Mindset with Laughter

Another great thing to practice that can help you in shifting state is LAUGHTER! It is truly like having an instant vacation.

It also has been proven to support creativity via scientific evidence.

Laughter uplifts us to better moods through the increase of neuro-chemicals production. Those include dopamine, oxytocin, serotonin, and all the feel-good hormones.

Laughter increases the production of endorphins, which acts as a natural pain-killer. It helps us to relax more and boost our immune system as well. All of this helps in better creativity. (Many people can get stressed at times when they are close to submission regarding their creative process and work. Having a good immune system decreases the chances of being sick and delaying delivery of the scheduled time.)

Set your intention and enjoy the process. Laugh and breathe more while working on your creative projects.

All of this will make your creative journey more delightful and connect you with your constructive and creative mindset.

Remember...

"You can't use up creativity. The more you use, the more you have." ~Maya Angelou

Chapter 6:
Breathe and Laugh to Creativity

In this chapter, you'll discover...

- Breathing for Creativity and Life

- Dr. Marilyn and how BREATHWORK changed her life

- Laughter is a Superb Remedy for Creativity

Breathing is a lot like creativity. Like an inhale, you receive an inspiration, you let it run through the unique magnificence of who you are, and then you release it into the world, letting it go, unattached to the way it needs to look." -Jill Badonsky

Breathing, as simple as it sounds, is a good exercise to practice, and with intention. Breathing is fundamental to life, and without OXYGEN, there is no life! Breathing is also a foundation for the whole body and every organ.

Research supports that DEEP BREATHING exercises and balanced oxygen levels. It can have a POSITIVE IMPACT on stress, anxiety, blood pressure, lung capacity, muscle tension, heart disease, and so much more. Breathing stimulates the vagus nerve (the longest nerve in one's body, running from the brain to the gut).

Deep breathing has an opposite effect versus that of SHALLOW breathing (which can hurt our creative side).

A very important reminder to all of us, as we all breathe naturally, however, (many according to healthiest breathing techniques) breathe wrong for optimal lung health and balanced oxygen circulation.

There are different recommended breathing techniques. Depending on what and how they are used, that can be of great assistance and for better well-being.

"Being aware of your breath forces you into the present moment - the key to all inner transformation. Whenever you are conscious of the breath, you are absolutely present. You may also notice that you cannot think and be aware of your breathing. Conscious breathing stops your mind." -Eckhart Tolle

Meet Dr. Marilyn Scott "The Amazing Doc"

That brings me to share the story of a dear friend, Dr. Marilyn A Scott. I have been connected with her for a few years. I was happy to spend time in person with her at the *Wow Book Camp 2018*. I was able to discover and know more about her on a personal level. The following year, in November 2019, my co-host Dr. Bob Choat and I invited her to be a guest on the *MEET THE AUTHOR* show. It aired live from the Wisdom Café Facebook group and, most recently, on the YouTube platform.

We discovered that "The Amazing Doc" held a degree in vocal performance and sang her way through college.

Noticing that since we met, Dr. Marilyn has been quite active. This includes the recent launch of her online radio show, *"Healthy Living w/Marilyn"* at *Tokovlradio.com*, publishing three books, speaking, conducting workshops and seminars, and later teaching and speaking on **Breathwork.**

"Um, I would love to pick her brain on that topic," I thought to myself. Especially about its relationship to creativity as that was an area she was teaching on. I wanted to find out how Breathwork influenced her creative journey. All I could do is ask if the Amazing Doc would be willing to share her story with all of us, and without any hesitation, she agreed. A few days later, she emailed her story.

Dr. Marilyn is also an involved and engaged mother/grandmother as well as a committed wife who loves her family.

I was grateful for her making time to contribute, especially with all her commitments and a busy schedule. She was and still is managing to pass it forward by helping others gain insights, manage their stress levels and emotions through her breathing teachings.

Embracing life through Breathwork!

By Dr. Marilyn A Scott, ND RMT

"Every moment of every day, I work on de-stressing my life. It was challenging in the beginning as I would remain quiet and start breathing with my eyes closed. I found out this was the way I was enjoying a calmer state, and the stress would dissipate. Breathwork!

This is not a new concept since we all breathe. It is a certain way to use your breath to enjoy an easier day. It's just like letting the stress roll off my back, shaking the feeling to the ground by taking a huge inhale, holding it, and then exhaling. I did this several times and felt my stress disappearing. Voila!

I felt relaxed and euphoric. The worry about that particular moment was gone. I could now move on with a smile on my face.

Living in the holistic world has offered me many natural ways to heal. I would walk other people's journeys as they enjoyed better health while learning about the different healing modalities, I would enlighten them about.

Since this was the easiest way to reduce my stress, I decided to delve into it further. It was to see how creative I could be when stress was not an issue.

I was not disappointed with the personal findings. This is because I became more creative while writing my two books, enjoyed more playtime with my grandchildren, and found fun times with family and friends more enjoyable.

We all live with stress, and breathwork is an easy way for me and many of my friends and students to rise above into the spiritual realm of creativity and life.

Breathwork supports me in a way in which I find activities such as painting a picture, doing a puzzle with my grandson, knitting, or sewing helps me stay focused and more creative.

Getting my brain out of the way through breathwork, finding contentment in the creativity in my life as well as others makes me realize what life is all about.

We live in such a negative society, and staying positive through breathing properly helps rid my body of toxins, stress, and keeps me in a state of CALM.

The last Breathwork seminar I hosted helped those in attendance enjoy ninety minutes of "Me Time." This was where they could just delve into their issues by learning breathing techniques that they can take with them wherever they go.

Sometimes a memory would pop into my head out of the blue when I am driving. "Where did that come from?" I would ask myself. Who knows! However, I now know to eliminate those memories, and I can breathe at a moment's notice.

The memories are still in my memory vault, but the breathing is crucial for me as I have a strong desire to stay in a positive mode, enjoy life, be more creative, and love ME!

"Staying focused, calm, and relaxed helps me be a more creative person. As a result, I move smoothly through the day. One participant in my last seminar told me how she felt rejuvenated! Another participant said that they managed to get a negative episode out of their thought process. He felt a calming sense wrap around him. I have been able to get my seminar attendees in a calmer state of being, more rejuvenated, relaxed, creative. I have been able to help them find a more spiritual way of living. This will help me be successful in my mission to help those who enter my sphere of embracing life to the fullest." Dr. Marilyn A Scott, ND, RMT ©

Pretty COOL! I love how The AMAZING Doc describes stress "rolling off her back," and then shaking that heavy feeling to the ground. It's achieved by taking a huge inhale, holding it, and then exhaling. Then after several repetitions, she felt her stress disappearing.

This included memories that she did not want to revisit. That led to her shallow breathing*. The shallow breathing probably opened her up to recognize those intrusive memories. Her awareness of those memories and applying her breathwork, allowed her to be more focused on her priorities, needs, and current reality.

*Shallow breathing is an upper chest breathing that normally occurs when we get anxious, stressed, or depressed. If you notice that your shoulders rise when you take a breath, then you're breathing shallow.

Breathing patterns can predict our emotional state. When we are aware of them, it is easier to take charge of them. This happens, firstly, by being aware and fully present in the moment, and secondly, by consciously and constantly breathing deeper and better.

Breathwork helps expand the mind to new awareness, which stimulates our brain and shifts our consciousness. It helps us more in areas of critical thinking, creative thinking, and becoming better at problem-solving.

Learning proper breathing can sure contribute to greater available energy. As a Certified Laughter Yoga instructor, stretching and deep breathing were the first things we learned. Getting the lungs prepared was an important part before commencing the laughter exercises.

It's interesting knowing how Breathwork had such a profound impact on Dr. Marilyn's life. After sharing her story, I see why she is the AMAZING woman that she is.

Living a holistic lifestyle and having learned and applied several modalities in her journey (as she was learning, teaching, and treating), she was able to draw off the experience and tap into, to build and create new possibilities.

However, Breathwork, as she mentioned, was the easiest and fastest of all. It was after practicing it in both calm and stressful situations. This is why she dove further into it, then created and led seminars to teach others how to do the same.

Breath is the bridge which connects life to consciousness, which unites your body to your thoughts. Whenever your mind becomes scattered, use your breath as the means to take hold of your mind again." ~ Thích Nhất Hạnh

Takeaway Learnings from Dr. Marilyn Scott

1-Something as simple as breathing techniques can help you increase your overall energy, and bringing more resources that can be directed towards creative projects.

2-Get more creative by putting a stop to overthinking. Use Breathwork to help foster relaxation and energize you so you can open up that creative side.

3-How you breathe can help your emotional state of well-being and engage higher-level consciousness.

"I have a strong desire to stay in a positive mode, enjoy life, be more creative, and love ME." ~Dr. Marilyn A Scott via Dr. Sofie Nubani

Breathing is informally linked with mental functions. It helped Dr. Marilyn Scott strengthen her mental flexibility/adaptability, keeping her out of the shallow end in both areas, which are breathing and creativity.

Meanwhile, there are many available breathing exercises that you can choose from. I recommend you hire a Practitioner that specializes in breathwork to help guide you.

For basic access and assistance right now, I would like to introduce you to a few simple and basic techniques. They will help get you started. Keep in mind, there are many types of Conscious Breathing Techniques, and at the same time, apps for breathing, that you can download.

Box-Breathing: A Powerful Tactic for Rapid Response

I was introduced to Box Breathing two years ago by Dr. Bob Choat, Ph.D., and later on *Thrive Cafe* (a Facebook group) by Dr. Lori Shemek, Ph.D.

Box-Breathing (aka tactical breathing)

A NAVY SEAL TECHNIQUE YOU CAN USE TO BEAT STRESS

A very powerful technique which is known as "resetting your breath" or "Four-way Breathing" is a relaxation technique that aims to return breathing to its natural rhythm. This breathing exercise will help you to clear your mind, relax your body, increase your mental alertness, and focus; besides, it will make you feel more grounded.

It is a great technique to adopt for individuals in a high-stress career or stressful situations. It is used by military personnel as well as police officers.

Lt. Col. Dave Grossman, the author of *"On Combat,"* described how our heart rate affects our physiology and cognition. The normal resting heart rate is 60-80 beats per minute. When the heart rate reaches 115, the fine motor skills tend to deteriorate. It is like trying to put a thread through the eye of a needle, and it's almost impossible to accomplish that. At 145 beats per minute, the complex motor skills break down. Most sports use complex motor skills. At 175, cognitive functions tend to break down, and this includes creative thinking. Box-breathing helps to reduce the heart rate and, therefore, able to engage in activities, especially cognitive ones, more effectively.

Box-Breathing is very effective in combat. It's a very simple technique, fast, and easy to use, as well, to follow. It can be used anywhere and by anyone. You may be stressing out during your creative project, standing in line to pick your material or stuck in traffic, and more. It is then that Box-Breathing is very effective.

One of the goals of boxed square breathing is to bring the respiratory system back into alignment or homeostasis. To practice Box-Breathing, you follow a specific controlled pattern.

The count of breathing depends on each person's ability to hold their breath. Four counts/seconds is a good base to start. But depending on each person's tolerance levels, the amount of holding in seconds can vary. You can start with a one-second or count for each side when you do box-breathing and then work up to something between four and seven seconds per side.

A full effect cycle must be repeated for at least five minutes. Once someone is used to the technique, then they may choose to count to five or six or seven per side.

The Step-By-Step Way to the Box-Breathing Method...

You can do this technique with your eyes closed or open, depending on your preference. Sit upright, with your feet flat on the floor, if you're able to for the best results. You can also do this standing up.

Breathe in for a count of 4,

Hold for a count of 4,

Exhale for a count of 4,

Hold for a count of 4.

Repeat as many times as necessary to get to that state of homeostasis.

"The Box Breathing technique helps to trigger the parasympathetic nervous system to calm and stops the 'flight or fight' response in its tracks." ~Dr. Lori Shemek, Ph.D.

The nice thing about conscious breathing is that there are plenty of techniques from which to choose. You can start with Box-Breathing. Practice and develop a habit using it daily or as needed. You can do so if you feel that's what works best for you.

Furthermore, you can try:

Brain "NOSTRIL BREATHING" exercises that can help boost your creativity...

Breathe Through Your Left Nostril (Increase oxygen to the right brain)

Alternate Nostril Breathing (ANB)

Left Nostril Breathing:

Breathing just through your left nostril by blocking off your right nostril, can direct oxygen flow and energy into the right hemisphere of the brain. That part is responsible for different roles in the brain. That would turn on the parasympathetic nervous system helping you to relax and generate more space for creativity.

Breathing through the left nostril stimulates the 'feminine' (emotion and creativity) aspects of our body.

-Close off your right nostril with your right thumb.

-Breathe in through your left nostril only.

-Exhale through the right nostril.

-Use slow, steady, deep breaths, both in and out.

-Inhale fully before exhaling and then exhaling fully before inhaling again.

Repeat this breathing practice for three to nine minutes.

A 1994 study showed that when you are breathing through your left nostril, the right side of your brain becomes more active and dominant. The same is true when you reverse the process and breathe through your right nostril. At that point, the left side of the brain becomes more active.

The nasal cycle—the fact that most people only breathe out of one nostril at a time and the body tends to switch the dominant nostril every four hours or so— was first noticed by a German nose specialist in 1895.

Another study in 1993 showed that when you are breathing through your right nostril, you will use significantly more oxygen as compared to when breathing through your left.

Since then, studies have shown that different things occur in the body and brain, depending on which nostril you are using.

Our nose is directly linked to both our brain and nervous system. Each nostril side breathing technique has a different effect. You can compare the left nostril breathing to the right nostril breathing. If you're curious, set some time aside and learn more about it.

The Pranayama Way of ANB

Alternate nostril breathing is also called "anuloma viloma" or "nadi shodhana" (in Sanskrit, the ancient language of yoga). In a fable that describes Pranayama (the marriage of Prana and Yama), twin girls, Anuloma Viloma and Nadi Shodhana were born. Nadi always looked for balance and was expressive while Anuloma was the same regarding balance and was introverted. Breathing, using ANB, helps to create that balance.

It's a great breathing technique that improves lung function and respiratory endurance, lowers heart rate, relieves stress, and anxiety. It creates whole-brain functioning, by balancing all hemispheres of the brain, and at the same time calming and centering the mind. This leads to a good foundation for healthy, creative solutions, and innovation.

In an interview with Anderson Cooper on CNN, former Secretary of State Hillary Clinton describes the practice of ANB on page 27 of her newly released memoir titled "What Happened" as a key way to recover from the stress of losing a lifelong dream of becoming President of the country.

She shares how she used ANB after her loss of the 2018 United States Presidential election to manage both stress and anxiety. She highly recommends it. She also endorsed it to viewers of CBS Sunday Morning. She said the practice is "very relaxing and kind of calms you down."

Additionally, there's clinical evidence of ANB's benefits. A 2013 study concluded that ANB can alter brainwaves and assist the brain in performing better on tasks that require undivided attention.

"When you practice breathing, it neurologically calms your whole system."- Dr. Belisa Vranich, author of several books, Breathe - Breathing for Warriors, and a children's book: The Belly Breath.

Create a routine for your ANB exercise

-Set both time and duration for your breathing techniques.

-Practice each breathing technique separately. Depending on what you want to accomplish, stick to one regularly, and feel free to use more than one routinely.

-You want to reach at least to the five-minute range a day at minimum per session if you're in good health confections. Depending on your health condition, less might be recommended. Make sure to always check with your health consultant or doctor first in that case.

If you're healthy, that should be a good base. If you like to challenge yourself and increase your counts, do so sensibly.

How to practice ANB

-Sit in any comfortable seated position. Relax the body and breathe naturally for a few moments, allowing both your mind and body to wind down.

-Rest your left hand on your lap or knee.

-Make a "peace sign" with your right hand. Fold the two extended fingers toward the palm. You can also rest them lightly on the bridge of your nose. Place your thumb gently onto your right nostril. Place your ring and little fingers gently onto your left nostril.

-Close your eyes and start by softly closing your right nostril (using your right thumb) and inhale slowly, deeply, smoothly, gently, and without strain through your left nostril.

-Close your left nostril (using your ring and little fingers) and then release closure of your right. Exhale through your right nostril. Inhale through your right nostril.

-Close your right nostril and release closure of your left. Exhale through your left nostril.

This completes one round. Continue the pattern from steps four to seven for as long as you wish.

When you're finished with the exercise, relax both arms, sit and breathe naturally for a few moments before opening your eyes.

According to an article, *"3 Reasons Everyone Should Try Alternate Nostril Breathing"*, by Dr. Paula Watkins on **MindBodyGreen**, she explained the process of ANB:

ANB session typically involves gently pinching one nostril closed with your fingers and then taking three long inhales and exhales. Then plug the other nostril, and repeat the process. Do the complete rotation three times.

If you find you need PEACE and BALANCING, then start inhaling through your LEFT nostril.

If you need ENERGIZING and ACTIVATION, then start with the RIGHT nostril.

More recently, scientists have even shown that it even makes a difference which nostril you start with. The first breath in 'Nadi shodhana' is usually through the left nostril. This traditional variation has been shown to reduce both heart rate and blood pressure while increasing reactivity.

Conversely, starting with the right nostril, was shown to increase both heart rate and blood pressure. In other words, this affects stimulating the sympathetic side of the nervous system. It could also be the 'masculine' aspects of our energetic body found in traditional thinking.

You can develop a conscious breathing habit in the morning for a good start of the day. You can then do it before going to sleep for a deeper, more restful nighttime sleep.

Twice a day is a good practice. As you develop good deeper breathing habits, you will value using them at different times when needed (between breaks, traffic, during projects, stressful, and when you feel anxious). It's a great antidote to stress!

"Just like The Eyes are The Window to the Soul, the Nose Is a Window to the Brain."-Dr. Sofie Nubani

If you or someone you know is suffering from asthma or COPD, then I would like to share a breathing exercise that is safe and very helpful for both you and them. It is called Pursed Lip Breathing.

According to the most recent article by the American Lung Association, Pursed lip breathing is a technique that helps people living with asthma or COPD when they experience shortness of breath. Pursed lip breathing helps control shortness of breath, and it provides a quick and easy way to slow your pace of breathing, making each breath more effective.

Great questions and answers by Healthline on Pursed Lip Breathing PLB.

Why do Pursed Lip breathing?

Pursed Lip breathing can help improve and control your breathing in several ways, including relieving shortness of breath by slowing the breath rate by keeping the airways open longer. This decreases the work that goes into breathing and improving ventilation by moving old air (carbon dioxide) trapped in the lungs out and making room for new, fresh oxygen.

Other than the lung benefits you can get from Pursed Lip breathing, you can experience overall relaxation. This is accomplished by taking consistent, deep breaths. This can calm the central nervous system, which has a relaxing effect on your entire body. This can help reduce stress and anxiety.

What is Pursed Lip breathing used for?

Pursed Lip breathing improves lung mechanics and breathing all at once. This means that you don't have to work as hard to breathe well. This is particularly helpful for people who have lung conditions that make it more difficult for them to breathe. These conditions can include obstructive lung disease, such as asthma, and restrictive lung disease, such as pulmonary fibrosis (PF). This is a type of interstitial lung disease (ILD).

Pursed Lip breathing is also used as part of the treatment for chronic obstructive pulmonary disease (COPD). People with this condition have severely declining lung function and breathing ability. The disease progresses to overinflated lungs. It reduced the ability to exhale air. It can make breathing so difficult that it impacts the quality of that person's life.

There are significant health benefits for people with COPD who practice Pursed Lip breathing. One study, Trusted Source, found that Pursed Lip breathing reduced dynamic hyperinflation in people with COPD. Furthermore, it significantly improved their exercise tolerance, breathing patterns, and arterial oxygen.

COPD can only be delayed. The damage can't be repaired once it happens. For that reason, breathing exercises to improve lung function are important. They can make breathing significantly easier.

How does Pursed Lip breathing work?

159

Pursed Lip breathing should be practiced until it becomes second nature to you. It's most effective when you're focused or relaxed. You can practice it in the following way:

1-Sit with your back straight otherwise lie down. Relax your shoulders as much as possible.

2-Inhale through your nose for two seconds, so you can feel the air move into your abdomen. Try to fill your abdomen with air instead of just your lungs.

3-Purse your lips like you're blowing on hot food. Then, breathe out slowly, taking twice as long to exhale as you took to breathe in.

Then repeat. Over time, you can increase the inhale and exhale counts from two seconds to four seconds, and so on.

Stay curious and explore other techniques to know what else might help you or someone important to you, and share this information with.

Learn more about:

Coherent Breathing

Diaphragmatic Breathing

Yogic Breathing

Remember to take DEEP BREATHS, so you enjoy LESS STRESS. It's worth a try!

> *"Let your breath be your ANCHOR, allowing the flow of life through you, as you are WITNESSING every inhale and exhale. It is reassuring that you are still alive and have the power in this present moment to CREATE." ~Dr. Sofie Nubani*

Laughter

Another great thing to practice that can help you in shifting state is laughter. It is truly the shortest distance between two people. I would add the shortest distance between your tensed-up self and uplifted self. If you want to experience an internal organ massage. This is the one that will help release toxins out of your body, then have a good belly laugh. You'll see how your spirit will just feel so uplifted, and your body will feel OH just so relaxed.

"The person who has a sense of humor is not just more relaxed

in the face of a potentially stressful situation, but is more

flexible in his approach." -JOHN MORREALL

Laughter is a mood lifter, and emotional booster, uplifting our moods through increasing the production of neurochemicals, such as dopamine, oxytocin, serotonin, and all the feel-good hormones, makes laughter a powerful medicine, a great healer and a good ally to have during good or challenging times.

Laughter also has been proven to support creativity through scientific evidence. It increases the production of endorphins, which acts as a natural painkiller, helping us to relax more along with boosting our immune system.

A lot of people can get stressed when they are in the final stage of a creative process. Having a good immune system decreases the chance of getting sick and delaying the delivery of the scheduled submissions.

Laugh More For Increased Creativity And Health

Add more humor to your life, TODAY, in both your personal as well as your professional life. Watch more comedies, tell more jokes, find more jokes, and be around funny people.

Book a *Laughter Mindset Experience* and/or sign up for a laughter yoga class. Feel free to join the *Laughter Mindset* group on *Facebook* and other groups that deliver good humor content on social media platforms. You can also follow humor and comedy Channels on YouTube and more.

I am very passionate about the power and importance that laughter brings and contributes to the world. I believe that a lot of political, medical, mental, psychological, and sociological problems will be reduced or even totally resolved with laughter.

Viktor Emil Frankl story and his thoughts on laughter

Viktor Emil Frankl was an Austrian neurologist and psychiatrist as well as a Holocaust survivor. He survived Theresienstadt, Auschwitz, Kaufering, and Türkheim. He was also the author of the famous book, *"Man's Search for Meaning,"* which is a MUST read. (Frankl's book has been widely cited as one of the most important and inspirational books of the 20th century.)

Man's Search for Meaning is a 1946 book by Viktor Frankl. It chronicled his experiences as a prisoner in Nazi concentration camps during World War II and describing his psychotherapeutic method. That involved identifying a purpose in life to feel positive about and then intensively imagining that outcome.

According to Frankl, the way a prisoner imagined his future affected his longevity. The book intends to answer the question, "How was everyday life in a concentration camp reflected in the mind of the average prisoner?" Part One constitutes Frankl's analysis of his experiences in the concentration camps. Part Two introduces his ideas of meaning and his theory called logotherapy.

I learned more about this AMAZING man while reading about him in an article from *GoodTherapy*, from which I will share some information. All I can say is, there are not enough words to praise him as well as describe the respect and appreciation I have for all his contribution to humanity, but mostly for his wise and loving soul.

This is a man whose brother, father, mother, and wife all were killed at the concentration camps. Yet his attitude to life and a sense of purpose allowed him to transcend his unbearable situation and gave him fuel to serve his bigger WHY.

He was a professor of neurology and psychiatry at the University of Vienna from 1948–1990. He directed the neurology department at the Vienna Polyclinic Hospital between 1946 and 1970. Throughout his career, Frankl published numerous books, received dozens of honorary degrees, lectured around the world, and served as a guest professor at universities, including Harvard, Southern Methodist, and Duquesne.

Frankl thought that during extreme physical circumstances, a person could escape through his or her spiritual self as a means to survive seemingly unbearable conditions. He believed the spiritual self could not be affected by external forces. Frankl spent most of his later career studying existential methods of therapy.

Viktor's thoughts on laughter: Humor Souls Weapon For Self-Preservation

"To discover that there was any semblance of art in a concentration camp must be surprise enough for an outsider, but he may be even more astonished to hear that one could find a sense of humor there as well; of course, only the faint trace of one, and then only for a few seconds or minutes.

Humor was another of the soul's weapons in the fight for self-preservation. It is well known that humor, more than anything else in the human make-up, can afford an aloofness and an ability to rise above any situation, even if only for a few seconds." -VF

"Never would have made it if I could not have laughed. It lifted me momentarily out of this horrible situation, just enough to make it livable." ~VIKTOR FRANKL

If the incredible Victor Frankl did not have a Laughter Mindset, just like he mentioned: HE NEVER WOULD HAVE MADE IT!!!

Not only did he make it through such horrible conditions, but we are also talking about a man who lost his family, home, friends, and all professional positions, yet he mastered applying supportive thinking styles that regularly boosted his creative solutions.

A Laughter Mindset helps you rise above your circumstances, challenging situations even if it is only for a few seconds. It allows enough distance for us to view our suffering from a different perspective.

Even the anticipation of laughter can lower our stress hormones and boost our happy/healthy hormones. No condition in which we can find humor will ever prosper over us.

Why is humor good for creativity?

Recent research shows that people in a lighter mood experience more "eureka!" moments along with greater inspiration.

According to Psychology Today, while at Northwestern University, Karuna Subramaniam studied two groups of participants that watched two different movies. One group watched a comedy, while the other watched a horror movie (The Shining). Or worse yet, a lecture about quantum electronics.

Immediately after, she gave both groups a word association puzzle to solve. She found that the group that watched the comedy was more creative solving the puzzle than the other group (we already know that negativity is bad for you). She confirmed her results using MRI equipment that showed increased activity in the area associated with creativity, that is, the anterior cingulate cortex, in those people who watched the comedy.

Comedies/ Health & Creativity

Watching comedies can not only make you more creative, but it can even support your overall health and boost your immune system. The viewing of comedies was reported as the main result in helping some people. That included those with terminal, and deadly diseases recover while laughing their way to health.

Optimize Your Creative Mindset

Read the following article written by Jaimie Licauco from Inquirer.net and see for yourself how Norman Cousins showed laughter to be the best medicine.

About 25 years ago, Norman Cousins, editor of the respected literary magazine Saturday Review in New York City, was diagnosed with Ankylosing Spondylitis, an incurable and fatal spinal column illness of unknown cause.

He tried all sorts of alternative remedies, including Vitamin B-17 or laetrile, large doses of Vitamin C, and several others, with little or no effect on his condition.

So, one day, against the advice of his doctors, he left the hospital and closeted himself in his apartment for one month doing what he enjoyed most—reading humorous stories and jokes, watching comedy movies, and reading his favorite comic books.

He did nothing but laugh and laugh each day for one whole month. He also wrote original jokes which he would read aloud to himself then laugh like crazy. He noticed that every time he laughed; his pain was eased.

At the end of one month, Cousins returned to the hospital for a checkup. To the surprise of the medical staff who examined him, they found no trace of the dreaded disease. He was completely cured!

So, they asked Cousins what medicines he took that cured him. They would not believe him when he replied he had not taken any medicine since he was told his ailment was incurable.

They said, "You must have done something you never did before."

He finally replied, "All I did was to laugh myself to health." He became known as the man who cured himself through laughter and was even appointed a faculty member of the University of California Los Angeles School of Medicine, although he was not a doctor.

Later he told his incredible story in a book, "Anatomy of an Illness," which was made into a movie.

At that time, medical science did not believe there was any connection between the mind, the emotions, and the immune system. The immune system was thought to be independent of and not subject to the directions of the mind or the vagaries of human emotions.

In the near future, more progressive physicians will be asking their patients not only about the symptoms they have but also the following: "How do you feel about your life? Your wife or husband? Your Job? Your mother-in-law? Your living space home/work-office, team, Boss? What upsets you or makes you angry? Do you get enough sleep? Etc."

They may prescribe not just drugs or surgery but also meditation, visualization, yoga, Qigong, Tai Chi, or even laughter to fight disease.

You see, when you laugh, you're in a state of ease, joy, and your whole body immediately becomes less tense, anxious, and more relaxed. A much better base to create from!

Reading about heroes like Victor Frankl, Norman Cousins, and more always had inspired me and gave me intrinsic motivation to add more humor to the world.

I Co-Led *Laughter Mindset Experiences* (Workshops) with a lot of positive feedback. I am an admin of the Laughter Mindset Facebook group and Co-Founder of The Laughter Mindset Program.

The best way I can describe The Laugher Mindset Experience is with the Laughter Mindset slogan:

"The Laughter Mindset, a place you don't just visit, You'll SHIFT state right away.

Very Good

Very Good

Yeahhhh!!!

Now breathe and laugh Ahhhh HA HA HA" —Laughter Mindset

Yes, you do shift state right away when you are laughing. Yes, it is also very good for you to engage in. And, yes, you want to preferably breathe, and then laugh (especially if you are practicing laughter exercises to prepare the lungs for laughter as they will expand). On this note, let's laugh together now! ARE YOU READY?"

An eight-year-old boy came home excitedly, telling his dad that a school play is gonna be held next month

Dad: That's great! What role did you get?

Son: I'll be the husband!

Dad: (*sigh*) Tell your teacher tomorrow to give you a different role with more lines.

Ha Ha Ha poor kid he is learning a new thing about a husband's role in a marriage at a very young age!!!

Laughter And Creative Thinking:

"It's no accident that AHA and HAHA are spelled almost the same way." - Mitch Ditkoff

In an interview from an article in Forbes by Jacquelyn Smith on Michael Kerr (an international business speaker, president of Humor at Work, and author of The Humor Advantage titled: Why Some Businesses are Laughing all the Way to the Bank -Dec. 2013.) stated:

Ha + ha = aha! "Humor is a key ingredient in creative thinking," Kerr says. "It helps people play with ideas, lower their internal critic, and see things in new ways." Humor and creativity are both about looking at your challenges in novel ways and about making new connections you've never thought about before.

You can build trust with the effective use of humor because humor often reveals the authentic person lurking under the professional mask," Kerr says.

He explains that numerous studies suggest that people who share a healthy and positive sense of humor tend to be more likable. They are also viewed as being more trustworthy. "Humor is also viewed as a sign of intelligence," he adds. "All of these characteristics, as well as the fact that humor is a fabulous icebreaker and can tear down walls, can help people build relationships in the workplace, and especially these days, relationships are critical to success."

He added: "People who laugh in response to a conflict tend to shift from convergent thinking where they can see only one solution, to divergent thinking where multiple ideas are considered."

Having said that, I encourage you to watch more COMEDIES:

In 1987, psychologists Isen, Daubman, and Nowicki found that "people who watched a comedy film were more likely to solve a problem requiring a creative solution than people who watched a neutral film."

They cogitate (deeply thinking, reflecting) indicating that this was because positive emotions help to stimulate creative thinking. Additionally, researchers from the University of Maryland also discovered that comedy improves our mental flexibility by engaging our brains in ways that it does not expect.

The mere act of watching comedy can more than double our ability to solve brain teasers.

SIGN UP FOR AN IMPROV CLASS... SECOND CITY IS WAITING FOR YOU!

Did you ever consider taking a comedy or improv class?

It would help to stretch your imagination and in ways that you've never thought possible. It will invite you to engage in activities that will inspire your creativity.

I remember signing up for acting class in my early twenties because I appeared to be very social and open.

When I had to speak to a group of people or stand in front of an audience, I felt quite nervous at the beginning. I discovered that about myself years ago. This was when I was a narrator for Shakespeare's play 'Romeo and Juliet' back in high school. Right from the first performance, I froze right after the two-minute introduction. I never continued narrating as I blanked out and could not recall any of my lines. My theater teacher noticed as she started clapping, and everyone else followed her, and, hence, I was able to exit off the stage.

I remember feeling very embarrassed and tense. During my high school years, I went to an all-girls Christian Protestant school. It was one of the oldest and best high schools in Amman, Jordan, called CMS. They followed the British System, which was different from my prior education in an American school.

However, during this play, we had the other branch of School for Boys to participate in. It became even more embarrassing to my young teenage soul.

The play was performed a few times. I remember asking my theater teacher to assign another narrator for the next shows, but she insisted I would try again and explained there was not a ready replacement.

Well, I did a lot better on the second performance, which was in front of our families. I remember telling my mother to have her dad and brother sit upfront so I would feel more comfortable. They did. Therefore, I did feel more at ease as I performed much better.

It wasn't until years later when this feeling of tension in my stomach revisited. During my career as a vacation consultant, I had to stand in front of the room and present in a morning meeting talk about my experience, to all the representatives there. I had to explain how I was able to help the family who signed up with me the day before and joined the program, with every excuse and reason that made sense for them not to join, and they still joined.

Though I was very interactive with most of my coworkers and teammates, yet, as I stood there presenting and them watching me, it made me feel nervous (they probably heard it in my voice). In the end, I was able to continue and share all the information more comfortably.

I thought a few years later that being more seasoned in the business and interacting with even more employees that I didn't think I would have that feeling again, but I did.

I was assigned as part of a VIP panel for a sales training years later while working with, (Starwood Resorts and Hotels at the time, currently after the merger is Marriott Hotels) to speak on how to sell ELITE packages to exciting owners. That was their high-end ticket item to clients. An area I loved sharing my knowledge in, as I knew it was the best value back for the purchaser's investment, giving them the best benefits and vacation experience in their system.

I remember how enthusiastic I was about the topic when other reps would pick my brain and ask questions between breaks. This happened while I was presenting it to potential new owners.

"How could everyone not be showing and presenting it," I often wondered. It's the best product the company offers with the most privileges as well as flexibility.

I was very excited to be part of the panel, and that even got me to such a high feeling from the night before and the morning off.

I didn't need to practice as I would be sharing everything I do daily. It was my process. Now how could this be complicated??? Well, sure enough, I was able to pull it off, but boy did I get nervous the first few minutes. "Again," I thought to myself. Even when I had everything down packed!

Regardless of the beginning, as I continued sharing with all attendees. I managed to engage with them and felt a lot better. They probably felt it in my voice. Since there were few familiar faces from my actual department that attended, they started asking questions. The participation transitioned me back to being more relaxed and into my passion for the topic.

However, it was after that last experience that I got to take action on this. I decided to take an acting class. After all, I would push myself out of my comfort zone and more into my confidence in that area.

I signed up at that time with Ariza Talent agency intending to get more comfortable speaking in front of an audience. Well, I must say it was not as easy as I thought it was. Memorizing your lines and being in character required focus, and, on several occasions, we had to improvise.

All this with practice and time helped me feel much better and a lot stronger. Not long after I graduated from my acting class, I was on the Business Professional and Social committee board of AACC association with more of a speaking role. That included introducing speakers to events. I was not feeling nervous about all of this. Instead, I felt excited, and it became something that is no longer of a big concern to me.

Taking an improv, acting, or comedy class can truly help you become a better speaker and presenter. You'll have fun and be challenged to open yourself up. In improv workshops, two words are a foundation for all improvisation; **"Yes, And."** According to Kelly Leonard and Tom Horton, authors of a book by the same name and who are a part of The Second City leadership, "Creative breakthroughs occur in environments where ideas are not just fully explored but heightened and stretched to levels that might seem absurd at first. That is where the best comedy comes from, and that's where invention is realized."

Do what you fear most. You shall then dissolve one more wall standing between you and your best potential.

"Improvisation, if you play it at the top of your intelligence, leads to a kind of truth that people find really accessible." -

Bonnie Hunt

Invite more Play into your life, BE THERE & CREATE:

Inviting fun activities to build your confidence and enhance your creative skills is very smart to do. If you can be mindful of laughing more during the process, it just becomes more joyous and even easier to apply.

Set your intention and focus on having fun, laugh, and breathe, while working on your creative projects.

"Laugh my friend, for laughter ignites a fire within the pit of your belly and awakens your being." ~STELLA

MCCARTNEY

Laugh more while you're creating and create from a base of bliss. All of this will make your creative journey more joyful.

Find Humor Even Through Social Media Misunderstood Messages

Let me start with a story that I experienced with one of my LinkedIn connections, who became my friend over time. Mian Mohsin Zai, who is an International Award-Winning Author, Speaker, Spokesmodel, Publishing and Marketing Specialist, and with his permission, I will be sharing a conversation we had via LinkedIn messages:

Mian:

Dear Dr. Sofie,

Would you be interested in reading and reviewing my award-winning book, *"Wrinkles: A True Love Story"*?

If yes, then please write me your email address so I can send a PDF of my book.

You will be requested to post your review to Amazon and give a stars rating.

Awaiting your positive response.

Much love, MIAN!

Me:

Sure, you can send it... I will be busy till Feb as I also have 4 other book reviews to submit from prior commitments

I love to support you if you give me a summary of your book. I may be able to do your view faster ... just about to launch my book too and in the last chapter as we speak... lots going on, so reading a whole book will be a big-time commitment.

You can send PDF to:

369 Tesla Vista Dr.

Orlando FL 33096

Mian:

The PDF ebook is sent via email, my dear.

Please write your email.

Me: LOL

The funniest joke for the start of a decade!

Here is my email address ha ha ha

abundancenow888@icloud.com

I must have been so consumed in my book series and not fully focused on my response to Mian. But we both sure had a good belly laugh from my response.

Yes, I did not read "email address" before the address in the original text before I responded to him. Reading fast and thinking of the book being in the form of a document/ package sent to my home address in paper form to read was what I envisioned. It was because many of my author friends who gave me signed copies of their books did just that.

Yet I still wrote, "Send the PDF to my home address," hahaha. You know I was just tired, working so many late nights and early mornings on my book series. At the same time, I was still making an effort to be there for those who needed me as much as I could. However, this was an eye-opener, as I reduced my communication and interaction with lots of people afterward, so I can remain FOCUSED on WRITING.

Never lose your sense of humor, even when you make mistakes. Laugh them off as you learn from them, by taking action to course correct for better results.

I figured sharing some of my personal stories could get you to start laughing, this is only one of many. I will be looking forward to sharing more with you in book 2 and 3 soon.

Don't take things personal in life and have fun while you learn from both feedback and mistakes. MIAN and I laughed a few days later when he called to check if I received the email and had gotten a chance to read his book. We joked about sending my home address instead of my email address. However, at the end, January 3rd 2020, was a day I will remember, that started my new decade with some laughter.

"A person who knows how to laugh at himself will never cease

to be amused." ~Shirley MacLaine

I laughed hard then and now while writing and sharing the story with you. Did you ever have a similar experience? Well, if so, you're probably laughing in your head now. If you have, how about sending me an email and sharing your story. FYI that would be to my **EMAIL** address, not my **PO BOX** address.

Imagine you lived a perfect life and always right, you then may just not have enough funny memories to reflect on or share.

So next time you mess up laugh it off...unless you intentionally messed up, in that case, go to your closet, ask for forgiveness and repent lol

> *"IF LAUGHTER CAN'T SOLVE YOUR PROBLEMS, IT*
> *WILL DISSOLVE THEM BY CHANGING YOUR*
> *BODY CHEMISTRY AND MINDSET SO YOU CAN*
> *FACE THEM IN A BETTER WAY."*

> *"There is no laughter in the medicine, but there is a lot of*
> *medicine in the laughter."*

> *"When you laugh, you change. When you change, the whole*
> *world changes."*

> *"We are paying a very high price for taking life seriously, now*
> *it's time to take laughter seriously." ~ Dr. Madan Kataria*

Laughter and cheers to Dr.Madan Kataria and to all the great work he has done around the globe in spreading humor through Laughter Yoga exercises.

Dr.Madan Kataria, a medical doctor from Mumbai, India, is popularly known as the 'Guru of Giggling' (London Times). He is the founder of the Laughter Yoga Clubs movement that started in 1995. Beginning with just five people in a public park in Mumbai in 1995, it has grown into a worldwide movement of over 6000 Laughter Yoga clubs in more than 60 countries. I was certified by him as a *Laughter Yoga Instructor*. In my heart, I feel a combination of laughter, creativity, and spirituality can enable many to truly transcend their Mental, Physical, and Soul exhaustion.

Celebrate life by honoring your breath and giving it YOUR BEST.

Your best intentions

Your best effort

Your best contribution

Your best peace

Your best joy

Your best self!!!

I believe that every occasion and situation need its special attention. Some will require focused attention and mindfulness, like a surgeon during an operation. Firefighters, Paramedics, and Law Enforcement Officers are not expected to be laughing while answering calls, especially in an emergency, such as a 911 call. But, with such demanding jobs, they too NEED to laugh MORE to keep their sanity and have a better balance in life. I remember Dr. Bob Choat told me stories of his time as a Los Angeles Police Officer. In the Marines, he said that laughter certainly made a difference during the aftermath of stressful events.

"I remember an incident back in my LAPD days 40 years ago while working patrol in the West Valley Area, me and my partner were engaged in pursuit down Valley Circle Blvd. Driving at high speed, all of a sudden, our unit (police car) started slowing down, and there were sparks flying up behind us. The driveshaft had broken off from the rear differential, and people on the sidewalks were cheering, laughing and whistling. All I can say, it was quite embarrassing. The suspect we had been chasing got away, and we ended up stuck on the side of the road waiting for a tow truck. Later, we both were back at the station, and other officers were laughing like crazy. We joined in. It was hilarious thinking about what happened. We looked at it as a police comedy show. HA HA HA!

Laughter helped alleviate an embarrassing situation as well as

the stress from it." ~Dr. Bob Choat

While you're serving others, make sure you add a dose of sunshine and create some "ME TIME" to relax and add more giggles to shift your state from possibly a "cloudy day" or negative emotions to a "pick me up" positive state.

When you understand the science of laughter, you will intentionally want to integrate it into your wellness plan.

There is a lot of scientific evidence and research supporting the benefits of laughter to our overall health, including its aid in memory recall, lowering blood pressure, stress levels, enhanced creative abilities in addition to giving your diaphragm the only BEST exercise. Knowing this, YOU WOULD WANT TO LAUGH MORE, wouldn't you?

Laughter, Spirituality, and Creativity are Superfoods to our Soul that can shift a mental state instantly. A consistent input of those three into our holistic self-strengthens the immune system of our whole being. I recommend it to be a daily dosage for a healthy body, mind, and soul.

When you understand the conclusive contribution of laughter, you will add it to your emotional gym exercises more often.

So, I studied the science of laughter, got certified as a Laughter Yoga instructor, and later became a Co-Founder of the Laughter Mindset Program. Since then, I've gone through some big losses in my life. That includes my mother, my beloved angel cat Giovanni, my grandmother, Dr. Wayne Dyer, and later my son's very close friend/brother, "Frenchy".

I made sure to not let my body go without laughter fitness exercises. I engaged all hemispheres of the brain for optimal mental health and clarity. This wasn't the case because I found things funny, nor because I was living in denial, or not because I was feeling sad.

However, I still brushed my teeth every morning and before bedtime. Just like I had to eat even if I was not hungry or felt like eating. I knew my lungs needed laughter exercise especially understanding the science of laughter and its positive influence in our body. I knew that there is nothing that will work my diaphragm as laughter would.

It sure lifted my mood, helped boost my immune system, especially in such trying times. Laughter shortened the period of my grieving or at least helped me cope better in several ways.

This way, I can be able to be there for myself, my loved ones, serve my purpose, and know that all my angels in heaven are a part of me that will always be alive, remembered, and loved. They may leave our homes but never our hearts.

You see that in life, you will invest in learning skills that will better equip you during your life journey. Similarly, you want to make sure you're SOUL SKILLED in times of crises, facing adversity, or unexpected life events.

I miss all my angels in heaven, each in their own special way. I miss each of them in their own special way. But throughout the years, I learned a lot about myself, and a lot of different energy healing modalities, mindsets, thinking styles, and systems. Not that they made me immune or numb from feeling the pain, but they helped me understand, direct, and regulate the pain much better. I understood the laws of nature, creation, detachment and the universe. I looked at life with a different perspective and clearer insight.

Understanding the relationship with my CREATOR better increased my faith, and my feelings of detachment were eased. Furthermore, my acceptance of what I can't control was accepted and respected. My inner peace was more sustainable.

"A sad child means an ill child, and a laughing old man means he is still young. Even death cannot make him old, nothing can make him old. His energy is still flowing and overflowing; he is always flooded. Laughter is a flooding of energy." ~Osho

Surround yourself with more childlike playfulness, give yourself permission to play, create, laugh, learn, and grow. Be around happy, joyous souls and laugh a lot more TOGETHER.

Laughter is said to be contagious; WE laugh up to 30 times more when we are in the company of others as opposed to when we are alone.

Go out there and spread the LAUGHTER VIRUS. It is the only uplifting and healthy virus to be passed around in a crowd. Stay contagious! Keep tossing some Laughter Cocktails and boost your endorphins, creativity, and adaptability to life. Can I say Cheers to that?

Remember This...

Breathe and Laugh to Creativity

"Laughter is a form of internal jogging. It moves your internal organs around. It enhances respiration. It is an igniter of great expectations." ~Norman Cousins

Go out there, have more fun, laugh more, BE PRESENT, and CREATE!

Chapter 7:
The Science of the Brain and Creativity

In this chapter, you'll discover...

- Individual Creativity
- Collaborative Creativity

"Honoring your INDIVIDUALITY allows you to walk CONFIDENTLY into your CREATIVE SELF by TAP DANCING along the Timeline of YOUR LIFE." ~Dr. Sofie Nubani

Individual Creativity

Individual creativity is more akin to ideas generated that are not yet a reality. This includes concepts, which are implementations and inventions that produce results that are created by a single individual.

For example, this would include a chef creating a recipe, a sales leader creating a training manual, a singer writing his or her lyrics, an engineer inventing a railway station, and so forth.

Individual Creativity has advantages such as:

- Setting your environment.

- Freedom of start and end time.

- Adjusting your preferred climate. (You may prefer slightly cooler or warmer temperatures).

- Choosing soundtracks or frequencies, you enjoy listening to while working on creative projects.

- Being Self-Entertained and having something to look forward to.

- INCREASING your Self-Esteem, independence, creative confidence while DECREASING your Self-Doubts, dependence, and limitations.

- No dress code required; you may choose to dress down, be in something comfy, go barefoot, wear shorts and a t-shirt.

- No external distractions or influences on your thoughts, choices or actions

- You step back into your memory and collect/connect dots from your past experiences, beliefs, values, principles, learnings, knowledge, divine channeling, and individual intuition. This will allow you to tap freely into your creative abilities.

Being able to think creatively and create individually is such an empowering skill to have. Creativity is the motivator of social progress, and it affects all aspects of human life.

If we understand how our brain functions and how we can build new neural connections and pathways based on our thoughts, ideas, associations, and connections, with practiced curiosity, new experiences, and flexible perception, it all can BOOST our creative state.

Bypassing old patterns and incorporating new ones and, at the same time, expanding our experiences and association cortex WILL hold a powerful influence on optimizing our creative mindset.

Our brain builds HIGHER COGNITIVE functions by:

1. associating

2. linking

3. connecting

If we learn the organization of our brain and how it operates during our creative process, it will give us insights and better clarity on how we can best implement them within ourselves. Furthermore, it will allow us the possibility to recreate that same process in machines.

Also, it will enhance our creative experiences and clarify (based on one's brain functions and abilities) why some may apply their creativity better than others.

Creativity and the Right Brain Myth

The Myth about the Creative Right Brain:

THE HUMAN BRAIN DOES NOT HAVE ONE CREATIVE CENTER.

Creative people use the WHOLE BRAIN during their creative process!!!

Creativity is the result of different sections of the brain, communicating and interacting with one another to generate novel patterns through the use of existing ideas or concepts.

Ned Herrmann was the head of management education at General Electric and founded the Ned Herrmann Group in 1980. Ned was also an educator and consultant who has spent two decades developing models of brain activity and its relationship to the creative process. He shares an interesting view of creativity residing in the RIGHT hemisphere of the brain. I like his response to a question that was asked on a blog post at ScientificAmerican.com.

In addition to Ned Herrmann's idea of a creative process, I would like to introduce you to an early 20th Century model by Graham Wallas known as "The Creative Process Model" further down below.

Question:

Is it true that creativity resides in the right hemisphere of the brain?

Ned Herrmann's answer:

The role of the right hemisphere is essential to the creative process. But it supplies only a quarter of the thinking needed to realize the full creative process. We also need the left hemisphere and both halves of the limbic system to optimize creative output.

For example, he mentions the creative process in each stage using the idea of whole-brain creativity.

The most understandable description of the creative process consists of six phases:

- Interest
- Preparation
- Incubation
- Illumination
- Verification
- Application

Each step of this process has its distinguishing brain waves.

From a left brain/right brain perspective, the creative process can be diagnosed as follows:

1. Interest (left and right).
2. Preparation (left)
3. Incubation (right).
4. Illumination (right).
5. Verification (left)
6. Application (left and right).

It is a balanced process--four "lefts" and four "rights."

When it comes to brain function, in particular, realize that it's not a one-side hemisphere function as shared above. Creative thinking involves increased communication between brain networks that usually work independently. Creativity is enhanced by increased use of the whole brain.

Several different parts of the brain are important for creative thinking, including the frontal cortex, hippocampus, and basal ganglia.

1. **Frontal Cortex**: (The prefrontal cortex (PFC) is the part of our brain located at the front of the frontal lobe. It is implicated in a variety of

complex behaviors that include planning. It greatly contributes to personality development and houses most of our higher cognitive function). The frontal cortex has long been thought of as the hub or center of creativity. It controls important cognitive skills in humans, such as emotional expression, problem-solving, memory, language, and judgment. It is, in essence, the "control panel" or "inner CEO" of our personality as well as our ability to communicate.

Besides, it seems to be responsible for many of the functions that contribute to creative thinking. Those include working or "short term memory," abstraction, planning, and cognitive flexibility.

Recent research has concluded that the frontal cortex is critical to creative thinking and having the ability to develop STRATEGIES, which is a key part of creativity. For example, when we think of new or unusual ways to use common objects such as nail polish to stop a run in a pantyhose, or a makeup brush to clean in between keyboards to clean dust or crumbs.

2. **Hippocampus**: The hippocampus is best known for the memory of things that you can declare, such as facts and experiences. The processes that the hippocampus performs to process these memories involve storing and retrieving the pieces of these memories from where they are stored in the cortex. In the creative process, it is similar to REMEMBERING experiences by pulling together different parts of the experience. The hippocampus may be used in IMAGINATION to pull together ideas in ways that you have not thought of in the past.

Albert Einstein once said: "Imagination is more important than knowledge. Knowledge is limited. Imagination encircles the world."

Just as creativity is an important 21st Century Skill, so is IMAGINATION.

"The true sign of intelligence is not knowledge but imagination."

So, the hippocampus is the brain region that allows us to imagine a future. It also is the same brain region involved in recalling/remembering the past.

Creative processes in the brain require the concept of internal representation. Internal representations are instantiations of ideas, concepts, or images that the brain stores for some time, however brief or long.

New research demonstrates the critical role our hippocampus performs concerning creativity.

In one study, it was shown that participants who had damaged their hippocampus had lower scores of divergent thinking as measured by the Torrance Test of Creativity [2].

In a second study, it was shown, using the RAT, that convergent thinking was also impaired in patients with hippocampal damage as described above [3]

3. **Basal ganglia**: The basal ganglia are structures deep within the brain. They are associated with a variety of functions, including control of voluntary motor movements, procedural learning, habit learning, eye movements, cognition, and emotion.

Cooperation of the basal ganglia, cerebellum, sensory cerebrum, and hippocampus will lead to possible Implications for cognition, consciousness, intelligence, and creativity.

The basal ganglia process the memory of skills and how to do things. These are often things that we do not have to think about directly, such as riding a bike. You get better at doing creative tasks with time and practice.

4. **White matter**: White matter makes up the connections between various brain structures. The better connected the areas of the brain are, the better and faster the brain is able to process information. In the

creative process, having a well-connected brain may allow you to bring together more ideas, more quickly.

Stress reduction, walking, dancing, exercising, learning new skills, and learning how to juggle all increases the amount of white matter in the brain. This all results in better neural connections and creativity.

The UC Davis Health System describes it best: the gray matter (nerve cells) of our brain is the computer, and the white matter are the cables that connect everything and transmit signals.

Creativity is a sum of ALL the NEURAL NETWORKS that our body is made up of, shaping, framing, and creating our experiences from the top of our head to the bottom of our feet.

Taste, sensations, touch, sound, and smell all influence our creative expression. A certain smell may spark thought. It could also be a new association between the smell and location at the time that may spark words for a new poem. Maybe, the sound of children playing in the background may spark a memory, a new idea, or design for a new children's playground at a park.

The more ideas, the more experiences, the more available neural connections we have access to will allow our neural body function and network communication to assist us in our creative process.

"The world always seems brighter when you've just made something that wasn't there before." ~ *Neil Gaiman*

It's about being "in The Zone" and achieving a state of flow as our brain waves transition from beta to alpha and then theta. In such a state, our SENSE OF SELF starts disappearing. We experience a temporary deactivation of the prefrontal cortex.

An article in Psychology Today titled, *"Flow States and Creativity"* by Steven Kotler in his column *"The Playing Field,"* affirms how a state of flow is influenced:

This has huge consequences for creativity. For example, during flow, the dorsolateral prefrontal cortex (the part of the brain charged with self-monitoring and impulse control) goes quiet. The DLPFC is our inner critic, that voice of doubt and disparagement. As a result, with this area deactivated, we're far less critical and far more courageous, both augmenting our ability to imagine new possibilities and share those possibilities with the world.

During flow, the brain releases an enormous cascade of neurochemistry. Large quantities of norepinephrine, dopamine, endorphins, anandamide, and serotonin flood our system. All are pleasure-inducing, performance-enhancing chemicals with considerable impacts on creativity. Both norepinephrine and dopamine amp up focus, boosting imaginative possibilities by helping us gather more information.

They also lower signal-to-noise ratios, increasing pattern recognition, or our ability to link ideas together in new ways. Anandamide is a potent antidepressant and is noted for inducing "blissful" sensations and is known as a natural, reliable mood-enhancer. Anandamide increases lateral thinking—meaning it expands the size of the database searched by the pattern recognition system.

Anandamide can be increased by consuming dark chocolate with high cocoa content in addition to CBD. CBD is especially helpful for those people who have a hard time increasing the levels of anandamide by themselves. Exercising, especially running, is another great way to boost levels and change moods.

"Eating chocolate boosts anandamide in two ways – by stimulating the endocannabinoid receptors and by blocking anandamide's breakdown. In fact, some researchers say that the simplest way to increase anandamide levels is by eating dark chocolate." ~Meredith Patterson

So, now that you're aware of the areas of your brain that are responsible for enhancing the creative process. Those include the importance of hormonal balance towards a better state of flow. Knowing all this, you'll start to engage in those so-called "PEAK EXPERIENCES" more often. Abraham Maslow, the creator of the Hierarchy of Needs, referred to this as "extraordinary experiences."

It could be ARTISTIC CREATIVITY or SCIENTIFIC CREATIVITY. The process of creating can consist of generating new ideas, imagining possible outcomes, problem-solving, visualizing new realities, or simply connecting the dots between two existing concepts helps express one's extraordinary experience.

This could've been created by using a formula of (multiplying, dividing, or subtracting). Thus, it could have resulted in inventing a new product or service.

Such experiences create beautiful 'aha' moments connecting one to their feeling of intrinsic motivation. This boosts their creativity and increases their productivity.

This will energize them as they feel a sense of trust in their abilities, accomplishments, and adds positivity and optimism towards creating more in the future. Having Peak Experiences (as referenced above) a state that is generated effortlessly, leaving us less judgmental, more energized, and creative.

"If you can't describe what you are doing as a process, you don't know what you are doing." ~W. Edwards Deming

The Graham Wallas Creative Process Model

THE CREATIVE PROCESS MODEL of the Creative process as defined by Graham Wallas, the scientist, and author of "The Art of Thought," is laid down as follow:

1. Preparation

2. Incubation

3. Illumination

4. Verification

Researcher Graham Wallas, many years ago, set down a description of what happens as people approach problems to come up with creative solutions. He described his four-stage process as follows:

1. In the **preparation** stage, we define the problem, need, or desire. We then gather any information that the solution or response needs to account for. Finally, we set up criteria for verifying the solution's acceptability.

2. In the **incubation** stage, we step back from the problem and allow our minds to contemplate and work it through. Like preparation, incubation can last minutes, weeks, or even years.

3. In the **illumination** stage, ideas arise from the mind to provide the basis of a creative response. These ideas can be pieces of the whole or the whole itself. This means seeing the entire concept or entity all at once. Unlike the other stages, illumination is often very brief and involves a tremendous rush of insights within a few minutes or hours.

4. In **verification**, the final stage, one carries out activities to demonstrate whether or not what emerged in the illumination stage satisfies the need and the criteria defined in the preparation stage.

The first and last stages are left brain (Quadrant A and B) activities. The second and third stages belong to the right brain (Quadrant D and C).

This model of the creative process has been placed on Ned Herrmann's Four Quadrant model of the human brain. In that model, he adds **Interest** as a first and **Application** as the last. That makes it a six-step process as follows:

1. Interest

2. Preparation

3. Incubation

4. Illumination

5. Verification

6. Application

(Notes based on Ned Herrmann's book, *The Creative Brain*)

"The creation of something new is not accomplished by the intellect but by the play instinct acting from inner necessity. The creative mind plays with the objects it loves." ~Carl Jung

When it comes to Individual Creativity, it is very helpful to understand the different types of creativity and the actual psychology behind it in order to foster, cultivate, and optimize a creative mindset.

Creativity is considered one of the most complex topics to study, as noted by many psychologists. It is very interesting to note how only a few psychologists had fundamental insights, theories, and supporting evidence that helped many understand the psychology behind creativity. Their works and contributions are valuable and even to this day are helping others unlock the secrets behind it.

That leads me to Arne Dietrich, a professor of cognitive neuroscience. Dietrich studied the neuroscience of creativity, among other topics such as, consciousness. Dietrich argues that creativity doesn't stem from one easily definable process or brain pattern. His results also indicate that "emotion has a huge effect on the way our brains can be creative" and that positive emotion seems to be related to a deeper state of creative flow.

Earlier we had awareness about the different functions of the brain and their active role in creativity. Now we will learn about the 4 different types of creativity.

Types of Creativity

A 2004 research paper published in the Psychonomic Bulletin & Review, shared how Dietrich described the four different types of creativity based on where it resides within the brain. Dietrich created what he called the "Knowledge Domain" with four distinct processing modes;

1. Deliberate

2. Cognitive

3. Emotional

4. Spontaneous

1-Deliberate and Cognitive Creativity:

"Thomas Edison"

Thomas Edison, demonstrates an example of this type of a creative individual. Someone who has prior knowledge in a few domains, possesses skill and abilities to take action by connecting the dots of previous experiences putting together existing information in new and novel ways.

This type of creative individual usually is purposeful, has a high level of intellectual curiosity, and willingness to learn. Engineers and similar occupations tend to fall into this category. They are deliberately focused and with a high use of their cognition, drawing off of knowledge in this area, and forming connections from such information.

Edison believed to discover a good idea you need to generate many ideas.

"GENIUS IS 99% PERSPIRATION AND 1% INSPIRATION"

It took Edison over 50,000 experiments to invent the alkaline storage cell battery and 9000 to perfect the light bulb.

"I have not failed. I've just found 10,000 ways that won't

work."- Thomas Edison

Edison, who received no formal education, believed that the educational system programmed people to have certain assumptions based on what they studied. Which in essence led individuals to have fixed perceptions and a lack of expanded consciousness to other possibilities outside of their formal teachings.

Edison's Unique Hiring Style

Edison's experience led him to develop a hiring style prior to hiring a research assistant. Prior to hiring a research assistant, Edison would invite the candidate over for a bowl of soup. If the person seasoned the soup before tasting it, Edison would not hire the candidate. He did not want to hire people who had so many built-in assumptions into their everyday life that they would even assume the soup is not properly seasoned. Edison was definitely a Deliberate Cognitive Creative. "You consciously think about something and then piece together information to form an original idea." This type of creativity lies in the brain's prefrontal cortex (PFC), which allows you to maintain focused attention on a problem. In addition to this, you also connect information from your existing body of knowledge and different parts of your brain which results in generating novel ideas.

You can actually PLAN for this type of creativity. PFC FUNCTION in Deliberate Cognitive Creativity:

FOCUSED ATTENTION + BODY OF KNOWLEDGE = NOVEL IDEAS

2-Deliberate and Emotional Creativity:

"A-ha" moments

Insight, often referred to as an "A-ha moment," has been defined as a sudden, conscious change in a person's representation of a stimulus, situation, event, or problem. According to Dietrich, "Creative people who are classified as deliberate and emotional, let their work be influenced by their emotions."

If you've ever gone through a crisis (a world pandemic, a relationship break-up, got fired, gone through a bankruptcy) and then replayed the incidents, and reflected on what series of bad decisions you might have made that contributed to the crisis, then you may have experienced deliberate and emotional creativity. This type of creativity lies in the brain's AMYGDALA, responsible for human emotion such as fear, stress, and embarrassment. Such emotions can also be a motivator of creativity. Thank you, amygdala!!!

Though it is not the best environment to create from, it might just be what you needed at the time to get distracted from such a state and transition out of it (fear, stress, guilt, embarrassment etc.).

The almond-shaped amygdala forms part of the limbic system and plays a key role in the processing of emotions. This part of the brain also accords with emotional intelligence and intrapersonal awareness.

You can influence the amygdala by a variety of strategies, games, and brain exercise. Why not go for it?

3-Spontaneous and Cognitive Creativity:

"EUREKA!" A MOMENT OF A SUDDEN DISCOVERY.

Just like Sir Isaac Newton's "Eureka" (Apple falling on the head) moment. Similarly, in the case of Archimedes and his creativity that was shared throughout history.

Have you ever experienced a "eureka" moment? How did you feel? If not, let me explain. It is a moment that occurs when someone is working on solving a particular problem or challenge that seems too hard to iron or figure out. They then resume regular activities totally unrelated to the task at hand; like walking, talking to a friend, taking a shower. Then suddenly, after stepping away from the problem, they suddenly get a flash, vision, or deep insight into the correct answer, solution which helps them solve a particular problem. "Eureka!"

What truly happens to our brain in this type of creativity is explained in a breakdown in a blog article at The Grio regarding Spontaneous Cognitive Creativity:

"Spontaneous, cognitive creativity can activate when your brain stops working on something and shifts to your unconscious mind to work on it instead. Your unconscious work is done in the basal ganglia part of your brain. When you stop working on a problem and do something completely unrelated, you give your PFC time to make new connections among your existing body of knowledge without your focused awareness."

An example of SPONTANEOUS and COGNITIVE CREATIVITY.

Another insight that I like by David Burkus of Harvard Business Review explains exactly why breaks lead to creative breakthroughs:

"The researchers found that the group given a break to work on an unrelated task (the Myers-Briggs test) generated the most ideas...One possible explanation for these findings is that...When you work on a problem continuously, you can become fixated on previous solutions....Taking a break from the

problem and focusing on something else entirely gives the mind

some time to release its fixation on the same solutions and let

the old pathways fade from memory. Then, when you return to

the original problem, your mind is more open to new

possibilities -- eureka moments." (This type of creativity is

done in the basal ganglia part of the brain. Our unconscious

work is done in the BASAL GANGLIA.)

It is why, when it comes to creativity, RECOVERY is important. When you feel stuck or overwhelmed and just can't come up with a solution while facing a challenge or trying to solve a problem creatively, just STEP AWAY. This includes taking a break, resting your brain, even going to sleep. These are recommendations that will aid your creative process and may just lead YOU to your own Eureka moment.

4-Spontaneous and Emotional Creativity:

"Epiphanies"

An epiphany is an experience of a sudden and striking realization. Generally, the term is used to describe scientific breakthroughs, religious discoveries, or philosophical discoveries but it can be applied in any situation. This is the kind of creativity that you think of when you think about traditional creative careers such as, artists and musicians (creating from powerful spontaneous and emotional moments such as, a divine vision, religious experience or an epiphany.) Knowledge in such experiences is not necessary as it does not rely mainly on cognitive ability rather, on SKILL. A good level of skill is often needed such as; artistic skills musical, writing, painting etc. Such skills are required to create something from the spontaneous and emotional creative idea. This type of creativity stems from the AMYGDALA part of the brain as well.

Know that working in one mode of creativity, does not stop you from the other types of creativity. For example, a scientist might be studying research and experiment through deliberate and cognitive creativity, but might still experience spontaneous and emotional creativity while engaged in other creative endeavors.

A good example of this would be, the most influential scientist, theoretical physicist/mathematician Albert Einstein, who loved playing the violin and said: "if he had not gone into physics, he likely would have become a musician".

In reality there are conscious and unconscious agendas in the brain and both are important in the process of creativity and understanding the four different types of creativity. Understanding the creative process and the four different types of creativity will help you; prepare, relate, connect, and link different types of creativity in much better ways. Intentionally utilize every type, tool, strategy and use of CREATIVITY to its best value, benefit, novelty, functionality, and outcome. Learn your creative style/type, practice different thinking styles, explore YOU more often and discover new ways on how you can be more creative.

WANT TO LEARN MORE ABOUT YOUR CREATIVE TYPE?

Have fun with this free test: https://mycreativetype.com/share/visionary/

You can share what you've discovered with the OPTIMIZE YOUR CREATIVE MINDSET groups on social media platforms and interact with like-minded creative thinkers.

Drop by and say: "HELLO" to connect, celebrate, and grow with your creative soul tribe.

"It is when we understand our Individual Creativity (Creative Thinking Styles/Types, Processes, Experiences, Brain and Neural Functions that are influencing our creative behaviors and habits), that we can magnify the power of our creativity, sharpen our creative skills and optimize our creative mindset."—Dr. Sofie Nubani

It is necessary to guide your cognition in the most appropriate way. Leaky attention from outside influence may get you sidetracked and may decrease your creative productivity and focus. To be a successful individual (creatrix or creative) you must be able to self-regulate your thoughts, emotions, and behaviors. In addition to that, limit distractions and be flexible to shift mental sets (Shifting). For example, having characteristics that exhibit a delicate balance between spontaneous/cognitive control and flexibility/ stability.

According to an article in Psychology today by Hal McDonald, Ph.D.:

"Real-life creative achievement was associated with better

Inhibition abilities, indicating that an ability to "suppress or

override" certain trains of thought, even if they appear

inspirational, is necessary for productive creativity."

Furthermore, where real-life creative achievement was separated

into artistic and IT domains, people in the artistic, as

compared with IT, professions exhibited both; better overall

executive function and better shifting abilities. This suggests

that, while artists have demonstrably "leaky" attention, once

they are engaged in a creative task, they can usefully channel the

leak by inhibiting unrelated responses and shifting between the

task at hand and original ideas that may be related to that task.

Rather than being passively "possessed" by some external

inspiration, as Plato imagined, artists "may be able to actively

regulate their thoughts and behavior by guiding their cognition

in most appropriate ways." While a leaky attention makes them

susceptible to environmental influences beyond their control,

artists achieve a delicate balance between spontaneity and

control, exhibiting "characteristics of stability and flexibility, as

they are able to flexibly shift mental sets (Shifting), while also exhibiting the propensity to successfully regulate their thoughts

and behaviors (Common EF)."

Individual Creativity helps you cope with life better on many levels and in different areas, especially when dealing with uncertainties. It allows you to be more open minded, which will invite more experiences to your life and enhance your adapting skills.

However, to create best you must have creative awareness.

Creative Awareness

To consciously create anything, you must first focus your attention and awareness on the topic, and have some understanding of it. If we have no understanding about a topic, we have nothing on which to focus on. When our awareness shrinks, our creative abilities decrease. Therefore, creating will require both; awareness as well as understanding. The better you understand something, the better you can come up with creative solutions. The next time before you get frustrated while creating something, make sure to gather enough information, search, and research on its topic. Then ask as many questions as you need that will help you understand it better (for that you also would need to be patient with the process).

"Every human has four endowments - self-awareness,

conscience, independent will, and creative imagination. These

give us the ultimate human freedom... The power to choose, to

respond, to change."-Stephen Covey

ARE YOU A CREATOR OR A CONSUMER?

Although many of us will consume things however, a creator's mindset would think, "HOW CAN I CREATE A PRODUCT OR SERVICE THAT WILL BE FUNCTIONAL AND USEFUL?" That mindset will keep your creative zone ignited and your imagination boosted. Creative awareness helps you understand yourself better. If you learn more about your strengths and weaknesses, it will help build your confidence up which will make room for transformation. Creative awareness allows you to tap into your creative gifts freely making your individual creativity more unique. Acknowledge and celebrate your own uniqueness, diversity, and individual creativity TODAY!

Chapter 8:
C.O.U.R.A.G.E. | Section 1

In this chapter, you'll discover...

- The 7 Traits that will Optimize your Creative Mindset

"Creativity Takes COURAGE." -Henri Matisse

The Acronym C.O.U.R.A.G.E., was inspired by a research done by Gita Johar at Columbia Business School via a webinar interview that she gave a lecture on regarding "4 traits of creativity", which she explained in the Acronym C.O.R.E. It was very basic and brief, however, it inspired me to dig a bit deeper and research further.

I share this and invite you to remain open, flexible, and adaptable in life as you develop your creative skills. You will meet people, listen to webinars, lectures, and even music that can inspire you and can get your creative juices flowing. As you sharpen your *Association Cortex*, connect information and relationships, you will be able to create your own unique creative flair which will bring productive results.

In this case, I created an acronym where all the letters had a common thread. Each letter carries an important trait and has a strong pillar that will help you cultivate creativity, and will help you understand their influence on your creative process and flow.

The Acronym I created from the 7 traits that will Optimize your Creative Mindset is C.O.U.R.A.G.E.:

C-Curiosity

O-Openness (to Experience)

U-Uniqueness

R-Risk (Tolerance)

A-Attention

G-Gallantry (Courage/Boldness)

E-Energy

Understanding each word and trait in this acronym will guide you to create courageously, uniquely, and with spirit.

This chapter will cover the first three letters: C, O, and U.

Curiosity

Let's start with the C for Curiosity, what it means and why & how it is an important trait of creative people.

DEFINITION: A STRONG DESIRE TO LEARN OR KNOW ABOUT ANYTHING; INQUISITIVENESS.

Though curiosity and inquisitiveness are synonyms to one another, they are slightly different.

Curiosity can be described as a combination of: Creativity, Openness, and Inquisitiveness.

1-Creativity: Curiosity fuels creativity leading us into the unknown with a more positive attitude.

2-Openness: To find new experiences, which is why curious people seek out challenges and new experiences to expand their vision and broaden their horizons.

3-Inquisitiveness: Curiosity marked by various enquiries, which in particular relates to having intellectual curiosity.

Furthermore, having intellectual curiosity or inquisitiveness only happens when the search for information is a goal in itself.

That means, we are interested in a particular subject and our searching for information is guided by an intrinsic drive from our desire to know, learn, and understand. This is different from Information-Seeking, which can be motivated by either intrinsic or extrinsic drive.

"Intrinsic motivation refers to the spontaneous tendency 'to seek out novelty and challenges, to extend and exercise one's capacity, to explore, and to learn' (Domenico and Ryan, 2017)".

WHAT THE SCIENCE SAYS

"Research findings on the benefits of curiosity found that curiosity is one of the 5 strengths most reliably linked to satisfaction with life. Curiosity also is associated with happiness, health, longevity, and positive social relationships. Curious people are more attracted to activities that offer opportunities for growth, competence, and higher levels of stimulation. Thus, they are likely to report having personal goals aimed at self-improvement, such as wanting to know more about their character strengths! Curiosity is often the entry point to many lifelong hobbies, passions, and pursuits.

There are two key components to curious individuals: They are interested in exploring new ideas, activities and experiences, and they also have a strong desire to increase their own personal knowledge.

Curiosity is a strength within the virtue category of wisdom, one of six virtues that subcategorize the 24 strengths. Wisdom describes strengths that help you gather and use knowledge. The other strengths in Wisdom are creativity, curiosity, judgment, love of learning, and perspective." -VIA Institute

Curiosity is a behavior that arises from within you, driven by internal rewards. It is the opposite of boredom. Curiosity can lead to either happy or frustrating outcomes, depending on the original intention and motivation. Knowing the difference between healthy curiosity and destructive curiosity is what marks maturity and having wisdom.

- Do you recall a time in your life at which being curious resulted in an awful outcome?

- What was the root cause of that experience?

- What was the biggest lesson to take away from it?

- Knowing what you know regarding that experience, would you repeat the same action today?

I remember a time when I was 5 years old taking my 3-year-old cousin and 5-year-old neighbor's daughter to a long walk away from my grandma's house, where I was staying at for the summer. I had what was equivalent to the amount of a dollar in quarters. Me and my cousin and neighbor's daughter headed to a toy store that I enjoyed going to (located downtown). The toy store was about an hour walking distance away from my grandma's house.

It was such a thrilling adventure because I was so excited to buy a doll called "Sandy" at that time, for all 3 of us. YES, with one dollar, something the owner of the store did not accommodate. He probably felt uncomfortable to even have any transactions made, even if I had enough money to buy the whole toy store lol.

The biggest problem was that we did not inform any adults in our families that we were leaving and I was the one who led both of them to come with me which later on converted into a not-so-fun adventure.

After being noticed missing, my grandma tried to find us but couldn't. She then called my uncle to search for us. After asking different neighbors whether they had seen 3 little girls walking and a few people mentioning the last locations they had seen us at, she intuitively headed downtown and was able to find us as we were still at the big toy store trying to find Sandy dolls for all 3 of us.

43 years ago, things were a lot different and much safer, luckily for us. I mean, imagine 3 little cuties wandering around loosely on the streets today. BIGGG RISK!

My uncle was of course upset as he drove us all the way back home. I was the one who got in the most trouble, since it was my idea and I led the way to the store. Initially my dopamine levels rose (in anticipation of buying the Sandy Dolls) as we headed to the toy store, but unfortunately switched to high cortisol levels (as my uncle chastised me) as we headed back home!

A good advice: Never underestimate a 5-year old's curiosity and creative intelligence. In this case – memorizing directions to get to a place they really like. Obviously, my accounting skills were off on that one.

The good news is that later my uncle bought all 3 of us a Sandy dolly that we picked from my favorite toy store. He had told us that he would do so only I promised that I would not go someplace alone nor drag other kids along with me without first asking or being granted permission.

I remained very curious growing up and got myself in similar trouble through my teens. I always wanted to explore and discover more about things, more than what I was just told or thought they were. In fact, everything I was taught that was not good, piqued my interest to want to learn more about WHY it's was not good. Even if it was good, I wanted to understand WHY it was good.

That is exactly why and how, children could be challenging to impatient adults because of their ongoing CHARGED-UP curiosity.

Curiosity can cause unpleasant experiences/results sometimes just as it can cause the opposite, that being magical experiences/results.

As an adult today, I am considered to be a creatrix-intuitive existential spiritualist, I believe my intellectual curiosity, openness to new experiences and gallantry, led me to develop a lot of depth and awareness in many areas of my life.

What interests me in life is curiosity, challenges, the good fight with its victories and defeats." -Paulo Coelho

Were you a curious child in your adolescence?

I encourage you to AWAKEN your inner genius, curious mindset, and creative/curiosity intelligence. Start expressing your heart's intentions and passions to life, invite more vitality, energy, adventures, and a dab of intensity to your life.

Let those DOPAMINE levels rise, driving your CREATIVITY to new and undiscovered, exciting and soul charging heights!!!

Dopamine is associated with those "A-ha" moments we experience that are in turn linked with feelings of pleasure (for example, winning, accomplishments, problem solving, seeking-mode and creative projects etc...).

A scientific research paper done at the Medical University of Vienna, indicated a close correlation between dopamine, exhilaration, and creativity. It is probably what excites curious people to stay curious and feel the rewards from doing so. Researchers have determined that dopamine, the brain's reward chemical, is intricately linked to the brain's curiosity state. When you explore and satisfy your curiosity, your brain floods your body with dopamine, which makes you feel happier. Contrary to popular belief, dopamine isn't always about experiencing pleasure; now we know that it can be about SEEKING it too! In other words, for some people, the SEEKING is the pleasure, regardless of the result.

Optimize Your Creative Mindset

*"Dopamine makes the brain direct the body to repeat a
pleasurable behavior in order to get another positive reward.
Staying Curious will stimulate your brain and will optimize
your creative skills and cognitive abilities." –Dr. Sofie Nubani*

Leverage your CURIOSITY to learn more about yourself, as well as understanding others. This way, you will expand your consciousness and increase your self-awareness.

- Have you ever been curious about something and your inquisitiveness resulted in a happy and rewarding outcome?

- Do you remember the process of gathering your information and the state of your emotional openness that followed?

- How can you use your intellectual curiosity TODAY to create more positive experiences in your life?

- What topic piques your interest and curiosity enough for you to dive into and explore?

- From there how can you connect the dots and use your imagination to create something new after connecting them? (It could be a concept, product, service, or intellectual teachings)

If you are curious about something that you desire, or are simply just interested in and want to understand it better, then seeking information and knowledge is the right way to go. Asking questions and learning more about it will promote intrinsic rewards that will fuel your curiosity and charge your imagination. On the flip side, curiosity driven by unfulfilled desires, feelings of frustration, competitiveness or anger could lead to a destructive behavior and negative outcomes.

In any case, understand the different interests of curiosity; from there, pick your actions, and motivations wisely.

Ask yourself questions such as;

- What is the intention/reason behind my curiosity?

- Why am I curious about (what you're curious about)?

- Where could my curiosity lead me to?

Always ask questions to better understand the intention/motivation behind your curious drive, it will often set apart either pleasant or unpleasant experiences as a result.

"Intellectual curiosity describes the desire to learn and understand more about people, cultures, ideas, and concepts. This curiosity also provides the motivation to invest time and energy into the pursuit of knowledge. Some of the most revolutionary ideas and inventions have been a result of intellectual curiosity." (rampages.us)

In this book, the intention is to expand your awareness on curiosity, highlighting its importance and how it is linked to intelligence and creativity.

Even though there are different types of intelligences, most people are familiar with IQ, as mentioned in an earlier chapter of the Creativity Crisis. IQ, short for Intelligence Quotient, is a human mind's propensity that can be calculated by having the person take a particular intelligence test, often compared against their age group.

What many are not familiar with, is the importance of CQ, Curiosity Intelligence.

Though more research is still needed on it, I believe that it is one that needs to be included more when evaluating, testing, and selecting individuals on creative/innovative tasks and projects.

An article by Harvard Business Review stimulated my interest regarding this matter. The Article highlighted the importance of Curiosity and its connection to intelligence and how it is something just like EQ (Emotional Intelligence) and can be coached and taught to be well developed.

The Article stated:

"CQ" which stands for curiosity quotient, concerns having a "hungry mind." It has been linked to a sign of Intelligence.

People with higher CQ are more inquisitive and open to new experiences. They find novelty exciting and are quickly bored with routine. They tend to generate many original ideas and are counter-conformist. It has not been as deeply studied as EQ and IQ, but there's some evidence to suggest it is just as important when it comes to managing complexity in two major ways.

First - Individuals with a higher CQ are generally more tolerant of ambiguity. This nuanced, sophisticated, subtle thinking style defines the very essence of complexity.

Second - CQ leads to much higher levels of intellectual investment and knowledge acquisition over time, especially in formal domains of education, such as science and art (note: this is of course different from IQ's measurement of raw intellectual horsepower).

Knowledge and expertise, much like experience, translate complex situations into familiar ones. So, CQ is the ultimate tool to produce simple solutions for complex problems. Although IQ is hard to coach, CQ can be developed.

As Albert Einstein famously said: "I have no special talents. I

am only passionately curious."

WHAT DO YOU THINK?

PRETTY INTERESTING, ISN'T IT?

PRACTICE HEALTHY CURIOSITY

Practice healthy and supportive curiosity. Being curious and wondering why your neighbor's garage has been open for several hours after dark and informing them about it, is a kind act. Being curious about who visited your neighbor and how many hours their visitors stayed and why, is simply being NOSY and not the type of curiosity suggested in the **C.O.U.R.A.G.E.** acronym!!!

In the search for truth, curiosity is a very important trait. Both interest and inquiry will invite progress and awareness to results and outcome.

"Understanding revealed truths, discovered by one's openness to new ideas, willingness to learn, intellectual curiosity and intelligence, will invite better problem solving and creative solutions to his/her life." —Dr. Sofie Nubani

As you may have discovered by now, healthy curiosity leads to infinite creative possibilities.

Types of curiosity and their influence on creativity

There are different types of Curiosity:

1.   Cognitive Curiosity (includes A-Intellectual B-Scientific Curiosity C-Epistemic Curiosity)

2.   Sensory Curiosity

3.   General Curiosity

4.   Specific Curiosity

5.   Social/Interpersonal Curiosity

6.   Empathic Curiosity

7.   Diverse Curiosity

Understanding the different types of curiosity will help you train your brain to practice intelligent curiosity. Pursuing the right kind of curiosity can make your life a lot more fun and interesting.

However, the two basic types of curiosity are:

I.   Cognitive: Is the desire for new information.

II.   Sensory Curiosity: Is the desire for new sensations and thrills.

Please explore in more depth all the different types I shared above, if you feel curious enough to learn further.

Learn YOUR curiosity type

Did you ever discover your own curiosity type?

Have you ever wondered what your unique inquisitive abilities might be?

What drives your curiosity?

Learn more about your curiosity type and find out which one of the below you are:

Artist/Paintbrush and palette

Artists are **INTUITIVE CREATORS**. They are curious about the human experience and they express that curiosity by creating things that enlighten our awareness of the mind and of the world.

Inventor/Lightbulb

Inventors are **INQUISITIVE CREATORS**. They are curious about how things work and they channel that curiosity into creating things that improve the ways we interact with the world and with each other.

Explorer/Discoverer Backpack

Explorers are **INTUITIVE DISCOVERERS**. They are curious about the possibilities of the world and they engage that curiosity to discover new things through experience and participation.

Scientist/Test tube and bubbles

Scientists are **INQUISITIVE DISCOVERERS**. They are curious about the systems that shape the world and the universe, and they apply that curiosity to discover new things through observation and investigation.

If your curiosity is sparked, you can learn more about your curiosity type by taking the Britannica Curiosity Compass Quiz to know which of the four curiosity types (the Artist, Inventor, Explorer, or Scientist) you align with.

You can take The Curiosity Quiz at:

https://curiosity.britannica.com/curiosity-types.html

Britannica Group, Inc., is the world-wide leader at the forefront of the information revolution for 250 years. They have empowered the way the world teaches and learns, and they continue to pave the way in reimagining discovery and inquiry.

They offer many great tools for curious learners from students and families, businesses and governments, lifelong learners, educators, and administrators as well as college students.

"Curiosity is one of the most permanent and certain characteristics of a vigorous intellect." —Samuel Johnson

If you have not paid attention to the importance of this trait (curiosity) for your personal or professional growth, maybe it's time to engage in **PRACTICING** curiosity!

You see, by laws of creation, we are born and made to be curious. There is much wisdom learned when we are able to understand that. If that is not the case, then one's life timeline will be known to him/her and everything between the dashes.

210

Birth and death all would be revealed, everything would be known and expected. Religion would not exist in its form known to us today, as there will be no opportunity to repent, change course of direction towards pre-existing catastrophes, healing from a deadly disease, or preventing an accident. Everyone would live a life that is set in stone (good, great, challenging, or simply just bad, exhausting and/or overbuying).

There will be no hope, no excitement of discovery, no pleasure that comes from the anticipation of looking forward when something good is about to happen. All answers are known to us and destiny with every challenge, hardship, and disappointment is just to be expected and lived.

Imagine being born with a comprehension of what your later life will be like. Imagine knowing that at the age of 25, you'll end up in an accident that will physically disable you for life or you will have that accident at the age of 45 making you go blind. Most people won't know how to self-regulate and may begin their life with a pessimistic/negative attitude, leading to challenging mental health issues.

So, if our creator/creation meant to keep each day a mystery of its own unfolding, keeping us curious, surprised and having pleasure in the seeking of the unknown, then we have to know that there is a special power that CURIOSITY holds in our life and also in our minds.

By going back to creation, nature, life, birth, and death we can find many answers just waiting and demanding our attention. They are excited and ready to share with us ancient wisdom that is available, as it reveals the many layers of treasured truths, to all those on a quest, searching and seeking through their answers, hoping for a divine intervention.

THE NATURE OF CURIOSITY IN A HUMAN LIFE CYCLE

How about going back to the nature of a child, teen, and adult? We learned that infants are curious right from birth, we witness them applying their senses to communicate with their parents or caregivers right from the time they arrive in this world through their sense of touch, taste, smell, and hearing. As they continue growing, they take risks discovering new things that arouse their curiosity. They become more creative as they indulge in their inquiries and interests.

These same kids, now-teens, not having the support they needed to cultivate and support their curiosity, (by parents or teachers that might have shut them off, killed their ambition and curiosity) become less open to new experiences and become narrow minded as adults.

In such scenarios, in order for those same kids/teens to regain their natural curiosity ability, they will need to unlearn all what was applied and taught against their natural born curiosity, just so that they can tap into their innate way of being again.

On the other hand, having that same child grow into a supportive environment, one encouraging curiosity by their educators, parents and teachers, will tend to be more open, intellectually curious and is more creative as an adult.

In knowing that we, as a human race, were born with a spirit of curiosity. This led to a superpower that assisted our growth process prior to going into school and work systems (which limited our ability to learn and explore). In having awareness of this SUPERPOWER, we should take advantage of it, as it is an available resource that is within all of us.

Many may feel that they lost their sense of curiosity. This happened after many years of unanswered questions, and being discouraged from curious interests/behaviors by impatient parents, teachers, educators or authorities, who may not even have had enough wonder to explore their curiosity concerns. Are you that person who needs to reconnect with your "curiosity" superpower? The GOOD NEWS is you that you CAN start practicing curiosity, right away! If you forgot how to be curious just go hang out with a young child. Allow yourself to play and re-learn how to play from children. Ask more questions like, Why? How? Where? When? What?

"The self is not something ready-made, but something in continuous formation through choice of action." - John Dewey

Become curious about your own thoughts, universal signs, feelings, and physical sensations. Challenge yourself to the next level, surround yourself with others who know more than you, those that perfect their craft better than you. Then, learn from them, go the extra mile, investigate, explore, and learn. Continue to engage in intellectual conversations and mind stimulating discussions and dialogues.

STAY CURIOUS, CREATE, CHANGE, GROW, AND EVOLVE!

- Practice asking newbox-thinking questions (i.e., combining both inbox/outbox thinking questions) to get newbox thinking answers.

- Stimulate combinations, associations, relationships, and connections for better creative synthesis, answers, and solutions.

- Curiosity is also a very powerful leadership skill. Curious leaders are always looking for new and better solutions that will help lead others, increase engagement, gain collaboration, and fuel growth.

WANT TO INNOVATE?

PRACTICE CURIOSITY.

In a blog, Brian Grazer, Co-Author of A Curious Mind, shared an Interesting insight on curiosity:

"Curiosity is an incredible tool. But what I realized, what really inspired my desire to write A Curious Mind with Charles Fishman, is that most people don't use their curiosity with a sense of purpose and understanding—with insight about curiosity itself. Curiosity is the key to understanding people's personalities and motivations. Curiosity is a vital storytelling tool—and storytelling is the best way to engage and persuade other people, in your work life and your personal life. Curiosity is a fantastic source of courage. Curiosity is the best, most under-used management tool—a great way to create engagement in your fellow works, but also a great way to transmit values and priorities. Curiosity is the spark for creativity and innovation, the best long-term investment you can make. Curiosity is the best way to stay connected to those who are most important to you. Curiosity, in fact, turns out to be a quiet superpower that all of us have. You don't need an Ivy League education to use it, you don't need a high-speed Internet connection. What's curiosity done for you lately? We're betting it hasn't done enough."

Curiosity is the driver of creativity and innovation. However, with all the strength that intellectual curiosity may introduce and support in areas of creativity/innovation, let's keep humility at the base. Let's respect and understand other people's perspectives even if they are different from our own.

Let's apply our common sense and practical intelligence, while we soar in our curiosity. Gaining success through a discovery or innovation must not get to our heads. Regardless of how much we achieve, we must stay humble and keep moving forward. It is important that we find balance between humility and ambition so that we do not settle after small achievements and not become arrogant after pioneering discoveries. Staying hungry for knowledge and cultivating your curiosity and creativity will enable your continuous growth, and learning in life.

With all that being said, I would like to emphasize one very important point regarding "Curiosity" and that is: having GOOD INTENTIONS. Intention creates meaning and to have the right intention, is key in developing healthy levels of Curiosity that will serve a higher purpose and will also result in the best outcome serving yourself and others. The intention matters as much as the actions themselves.

Curiosity forms a basic foundation in the fields of Philosophy, Spirituality, Science, and Arts and it is the root cause Great Explorations and Big Ideas. Curiosity is one of the most fundamental and important foundations for Optimizing Your Creative Mindset.

"Innovators' curiosity is rewarded and renewed. It becomes a

lifelong passion. One that lends innovators deep meaning" -Dr.

KH Kim

Plant Curiosity to harvest Creativity, so STAY CURIOUS and allow your tasks to feel more rewarding and your outcomes more unique!

#BePresentNCreate

Next Trait of Creativity in C.O.U.R.A.G.E | Is the O for OPENNESS

Openness

There's a story that's told in Zen about openness:

> A university professor went to visit a famous Zen master. While the master quietly served tea, the professor talked about Zen. As the professor kept talking, the master poured the visitor's cup to the brim, and then kept pouring. The professor watched the overflowing cup until he could no longer restrain himself. "It's full! No more will go in!" the professor blurted. "This is you," the master replied, "How can I show you Zen unless you first empty your cup?"

Being open-minded allows for better communication with yourself and with others. The opposite of being open is closed-mindedness, and is most likely a subconscious anchor to one's fear, limiting beliefs, feelings of separation, guilt, shame, distrust, pain/hurt, or anger. The truth is: WITHOUT being open in heart, mind, and soul; one would live feeling restricted, limited, and would have a tunnel vision.

That, in itself, will decrease the strength of connection between oneself and a higher thinking self. It will restrict exploring and expanding in matters that need a broader vision, as well as look for better solutions and problem solving.

You must work on your emotional healing to "create" from a place of openness and joy. Perhaps, you have heard of the recovery slogan, H.O.W. (Honest, Open, and Willing). This slogan is a great anchor, guide, and reminder on how to stay positive and maintain emotional sobriety. Release anything that feels heavy on your soul and allow yourself to feel lighter. This will help you create with much more ease and with a state of wellness. Being open invites new experiences to one's life, which has been a common personality trait of many successfully creative people. Creative people are flexible and adaptable.

"A mind is like a parachute. It doesn't work if it is not open."

—Frank Zappa

215

According to a research study, "Openness/Intellect: The Core of the Creative Personality" stated, "Researchers have begun to uncover the specific cognitive, motivational, and neurobiological mechanisms that may account for the link between creativity and openness/intellect. The cognitive processes divergent thinking, working memory, reduced latent inhibition, and implicit learning all share an association with both creativity and openness/ intellect. Motivational processes linking openness/intellect include cognitive exploration, the reward value of information, and inspiration. At the neural level, diffuse white matter connectivity in the prefrontal cortex and functional connectivity within the default network may underlie both openness/intellect and creativity. Finally, dopamine, a neurotransmitter responsible for exploration and reward, is implicated in both openness/intellect and creativity. An integrated understanding of the basic neurobiological processes that underlie individual differences in openness/intellect and creativity can shed light on the purpose and function of these traits for our species." — Scott Barry Kaufman

Openness and the Big Five Personality Test

"The Big Five or Five Factor" model is the most scientifically sound way of classifying personality differences and is also the most widely used among research psychologists.

Results from "The Big Five Personality Test" give you more insight into how you react in different situations, which can help you to choose an occupation. Career professionals and psychologists use this information in a personality career test for recruitment and candidate assessment.

"Openness" is one of the five personality traits of the Big Five personality theory as well.

You can test your Openness by taking The Five Personality Test by going to: https://www.123test.com/personality-test/

You'll see how you stack up on 5 major dimensions of personality which are Openness, Conscientiousness, Agreeableness, Extraversion, and Neuroticism.

This personality test contains 120 statements. There is no time limit. Most people take about 15 minutes.

It indicates how open-minded a person really is. A person with a high level of openness to experience in a personality test enjoys trying new things. They are imaginative, curious, and open-minded. Individuals who are low in openness to experience would rather not try new things. They are close-minded, literal, and enjoy having a routine.

High openness means being creative and open to new ideas. Individuals with a high level of openness have a general appreciation for unusual ideas and unique forms of art. They can blend much better in diverse cultures and have better experiences during team collaboration.

They are usually imaginative, instead of pragmatic. They are creative which allows them to be open to new and different ideas, also allowing them to be in touch with their feelings.

Individuals who score lower in openness on a career test are generally more closed-off, resistant to change, and analytical. Fixed Mindedness is a barrier to Creative Output. Stay open and create space for receiving ideas. Just like the PROFESSOR and the ZEN MASTER in the story above, we learned how the professor's curiosity about Zen, using a monkey mind when speaking, asking, but not listening, left him no space to be open to receive information. He set the first lesson the Zen master wanted to teach him. It was to empty his mind and to remain open, in this case, through ACTIVE LISTENING, which includes three important components: the 3 A's; Attitude, Attention, and Adjustment. These three are important active listening skills.

Having an open personality is the key for all areas of creativity, including entrepreneurship. This is in contrast to other personality types who may fall into other career types.

According to Truity.com:

"Openness describes a person's tendency to think in abstract, complex ways, while agreeableness describes a person's tendency to put others' needs ahead of their own, and to cooperate rather than compete with others."

"What does your personality type have to do with being an entrepreneur? Quite a bit, according to a recent study."

"People in Illinois are competitive and less creative in their thinking while residents of Vermont are incredibly introverted."

"Deciding on a career is daunting, especially when you're not quite sure what you want to do for a living. To start you in the right direction, it might help to know your career personality type."

"According to data from Truity Psychometrics, "Thinkers," or those who are more analytical and logical, tend to manage bigger teams than "Feelers," or those who are more sensitive to other people's needs." Being Open will help you become more confident and stronger, as new experiences will add knowledge and familiarity to things that were not known prior. Being open connects you to a sense of freedom that is liberating to the soul. Reminding you of your free will and power of choice.

"We continue to shape our personality all our life. If we knew ourselves perfectly, we should die." -Albert Camus

There are also cases of some individuals, as well as famous artists who actually became more creative when they felt constrained and worked under high pressure, deadlines, and troubled conditions. Still, they had to give themselves permission to imagine and explore in order to create something for such results.

They had to be open to other possibilities that were available for them to tap into. By remaining open to new experiences, they are expanding their wisdom, knowledge, vision, and creativity. Their external world may be constrained sometimes, even their physical body, but all of that just gave them an extra boost. They charged themselves with persistence and positive discipline, serving their desired outcome. By remaining open to new experiences, you are saying "YES", to personal development; YES, to growth; YES, to soul expansion and exploration!!! What you need to be CLOSED-MINDED on; is FEAR of low self-esteem, doubt, fixedness, and limiting beliefs. Openness will increase your joy, faith, confidence, awareness, experiences, connections, opportunities, and will Optimize YOUR Creative Mindset.

YOUR THOUGHTS CAN CHANGE YOUR BRAIN AND PERSONALITY

Psychologists and neuroscientists used to believe that a person's personality was fixed for life, unable to be changed. We now know that a person's personality CAN change. How do we know that?

Optimize Your Creative Mindset

The answer is: through NEUROPLASTICITY!

According to Medicine.Net:

Neuroplasticity is the brain's ability to reorganize itself by forming new neural connections throughout life.

Neuroplasticity allows the neurons (nerve cells) in the brain to compensate for injury and disease and to adjust their activities in response to new situations or to changes in their environment.

"Because of the power of neuroplasticity, you can, in fact, reframe your world and rewire your brain so that you are more objective. You have the power to see things as they are so that you can respond thoughtfully, deliberately, and effectively to everything you experience." -Elizabeth Thornton

Norman Doidge, in his book, The Brain That Changes Itself, discussed in Chapter 8 (Imagination: How Thinking Makes It So) the power of mental rehearsal to make changes to the structure of the brain.

"...now we can see that our "immaterial" thoughts too have a physical signature, and we cannot be so sure that thought won't someday be explained in physical terms. While we have yet to understand exactly how thoughts actually change brain structure, it is now clear that they do, and the firm line that Descartes drew between mind and brain is increasingly a dotted line." -Norman Doidge

We know that "Neurons that fire together wire together" so WHY not use the power of NEUROPLASTICITY and your SUPERPOWER of CURIOSITY to develop more openness in your life?

You can literally imagine yourself into a personality and that can help raise your level of openness. It is important to get to know where you're at now in order to help develop a baseline, from how open you are to where you would like to be.

I suggest that you evaluate your level of openness through reliable self-tests or ask some of your closest people that you trust if they consider you open or not and why. Then, use your personal scale and your inner compass to get real with yourself. Ask yourself questions, dig deep and understand your sense of openness at a higher level. From your feedback, see how you can become more open. If you are already open to new experiences then, congratulations, you have one less area that you need to work at. Continue developing your creative skills to reach your highest creative potential.

"Creative experiences can be produced regularly, consistently, almost daily in people's lives. It requires enormous personal security and openness and a spirit of adventure." - Steven Covey

Uniqueness

I am reminded of a story from the book, More Ready-to-Tell Tales From Around the World, called 'You Are Beautiful as You Are" which tells the story of a crow who wasn't satisfied with the way he looked. The story goes:

There was once a crow who did not like his feathers.

"I wish I were a peacock!" he would say.

"You are beautiful as you are!" the other crows insisted.

"How plain and dull you seem to me!" he'd complain, and fly off to admire peacocks.

The peacocks strutted about with their colorful tail feathers outstretched. To the delight of the crow, some of the peacock feathers lay on the ground when the peacocks left.

The Crow flew down to the ground and stuck the feathers into his wings and tail. He attached a few sticking up from his head.

"Now I am as beautiful as a peacock," he exclaimed.

But, when he went to join them in their strutting, the peacocks poked him and pecked him. What a fuss!

"You are not a peacock," they said, "Don't imitate us!"

Bruised and still dragging some broken peacock feathers in his tail, he returned home.

After all his insults, no one wanted his company!

As he sat alone, the other crows said, "It's foolish to try and be what you're not. Learn to love the feathers you've got!"

We see many people in today's world trying to fit in by copying whatever is mainstream. They seek approval and validation even by living beyond their means just so they can stand out more in a crowd. While there is nothing wrong with admiring beauty and improving one's looks or style, as long as it is only coming from personal desire and interest. If it is motivated by peer pressure and trying to impress someone, then it is toxic and destructive.

It is true that we keep progressing in life and keep improving our living status by exploring more of the beautiful things in life. A lot of changes in our life are a direct influence from what creative people have to share with us, from being inspired by nature scenes, beautiful artistry, unique jewelry, home, art and cloth designs, to unique recipes, teaching styles, creative solutions and more. All that is normal, healthy and is fine. Enjoy your UNIQUENESS. It's a gift given to you and you make it stand out by sharing it more!

> *"From the very beginning you are being told to compare yourself*
>
> *with others. This is the greatest disease; it is like a cancer that*
>
> *goes on destroying your very soul because each individual is*
>
> *unique, and comparison is not possible." -Osho*

Trying to be a peacock when you are a crow could lead to depression, anxiety, isolation, and true loss of self-image and identity. Being curious, courageous, and open to new experiences is good when it is applied with EQ & CQ (emotional & curiosity/creativity intelligence). Admiring a superhero and being inspired and empowered by their character is good but trying to imitate Superman and jumping off a building is not.

There is a unique rational response to any particular body of evidence, as the Uniqueness Thesis holds, roughly speaking, according to M. Kopec (2016).

STOP BEING A CONFORMIST AND START ON THE ROAD TOWARDS SELF-EXPRESSION

Practice idea generation to become more creative and better in problem solving, applying your own unique insights, sharing your own unique perspective by your own unique self.

A self-expression coming from your own personal feelings and experiences is better than imitating someone else. We see this in people who conform to the norm, following celebrities and trends, trying to keep up with Jones's or remain submissive to others whom they wish to be like. Losing their identity in the race called life, they want to be like everyone else, but they never really take some time to discover their own passions, open their own gifts, and share their own unique expressions and dynamic personal flair.

Conformity limits one's Creativity, Self-Growth, and Self-Renewal; as well as an individual's unique potentialities.

"Conformity is the jailer of freedom and the enemy of growth." -

John F. Kennedy

Many creative people and artists embrace their own unique personality traits following their own path, pursuing their creative passions. They DO NOT conform. With that being said, as always, it's good to be open and learn that there are many possibilities to one existing problem, challenge, or conclusion.

There have been studies suggesting that Conformity can be creative, however, it is very important to first understand HOW you can best utilize and apply it properly.

I like how Thomas Ward, PhD, explains this topic best in an article he wrote in "Psychology Today", where he responded to the big question, "Can Conformity Be Creative?"

Dr. Ward's answer was:

"Copying others' examples promotes creativity if they

CHALLENGE your ASSUMPTIONS."

In the beginning, I was curious to see how Conformity could be creative. To me it seemed far from that, but as usual I like to be open about the views I hold and not be rigid. I read and learned to expand my own perception on things that piqued my intellectual openness and curiosity. I continued reading and was able to see how that made sense after understanding the results of the study he demonstrated on "How having examples helped stimulate creativity."

Looking at the study examples, which had a specific group expand their creative imagination from there, resulted in this group submitting more creative examples than the group that was not shown an example prior to the project.

Thomas Ward PhD explains;

"Clearly, seeing examples can limit people's approaches, but a recent study by Takeshi Okada and Kentaro Ishibashi, published in Cognitive Science, shows that when people (literally) copy examples it can sometimes boost their creativity."

He added, "Examples don't always constrain people. In fact, copying examples, or even just studying them carefully, can boost creativity and help people develop their own creative styles. But it has to be the right kind of example. To be really helpful, it's a good idea to work with examples that challenge your basic assumptions."

I totally agree, if the examples don't challenge your own basic assumptions, then you will only be copying and NOT creating.

In other words, examples CAN BE helpful and can serve as useful threads that may lead to sparks of new ideas, concepts, products, or services. They can guide, inspire, and motivate you during your creative process. Having EXAMPLES can be very appetizing and brain stimulating, giving you more clarity and better direction than without them.

In such cases, having examples could be a good base to start and expand from. Make sure while your imagination is boosted, passion is fueled, and actions are inspired, that you are using your own brush to paint your canvas and with your own soul expression to make your creative work more; unique, memorable, valuable, appreciated, and original.

There are no specific rules to follow when it comes to creativity. Depending on each individual's own imagination, personal skills, interest, practice, and experiences, they will progress to the next level of creativity. Some may create more examples; others may be giving the examples for many to start creating from.

An artist may teach a group through a drawing he created by his own imagination. However, each of the group members may be inspired differently, some may create better artwork of the same original image while others may create something totally different, yet equally beautiful. In such cases, having an example may be of great guidance that can help in optimizing each individual's creative mindset.

I believe, based on the level of creativity, a person has a mini c, little c, professional c or big c as shared in the study above. By using examples their creativity can be utilized much more effectively. It is similar to how there are levels of entry in many fields of interest, for example in education (basic, introductory, intermediate, advanced; in schools its elementary, middle school, high school then Associate degree, BA, Masters, PhD). The conclusion is that we comprehend better on each present level, as our minds have grown from previous educational levels.

That is why OPENNESS to new experiences is a very important trait in creativity and is part of the acronym, C.O.U.R.A.G.E. To encourage new ideas and possibilities it is necessary to explore things with an open mind that allows and makes space for challenging your basic assumptions. However, the art is to deliver all these new connections, ideas and conclusions with your own unique style and personal or professional branding.

The Power of Personal Branding

WHAT MAKES YOU, YOU, ARE WHAT MAKES YOU UNIQUE

The top celebrities know this secret of personal branding and so should you. From Oprah to Madonna to Elvis Presley and more, each one stood out because they were different and unique. They created a style that fits them.

In your case, it's the set of skills, experiences, personality, and more than that which makes you different from other people. It's okay to learn from others while building your skills and probably necessary, too. It's the same when an apprentice learns from a master. Then, the apprentice went on to add his or her flavor to what they were taught by the master.

Plato learned from Socrates. Aristotle learned from Plato. Yet, each one went out and formulated their pearls of wisdom that greatly contributed to Western Philosophy.

A celebrity who has defined her style and one that goes against social norms is Lady Gaga. In an undergrad research paper from 2010 (A Study of Lady Gaga's Brand, Branding Techniques, and Their Application to Other Brands), Megan E. Carter concluded this about Lady Gaga, **"Her brand makes people feel accepted, understood and a part of something bigger."** Lady Gaga is unique because she knows herself, her message, and what she stands for.

In a 2011 Forbes article by Judy Martin, she described Lady Gaga as "Mother Monster and Protector" The article expands on this, "Lady Gaga has made her mark as a feminine brand by taking one extra step; embracing her femininity as the perennial "mother" figure who is too fierce to let criticism throw her into a tailspin."

Modeling, Mimicking, and Copying

While it's okay as a foundation to adapt and extract, it's not okay when it comes to creativity leading to innovation.

Have you ever seen a business trying to duplicate a successful business model used by another business, yet even by using the same business model, they were unable to duplicate it successfully?

We see this happening in many organizations. They go blindly into teachings that instruct to copy and mimic everything another successful business is doing and expecting the same successful results. However, the result is actually surprising, they actually fail to duplicate that same successful business model.

We see many great motivational speakers, business owners, trainers, mentors, and coaches especially in the West, who have encouraged their clients or employees to find a successful personality to follow. They then ask their clients or employees to copy and model those experts fully, based on the results they wished to achieve.

Optimize Your Creative Mindset

Following the footsteps of successful leaders, may help many and could save others a lot of time and money, yet, without understanding the culture of an organization, the environment, and background of its leaders and employees will carry one big disadvantage and that is, these results possibly happened based on someone else's atypical vision, experiences, background, work ethics, mission, goals. (This example is specifically relating to creativity and one's unique expression).

With my full respect to many speakers and trainers, if every person models a successful person who achieved results they desired, and every company duplicated everything their successful competitors did, we may indirectly be muting the unique creative voice each person owns — something that is unique to them.

Learn from successful entrepreneurs, spiritual teachers, leaders, friends, mentors who are very supportive of your creative personal development, growth, and journey. But you can never be that other person no matter how hard you mimic, copy, model, and follow every little step they did.

"Immature poets imitate; mature poets steal; bad poets deface

what they take, and good poets make it into something better, or

at least something different." -T.S. Eliot

Out of a thousand people that may model, copy, or mimic someone successful, maybe only 5 may master their craft. Yet if they have not added their flavor, voice, creative talent that is unique to their soul projection, then, in the long run, they will not enjoy their progress in that direction or their success.

The source of their effort was mainly focused on duplicating someone else's results. They have never ventured in their curiosity and imagination, adding what could be more suitable, or deducting what may be better for their particular business culture and environment. Due to this reason, this leads to unfulfilled and unsustainable results.

The truth is in school when you learned about famous scientists or learned how to solve math problems, you learned about Shakespeare, but you did not have to imitate his personality or the others. You learned math problems and how to solve them, but you did not have to be Newton to graduate as the best math problem-solver.

So, learning from and about successful people is very wise, provided you do not strip away your uniqueness.

The popular mimicking someone else's behavior, copying someone else's business model, now even teaching/learning in school, to pass a test and not actually learning and understanding a subject, may serve a little purpose, solve a temporary solution, provide a little relief but are not going to provide sustainable results that are empowering and inspiring to a very needed skill in the 21st century, and that is creativity. In particular, creativity leading to innovation.

As per the Harvard Business School professor, Teresa Amabile, there are three components of creativity:

• Expertise

• Creative thinking skills

• Motivation

The most creative people are also innovators. They spend countless hours learning, honing their skills, sharing their gifts consistently, and that is how they are acquiring expertise. Mimicking, copying, and blindly modeling others does not involve components of creativity especially creative thinking style — the intrinsic motivation that inspires creativity leading to innovation.

In earlier examples, the only innovative results would have been accomplished by those who created the original model that everyone else is trying to copy!

Many models and systems that are practiced within organizations, schools, and companies are not encouraging creative thinking. Instead, they teach others to model exactly a successful model, taking out their opinions, feedback, and creative solutions. They raise a culture that leads and directs all its participants to conform rather than create.

Many motivational speakers and business models, I noticed especially sales-oriented company cultures follow this famous quote:

Optimize Your Creative Mindset

"If you want to be successful, find someone who has achieved the results you want and copy what they do and you'll achieve the same results." - Tony Robbins

I have much admiration and respect for Tony Robbins. I attended one of his events in my early 20s, I listened to his YouTube videos, TV, and radio interviews in the last two decades myself. I can say that he was very dynamic and definitely a very talented authority. No one doubts that he is very special and has a unique delivery style. Tony has created proven methods to accomplish successful results, he influenced many positively all around the world and has many great contributions that helped and saved countless lives.

However, my concern with that quote and message is that when it comes to a young teen, a new employee, or simply anyone getting this advice and applying it fully, they may lose sight of tapping into their imagination, thought process, and their creative mindset.

Their employer, boss, or teacher may have never asked them to add their personality, charisma, and sole expression while following this quote to its exact instruction. Or, they may have never challenged them to create or taught them how to adjust, adapt, or offer them something like tools or suggestions that may add greater value to the task in hand.

Ultimately, they end up following and copying by default the work of others. This becomes their living style and unfortunately their programmed mindset. Attending seminars, going to events, signing up for a class to learn about how a system works, and follow a proven, successful process is perfectly alright. Creating a training manual, setting strategies and teaching processes is all necessary for business success, provided that training manual is aligned with ITS companies, organizations, or school's cultures (success, creative, curiosity, practical, emotional, and social intelligence).

It is when we copy others, even in their success that we lose the chance to create new experiences that are only created by our imagination, intrinsic motivation, and relentless passion.

If that person's mission is aligned with yours and they are getting results that you are having difficulties to reach, then studying their process is alright, provided you do not lose your identity trying to copy someone else's success — later in life you may find out that this is not who you really are or who you wanted to be.

WE ARE ALL UNIQUE, EMBRACE YOUR UNIQUENESS, AND ALLOW IT TO THRIVE!

Even when God created the human race, he created us in different colors, looks, races, gender, sizes, and personalities, even identical twins and triplets may look the same but each remains to have their individual and unique personality. The same goes with ducks, penguins, eagles, and more.

Have you ever looked at a breed of Ragdoll Cats or German Shepherd dogs; again, they may all look so identical until you interact with one, you soon realize (as they introduce themselves to you) how each has their distinct personality and unique identity.

Did You Ever Wonder WHY?

How I see it from an existential viewpoint is — our creator chose not to fully duplicate identical beings, even though it would have been easier and faster. However, it's not the case, which then leaves our mind open to seeking the wisdom it represents to us. The teaching from The Laws of Creation, as we dig deep, trying to understand its purpose is…" What does it want us to learn?" *It's for each of us to embrace our individuality, identity, and uniqueness.*

"The Creator, in taking infinite pains to shroud with mystery

His presence in every atom of creation, could have had but one

motive — a sensitive desire that men seek Him only through free

will." — Paramahansa Yogananda

It is easier to copy and duplicate, but it takes courage, imagination, passion, action along with honoring yourself, your unique individuality, your gifts, and talents to create.

Optimize Your Creative Mindset

"Always be yourself, express yourself, have faith in yourself, do not go out and look for a successful personality, and duplicate it." — Bruce Lee

If more people believe in their unique abilities, identify their passions, have faith in their beliefs, dare to take action towards their dreams, those people will live different realities, enjoy being alive, and cannot wait to get up each day and to co-create.

If you need to ask for help, do it — seek advice, collaborate but never lose your unique core self, your vibrant flare, don't even dare!

From that space of creating, you can duplicate systems to increase your audience and target market reach, but with programs, systems, manuals that you created, and not hijacked from others. You can model behavior and systems that are successful but you need to do so in a different way than it is represented and understood by the mainstream.

For example, one of the strategies of NLP is to model how others think and behave, including those who are creative. As an NLP Master Practitioner/Trainer, I believe that there are important questions that need to be asked prior to deciding what person or company you wish to model.

An example of some good questions I like, if you want to "model a creative person" is from an article by Steven Handel, The Motion Machine on NLP and Creativity.

Questions to ask:

- What are the strategies a so-called "creative person" plays out in their heads?

- What is the structure of their experience, and what mental steps do they take before producing a creative outcome?

- Or, is it all spontaneous? And if so, how does one increase the chances of such a spontaneity occurring?

These are the types of questions an NLP practitioner would ask — they are the type of questions many need to learn to ask for them to be able to optimize their creativity and tap into their unique identity. They would ask higher-order questions that, in the interim, would help guide them to learn more about themselves, their unique identity, and their talents.

When people blindly copy, mimic, or model others, they will be losing the joy of participation in the creative process. This includes the ability to ask higher-level questions and has *Newbox* answers, the fun of exploration, building personal experiences, and personal growth in the beautiful process of creating.

You see, applying NLP during your creative process will add more to your individual unique experience. In addition, it will help you tap into many unusual ways of solving one problem.

NLP, or Neuro-Linguistic Programming, is a set of inter-and-intra-personal communication techniques first developed by psychotherapist Richard Bandler and linguist John Grinder (who worked together under the tutelage of British anthropologist Gregory Bateson). Its purpose was to discover the linguistic underpinnings of mental states and how they affect our behaviors and to later use this knowledge to modify our habits. It can be practiced through introspection (now more scientifically known as metacognition) or guided conversation.

So, how can you or your company be more creative? In chapter one, you learned about the different thinking styles, and how they can support your creative journey. Now, I want to introduce you to another tool for creative thinking that was inspired by Walt Disney, a creative genius who was very successful at turning fantasies into reality.

I wanted you to learn about Disney's creative strategy in this part of your chapter so you can anchor to it more. By practicing it, it will help you or your business to tap into the highest levels of unique creativity.

Based on a close associate of Walt Disney, he used to say "There were actually three different Walts: the dreamer, the realist, and the spoiler. You never knew which one was coming to the meeting."

Robert Dilts, author of the book "Strategies of Genius Vol. 1," and NLP EXPERT shares **On Walt Disney's ability to explore;**

Optimize Your Creative Mindset

"Walt Disney's ability to connect his innovative creativity with successful business strategy and popular appeal certainly qualifies him as a genius in the field of entertainment. In a way, Disney's chosen medium of expression, the animated film, characterizes the fundamental process of all genius: the ability to take something that exists in the imagination only and forge it into a physical existence that directly influences the experience of others in a positive way." -Robert Dilts

Inspired by Walt Disney, and the way he used to organize his creative teams to come up with ideas, NLP Expert Robert Dilts highlighted later modeled and developed 'The Disney Creativity Strategy' (sometimes referred to as the Disney Technique) as an NLP tool.

"The Disney Creativity Strategy" is a technique of organizing your company's thinking to have a better way to achieve goals and dreams.

You can also use the Disney Strategy as an idea generation method (you will need to change locations or take a break to create a clear distinction between three different phases) or with a group if you are a business or NLP trainer, guiding the group on best ways to think creatively in a more unique way.

The Disney Strategy separates idea generation into three distinct phases — a 'Dreamer' mode where all new ideas are encouraged, a 'Realist' or 'Implementer' mode which looks at how to make the ideas work in practice, and finally a 'Critic' mode which looks for flaws in the ideas and what could go wrong.

The Motion Machine on NLP and Creativity articles also adds:

"Dilts noticed that Disney had three separate approaches to his creative work and he alternated between these roles, which Dilts identified as Dreamer, Realist, and Critic. Each role has a distinct orientation concerning the creative process: the dreamer is the place of free association, brainstorming, and even fantasies; the realist is the place of action, of imagining putting the dreams into the physical world; and the critic is the place of testing the soundness of your ideas, checking in on what will or will not work.

Dilts believes that we each have a part of us that can identify with these roles. However, some of us are more of one than another. What happens if we are unable to find a balance?

"A dreamer without a realist cannot turn ideas into tangible expressions. A critic and a dreamer without a realist just become stuck in perpetual conflict. A dreamer and a realist might create things, but they might not be very useful ideas without a critic. The critic helps to evaluate and refine the products of creativity."

So, the main question is: throughout the creative process, how can we develop each of these roles? The answer Dilts provides says that we should set aside a time and place for each of these mental attitudes:

1. First, put yourself in the role of '**The Dreamer**'. Write down any ideas that come to mind. Make as many freely associated connections as possible, let your thoughts just flow without any limitation or just focus on putting these ideas into action.

2. Next, put yourself in the role of '**The Realist**'. Now ask yourself, "How can I put these ideas into a reality? What resources (money/time/skills) do I need?" Write these down.

3. Then put yourself in the role of **The Critic**. Now it is time to try and find the flaws of your strategy. What don't you like? What potential obstacles are there? What needs improvement? Write these down.

4. Now step outside your triangle of roles. Observe your reaction to each – are you being a good Dreamer, Realist, and Critic? How can you improve each?

5. Cycle through each role again. Using any insights from #4, cycle through the roles again, but this time, being an even better Dreamer, Realist, and Critic.

6. Take your ideas to action — do the above as many times as needed until you can begin putting your ideas to action. Even as you carry out your plan, keep these three elements in mind at all times.

How much time you spend in each session is up to you. I recommend at least 5-10 minutes of brainstorming, idea-jotting, and question-asking per role. When I first tried this strategy, I used to even light different-scented candles; which became a self-conditioned stimulus (an anchor, for those familiar with NLP lingo) to help me get into each mindset. You can use other habits (or "rituals") to help amplify your creative roles as you practice them more and more.

Real-world examples

Do you have a friend, family member, coworker, or acquaintance who you think makes a good Dreamer, Realist, or Critic? Why not use that as a resource to improve your creative process? You would be probably surprised about how much you can learn by pretending to think like someone else. How does your physiology change? How do your thoughts change? How do your motivations change?"

Now that you are familiar with different tools, thinking styles, and strategies that you can utilize, why not practice sharpening your unique abilities, both individually or with your group/team or company depending on what you need at the moment.

The fact that you are unique assures you, in addition, to a special place/special worth in your society and possibly the world.

That's why it is important to understand your unique skills and talents by engaging in projects that present meaning and offer value to your growth and provide a creative soul experience.

Remember, being different leads to innovation and Newbox answers, so go out there #BePresentNCreate

"Fitting in allows you to blend in with everyone else, but being different allows you to be yourself, to be unique and to be more creative." — Sonya Parker

Chapter 8:
C.O.U.R.A.G.E | Section 2

In this chapter, you'll discover...

- Fourth & Fifth Trait that will optimize your creative mindset
  - Risk Tolerance
  - Attention

Risk Tolerance

The Story of Two Seeds

Two seeds lay side by side in the fertile spring soil. The first seed said, "I want to grow! I want to send my roots deep into the soil beneath me and thrust my sprouts through the earth's crust above me. I want to unfurl my tender buds like banners to announce the arrival of spring. I want to feel the warmth of the sun on my face and the blessing of the morning dew on my petals!" And so it grew.

The second seed said, "I am afraid. If I send my roots into the ground below, I don't know what I will encounter in the dark. If I push my way through the hard soil above me, I may damage my delicate sprouts — what if I let my buds open and a snail tries to eat them? And if I were to open my blossoms, a small child may pull me from the ground. No, I should wait until it is safe." And so, it waited.

A yard hen scratching around in the early spring ground for food found the waiting seed and promptly ate it.

If you wait for the right time and fear taking risks, you may end up being swallowed up by life. It's important to take the step with your ideas and express them to their full potential. That is where growth happens regarding your creativity and your life.

"Cognitive risk tolerance is an individual's ability to formulate and express one's ideas despite potential opposition or negative assessment in regard to reputation, integrity, and honor, which is needed for creativity, innovation and global competitiveness."

(Charyton, Jagacinski, and Merrill; 2008)

There is a deep and meaningful connection between risk tolerance and creativity, one often overlooked.

The relationship between risk-taking and creativity is critical to understanding collective unity, group tranquility, social harmony, and innovation.

1-How is your attitude towards risk-taking?

2-How do you deal with uncertainty?

3-Do you have a tolerance for ambiguity?

The action of taking risks for the desired outcome requires COURAGE.

To embrace risk, we need to have the courage to make decisions, even if we have insufficient information. By using our best judgment at that moment then, we can later revisit and assess at a different time if or when we have more insights.

Creativity begins where conventional answers to challenges end. It's when facing a challenge that is not only beyond our current ability but also beyond what is possible at the moment.

The higher the challenge, the more it challenges our creative skills. There has been evidence showing a direct link between creativity and the direct level of challenge we undertake. The bigger the challenge, the higher our level of creative performance becomes.

We are still required to take action and many times without a previous example to follow, we do that. Starting...even with very small steps is a good place to begin building risk tolerance.

Any feedback is always good and makes room for improvement but by not being bold, willing to take cognitive risks, and start, nothing can ever happen.

Release your need to be right, instead have intellectual openness and curiosity, and see what unfolds from there.

According to a 2008 research, both, "Creative Personality and Creative Temperament were predictors of higher cognitive risk tolerance."

Successful creative leaders, entrepreneurs, mentors, even heads of households, have all started from a blank page at one point or a blank page over and over, they have that extra grit, baldness, gallantry, and risk tolerance in them. All of which are necessary creative success ingredients.

It's just like when doing your creative projects, "improvisation style" of action can help strengthen your creative skills. Stepping out of your comfort zone and getting comfortable with the idea of taking cognitive risk tolerance will sharpen your creative attitude and abilities.

Convergent — but not divergent thinking — is better when it comes to low risk-takers. So, when it comes to low risk-taking, you narrowing the possibilities, and making decisions with what makes sense to you as the best answer, is the style of thinking you need to apply. You need to qualify your ideas and choose the one that fits with your goals and will have a stronger impact when/if you select it.

The willingness to take risks determines to what extent you are prepared to accept victories as well as setbacks.

"The biggest risk a person can take is to do nothing." —

Robert Kiyosaki

The degrees of being patient, understanding, accepting results with no attachment to outcome both in victory or defeat, varies from one individual to another based on their tolerance level, soul set, mindset as well as their visual and flexible perception.

Many famous legends have been known for taking big risks in pursuing their creative ideas and innovations. You may have heard of a few, but let's dive into some of their insights, backstories, and areas of gallantry.

Legends, Entrepreneurs and Entertainers Who Took Creative Risks

1-Wright Brothers

Orville and Wilbur Wright were aviation pioneers, with a very curious nature. The brothers were the first to fly a plane heavier than air. To gain the right data (and experience), they tested kites and gliders. Starting in 1900, they used the town of Kitty Hawk, North Carolina, to develop their aircraft through a multitude of experiments. Years later, the United States government expressed interest in what they were doing and approached them to purchase a plane, as long as it met certain specifications. As they focused on creating a plane that was able to fly, their efforts paid off. In 1908, Orville piloted their creation. The first flight flew 120 feet and lasted a mere 12 seconds. This launched the aeronautics industry.

2-Albert Einstein

The relationship between risk and creativity is demonstrated quite well by the inquisitive genius, Einstein.

Two things about Albert Einstein that many never knew:

1) He was an eager sailor

2) He did not learn to swim

Many people consider Einstein as the greatest mathematician and physicist the world has ever known. However, his interest in sailing was not that well-known — this was for the simple reason. As a sailor, he had very poor sailing skills. His friends said that when he got into a sailboat, Einstein would get dreamy and forgetful.

Einstein said that he liked sailing because it gave him a chance to relax after all his hard work, thinking about equations and theories in his study. Those theories won him the Nobel Prize in Physics in 1921.

Yet whenever Einstein went sailing, his family was very concerned about him. Not knowing how to swim, or where he is going and without wearing a life jacket. Einstein would escape and relax in his boat many times not knowing where he was going, knocking masts and spars that run his boat aground. He was rescued a few times by children and boaters. Still, Einstein loved to sail and he sailed his whole life.

3-Henry Ford

The world-famous inventor of the automobile was very imaginative and willing to take risks. He slashed prices so steeply that he risked taking losses yet he managed to meet the crushing demand for Model Ts.

To satisfy consumer wants, Ford had to take it to the next level with a 'do or die' attitude. Henry Ford even cut down the working hours and increased minimum wages for his workers so that they could work for a longer period before quitting.

It was a very risky move that could be considered a mistake to most but was a strong reason why Henry Ford was able to conquer the automobile world.

4-Elon Musk

He co-founded PayPal, he created America's first viable fully electric car company Tesla Motors, started the nation's biggest solar energy supplier, and rolled the dice with NASA to launch his space exploration company SpaceX — all in the space of 15 short years.

He has managed to solidify Tesla Motors in a high risk, high-cost industry.

He faced the critics and haters when he founded his own SpaceX mission to Mars and was on the verge of company collapse when he played Russian Roulette between funding both failing companies Tesla & SpaceX, not knowing if both companies will fall apart or not. Elon Musk is known as this generation's well-known biggest risk-taker.

His net worth is estimated to be $38.3 billion and growing.

5-Beyoncé

Beyoncé previously revealed to Cosmopolitan magazine that the first risk she took came from branching off from her group and doing a solo album. "People don't realize that Destiny's Child started when we were 9. You just always have to take risks," she said.

When Beyoncé dropped her surprise, self-titled album at the end of 2013 "Drunk in Love," she admits that she was 'terrified' her surprise new album would flop:

"I was really nervous because this was a huge risk."

Queen Bey admitted that she went to great lengths to keep her fifth album a surprise. Showbiz reporter Jenni McKnight shared on Metro News, "We went through a lot of things to keep it secret, to keep the surprise,' she added. 'I really,

really wanted to surprise people, and for them really just to hear the art and not be about the hype and the promotion."

Today her album "Drunk In Love" sold millions of copies and Queen Bey is known to be one of the most Risk-Taking artists ever lived.

(The Harvard Business School even did a case study on the subject!) Naturally, though, the singer's album was huge, and Beyoncé went down as one of the most fabulous risk-takers in the history of music.

6-Bill Gates

After two years at Harvard, a young Bill Gates took a risk that would end up giving way to the rest of his (wildly successful) career: He dropped out of college to found Microsoft.

Today, Harvard's most successful dropout makes a point of urging students to stay in school ("getting a degree is a much surer path to success," he's said), but the idea behind his decision to drop out is still the same: Sometimes, a great risk reaps great rewards.

How about some businesses that took risks and their risk tolerance paid off on all their creative projects like?

- Google

- Dropbox

- Spanx

I share below *Inc.com's* interesting article about how taking risks paid off to all of these three companies' bigger success.

Google

Once upon a time, there was no Google. Co-founders Larry Page and Sergey Brin created the company while Ph.D. students at TK, and almost gave up on it all because it was taking way too much time. Page almost sold the company in 1997 for just $1.5 million. Later on, in 2006, when no one understood the potential of a little video service called YouTube, the tech company purchased it. The rest is history.

Dropbox

Can you imagine saying no to Steve Jobs? Dropbox founder Drew Houston did. Houston did not back down when Jobs told him that the cloud was not his — and now the file-sharing company is worth around $8-10 billion.

Spanx

Spanx founder Sara Blakely knew nothing about business, but all about how uncomfortable pantyhose were. After being told over and over that her idea was "so crazy," she wrote the patent herself and went for it. Now, their undergarments are everywhere.

As Zig Ziglar said, "You were born to win, but to be a winner,

you must plan to win, prepare to win, and expect to win." And,

of course, whether you are running an international firm,

bringing in billions or a small, one-man shop, you can set your

sites on staying afloat and just tread water instead, playing it

safe. But your business will appear as tired as it is after a while

and drown if you go that route.

Better to take smart risks and focus on winning, because if you

do not, your competition will!"

Great article insights and whether focusing on winning or focusing on accomplishing your goals, whatever resonates best with you, make sure you are enjoying and growing through the process. Be willing to take risks, but be highly strategic in taking it. Smart Risk-taking should serve your mission and definitely should not be reckless and incalculable. Ask yourself questions before taking risks to assess: If you should or should not.

1-Do you have the necessary tools or have access to them to accomplish your goal?

2-Is taking this risk aligned with your original goal, purpose, and mission?

3-Do you have the physical space to undertake such risk? For example — buying merchandise that will assist in your creative project but does not have the right storage space to keep them.

How emotionally equipped are you if things fail to pan out? Are your feelings of burden going to hold you back from getting up again and moving towards your goals? Be mentally and emotionally prepared for all possibilities.

Sometimes, you might need to change direction but definitely not your goal.

"Entrepreneurialism, to me, means being able to fail. And I believe that kind of leadership is not necessary only in business, but it's necessary for running countries, too. You've got to be able to believe in something strongly enough that you want to do it even if there's a risk of failure." – Bernard L. Schwartz

While writing this book, I had a 24-year stable job and doing my coaching. I worked a few hours in the day, and later in the evening mostly booked my coaching clients. I felt overwhelmed and unfocused, in September of 2019. I decided to resign from my first secure and financially stable job. I also took a break from coaching for a bit. I had no income for 10 months. I took a risk, a smart risk. I knew in my heart I had to write this book. My passion for writing was bigger than my fear of not being provided for. I lived off my savings mostly and had a few good surprises happen along the way.

I had a strong desire to share the content with all of you. I had faith that I was going to be okay, as I knew my intention was that of service and providing value to everyone reading. I was offered a few work opportunities during that time, but something in my spirit was keeping me focused and I stuck to my original plan, that was, no work until I completed all my book content.

It was my priority and that is where most of my attention was directed to. I declined many invitations to events, parties, and more. You see when you serve your bigger 'why' you become more assertive, your inner strength gets stronger, your faith increases, your doubts decrease, your courage takes the victory and your fears are defeated.

Yes, if I was surrounded by fake friends or uncaring family members, I may have lost my relationships with them. I was not social as they may have preferred me to be, however, I, deep in my heart, also knew that those who genuinely care will always be there, and I still do.

You see in life, you got to go for what sparks your soul, fuels your passions, and grounds your actions. Without having risk tolerance, you will not grow, evolve, or transform to the next best level of you. Today, what are some passions or interests you have, but you are delaying because you are afraid of risk and to step forward into the unknown? What are some possible solutions + plans that you can apply to overcome your fear of taking this risk?

My advice to you is to have patience when facing adversity, yet continue to be persistent with your mission. You will build resilience and be able to tolerate setbacks as you discover and learn new parts of your personality. You will be able to connect with your unique abilities to co-create and regulate/manage your emotions during your creative process better. Vibrationally: Fear repels. Faith attracts!

Stepping out of your comfort zone will never feel comfortable, it will require positive discipline, faith, courage, expanded vision, and risk tolerance. Feel grounded as you are taking a leap of faith, stepping into the unknown so you can stay vibrationally aligned with what you want to manifest and attract into your life.

"You must become tenacious going after your goals. Roar like a lion and charge every step you take with confidence and unwavering faith of the limitless possibilities that are waiting for you to explore." — Dr. Sofie Nubani

Attention

It is the ability to concentrate and focus on a particular stimulus selectively. Attention is the awareness of the present moment. It is important in learning and developing a creative mindset. Learning is most efficient when a person is paying attention. Research shows that attention and imagination are equally important for creativity. The role that attention plays in generating new and useful ideas is controversial among neuroscientists. Some neuroimaging studies have shown that creativity involves more cognitive control, or focused attention (2015).

Evidence exists that creative people do not necessarily differ in their predominant mode of attention, but can switch between various modes of attention more easily, and therefore have flexible attention. (Cognitive flexibility. Cognitive flexibility refers to the **ability to shift attention** between task sets, attributes of a stimulus, responses, perspectives, or strategies, Miyake et al., 2000; Zelazo, 2015). Creative people/creative acts are associated with distinct types of attention. To understand the type of attention, you may need to maximize the value of your time and energy as you are going through the process.

There are 11 types of attention:

1-Sustained Attention: Focus for a long period. It usually ranges between 5 min for a two-year-old up to 20 min for older children and adults.

2-Selective Attention: Focus on one thing at a time.

3-Divided Attention: Focus on two events at once.

4-Alternating Attention: Alternating your attention between two things is known as alternating attention. One task is entirely ignored while the focus is only on the other task and it is the exact opposite of multitasking.

5-Visual Attention: Having visual attention means blurring out all other stimuli and focusing only on the inputs received by eyes.

6-Auditory Attention: Paying attention to what you hear without interrupting. Attention employed by use of ears.

7-Controlled Attention: It requires us to pay attention and deliberately put in the effort. Controlled processing is intentionally done while we are consciously aware of what we are doing.

8-Executive Attention: Focus on completing steps to achieve a goal.

9-Automatic Attention/Processing - does not require us to pay attention, nor do we have to deliberately put in the effort to control automatic processes. Automatic processing occurs without us giving much thought to it. If we practice something long enough, it becomes automatic.

10-Active Attention - Active attention is where a person gives their full attention to a task at hand or another person. It also involves effort and the focus of attentional filtering — it is a type of concentration that requires conscious attention. It is similar to listening to a client fully and focused during a coaching session. Another instance could be a child's concern about a matter in school.

11-Passive Attention - Passive attention refers to the involuntary process directed by external events that stand out from their environments, such as bright light, a stinky odor, or a sudden beeping noise. "Engaging in an activity that draws your whole attention, without any effort on your part "Passive attention is involuntary. For example, enjoying a book you are reading and you lose track of the hours whizzing, or you are watching an interesting movie. Now that you are aware of the different types of attention, be mindful of what type of attention is required for a particular task and their application for optimal outcomes.

Let's answer some questions in order for you to better understand how attention plays a part in your life.

1-How paying the right type of attention (e.g. executive attention) can help you reach your goals?

2-Are you paying attention to what you need to tune out as well as to the not so obvious in order to gain understanding/insights?

3-Are you paying attention to your intuition, universal signs, and messages guiding you to a better direction and more clarity?

It is easy for people to pay attention to things that are interesting or exciting to them (attention happens when motivation and cognition are there) on the other hand, it is difficult for them to pay attention to things that are not interesting/exciting, be mindful of that.

Duration of Attention: Understanding Your Ability to Stay Focused

Once distractions are filtered out and you know what to attend to then, the right time, not too long or short is important to attend to the task at hand. This is called the duration of attention; also called focal maintenance (meaning a period maintaining or staying focused). Learn about the length of your attention span on different projects, and see what is the longest you can stay on one task before you can switch your attention to another. Different tasks may hold your attention longer depending on your interest level and urgency.

First and foremost, you need to know your attention span and focus tolerance. Test yourself to examine the maximum time you can sit still and remain focused without being distracted from internal or external forces on one given task. Just as we see individuals who multitask or have a habit of task switching, they may be easily distracted and have lower levels of focus resulting in depleted creative energy. We also know that some individuals possess an extremely short attention span, get bored easily and due to this reason, task switching is energizing for them while they are engaged in their creative projects.

Author and Psychologist

Doreen Virtue expressed her appreciation to the director of Hay House Radio giving her the flexibility of submitting her work not in an ordinary manner. Doreen shared that at times, she would be working on publishing 4 books and new deck cards at a time, going from one to the other till it was fully completed. Many artists shared similar feedback.

You must identify the best plan that works for you and follow through on it. Regardless of how many projects you are working on, for any of them to be complete, you need to realize the importance of being uninterrupted for blocks of designated times while working on that one task at hand.

Between creative work, network, and administrative work, you can easily get off track, and before you know, it feels like you are standing on a map that is unable to get you anywhere, yet you have no clarity or even enough energy to move forward to your desired destination.

Sometimes moving back and forth on the same roads may result in building a chaotic energetic field that is distracting from reaching your original goals.

So, where attention goes, energy flows — what you prioritize becomes the future you aspire to you are design. If you want to create a new product, course, or even new habits but if you are busy with everything else rather than focusing on them — in that case, you can never have enough energy to complete necessary tasks.

Your creative energy will be depleted and you will be mentally checked out. People vary in the amount of time needed to reach a state of centeredness and ability to focus on one task fully. Depending on the individual, personal space, environment, and health conditions, research says; for older children and adults generally, it may take anywhere from 20 to 35 minutes to stay focused and be able to concentrate on one task.

However, depending on the type of breaks e.g. stretching, breathing, the duration can go longer. Usually, 50 to 90 minutes is an average attention span one can hold. This is why you see lectures; presentations are always within that time frame.

Set your time limits and breaks

Be Intentional deliberant, focused, and conscious as you tap into your creative energy. Understand the difference between you setting time for your breaks vs you being interrupted while focused on the task in hand. One study shows it takes about 25 minutes to get back into the swing of things after you have been interrupted.

Check your phone notification setting, emails, and possible distraction from any electronics — all should be off. Also, disconnect from people that may disturb you, set boundaries, be assertive, and stay focused!

Learn the difference between getting attention and paying attention.

When it comes to attention, understand the underlying emotion and intention behind your desire. It is almost like listening and speaking — both are important — but in the long term, you will come to know that there was a very good reason you have two ears and one mouth right from the start. So listen actively and with curiosity.

Even if you are the teacher, the coach, the mentor who is speaking and teaching, without proper active listening, you will not have the right feedback and/or understanding to your students or clients. Realize that we not only "attend" with our eyes and ears — but with whole-body awareness. Our observation, cognition, and motivation all are important ingredients for our attention and connections.

So, while getting attention is a sign of strength, influence, and impact, either for good or bad, it is wise to pay attention to the new experiences you are inviting into your life. Employ and direct your attention to support your highest good and the good of others. Even a baby stops crying when you give them attention. Why not give attention to your creativity and let it flourish?

On that note, I would like to introduce you to Dr. Jo Anne White who has inspired many around the globe. To me, she is a soul sister. She has published many books and is an International #1 bestselling, award-winning author, speaker, and consultant. She's recognized as a Goodwill Global Ambassador for civil and humanitarian work in education, entrepreneurship, coaching, and women's issues.

With all the work she does and continues to do, I asked her if she could share her insight on how she can stay focused during her creative process, and how she was able to prioritize her attention to the different tasks in hand.

Dr. Jo Anne White's story

Awakening Creativity with Focus, Movement and Sound
By Dr. Jo Anne White

"Attention is vital to creativity. For me, the process of creating is a joy. As a writer, speaker, producer, consultant, and coach, I have a schedule with strict deadlines to adhere to. My attention has to be focused on production — the result, as well as on active creation — the ongoing journeying of the creative adventure.

During the creative process, my intuitions ramp up, although it's always in high gear.

Optimize Your Creative Mindset

I have learned to tune-out nonessential disruptions or distractions. This is necessary to attend to and complete a task or project. Everyone thinks their interruption is most important and warrants your instant attention. Unless it's an emergency or a responsibility you have to attend to, you do not have to give others your immediate focus. You can respond to their texts and messages later on. When you are creating, shifting your focus can ruin the creative thread. Why risk it?

I have learned through experience that I can move from one creative project to another. It works for me, especially when I am thinking through or incubating something that needs more time to gestate. As long as you make sure that you save and have a backup of whatever you are working on, it can give you the freedom to change gears. If this does not suit you, opt-out of it. It's not worth sacrificing your creative endeavor. For me, sometimes working with different projects stimulates new ideas or crossover insights that can be developed in both or something altogether new.

Often during the creative process, there may be lulls or moments when the information isn't forthcoming. I have a background in dance and have found a fun solution that works wonderfully for me. It may also work for you. Quick Reminder — you don't have to be a dancer to move your body!

If I am stuck, I get up from my desk or just stop whatever I was doing and dance. I move my hands and my body, sometimes with music and at other times without sound, unless that comes from within me. Sometimes it does. Mostly I am quieted by the movement. The movement and dancing ease my body and relax my mind which helps me gain further clarity and even expansiveness in my thinking.

The movement offers more fluidity and flexibility and helps generate novel ideas. It enhances not only my creativity — it helps me with concentration. After some minutes of moving, I feel freer and ready to return to the work at hand. I am not resisting. My body has been given a reprieve from the focused activity and so has my mind.

Yet movement also activates or turns on my brain. Often new ideas materialize and I am pumped and eager to return to my creative venture. Also, I have discovered another advantage. The movement quiets my inner noise so I can be receptive to the internal messages or inner guidance. I often receive intuitive/psychic information for my clients to support them. In this instance, the intuitive information aids me in nurturing and supporting my creativity. Upon returning to my creative project, the attention is there and I am more alert than before.

Often new ideas are generated and I am in a state of acute awareness. My focus is intensified. I seem to be a scribe, retrieving, and recording the information that flows through uninterrupted like a beautiful free stream. I also use the movement technique during a break in a workshop, the seminar I am leading, or hypnosis season. I encourage participants, clients, and students to move, stretch, and even use sound.

Another technique that I use is sound. Do you know you have a soul song that's unique to you? It's lovely and powerful when you can coax it out! Creating your sound that surges up from inside feels deep and moving and is so You.

The sound vibration offers balance to my mind and body and gives me a wonderful sense of peace and release. It silences other random, insignificant thoughts and once again primes me for more captivated attention. Refreshed, smiling, and feeling freer in many ways, I am now ready and eager to return to the creative venture at hand with more purpose, renewed vigor, strong intention, engagement, and attention."

Dr. Jo Anne is an Executive Producer and Host of the POWER YOUR LIFE shows, White's been featured online, in publications as Good Housekeeping, More, and WebMD and has appeared on Radio and Television Networks as NBC, CBS, FOX and Voice America sharing her expertise.

Both I and Dr. Bob Choat were guests on Dr. Jo Anne's Power Your life show. As co-founders of the laughter Mindset program, she interviewed us on the science of laughter and how important is laughter to our lives. She was an excellent and very seasoned host, with a beautiful sense of humor and such a big heart.

Learn from the diversified talented expert Dr. Jo Anne

1-How she learned to tune-out nonessential disruptions or distractions in her life, a step that she considered necessary to complete a task or project.

2-How she was able to move from one creative project to another, provided she made sure whatever she worked on was **saved and backed up**. That is what gave her the freedom to switch gears.

3-How movement and dancing eased her body and relaxed her mind which helped her gain further clarity and even expansiveness in her thinking.

4-How she had more fluidity and flexibility with movement which helped generate novel ideas, enhanced her creativity, and helped her with concentration as it quieted her mind chatter, which made her more receptive to her internal messages/inner guidance, and gave her more acute awareness, and intensified her focus.

5-How sound silenced random, insignificant thoughts as it helped her to be calmer and at peace, which primed her for more captivated attention.

6-How being assertive, staying focused, and using both sound, movement and dance all helped help captivate her attention.

Pay attention to the quality of your thoughts, ideas, standers, people, environment, food, information, discussions, dialogue, education, self-image, inner circle, social network connections, and household — something your future self will thank you for.

Everyone wants attention; attention creates connections. Connection invites bonding and promotes feelings of acceptance and safety. You want to be mindful of the quality of connections you are inviting with what you are giving attention to and why.

Take inventory of what is supportive of your creativity and what is toxic. Then be assertive and decide who must be removed and who is supportive and can stay in your life. Attention is likely to impact your happiness, so sharpen that skill.

Imagine if you had rotten food, would you still eat it, knowing it can get you sick and give you digestive problems? Probably not. Then why would you leave rotten energies around you, let it pollute your air, and mess up your internal organs? You need to raise your standards and the quality of your thinking/living. You can do so if you pay attention to what you are letting in your life at each given moment and what you are letting go of!

Questions that will help you gain clarity for your creative attention:

1. Why is attention important to your creativity?

2. What are some distractions that are affecting your attention that need to be removed?

3. Are all your senses engaged? Are you paying attention to how you are feeling about what you would like to create?

4. What fears are you giving attention to that may be holding you back from creating?

5. Is attention a matter of having the right habits? If so, what toxic habits do you need to toss out?

6. Are you seeking personal attention through your creativity by providing a service, helping a cause, or spreading a message or are you paying attention to the serving of your bigger why?

CREATE FOR A CAUSE NOT FOR APPLAUSE!

You must manage your attention and prioritize your time and regulate yourself emotions when it comes to optimizing your creative mindset.

"PRIORITIZE Your Time

MANAGE Your Attention

& REGULATE Your Emotions" —Dr. Sofie Nubani

To come up with better ideas. Practice paying attention.

Daring to Be Bold and Brave for Creative Success

Chapter 8:
C.O.U.R.A.G.E | Section 3

In this Chapter, you'll learn about

- The 6th trait Of Creativity In C.O.U.R.A.G.E, i.e., is Gallantry

Gallantry: (Nobility of spirit or action; courage)

"Adopt gallantry to live life creatively. To be creative is to take a new path that no one has taken. You have to have creative courage guided by your inner knowing, fueled by your confidence and driven by your intrinsic motivation." — Dr. Sofie Nubani

The Wolf and the Kid

A kid was perched upon the top of a house. Looking down, he saw a Wolf passing under him. Immediately, he began to revile and attack his enemy. "Murderer and thief," he cried, "what do you, here, near honest folks' houses? How dare you make an appearance where your vile deeds are known?"

"Curse away, my young friend," said the Wolf.

"It is easy to be brave from a safe distance."

(From Aesop's Fables)

Bravery and courage require stepping into the arena and coming face-to-face with adversity, even your fears, and taking action. Being true to yourself when you create requires this key ingredient.

"Courage is not the absence of insecurity, fear, anxiety, or despair, but resides in the decision to move through these feelings as constructively or creatively as possible." — Stephen Diamond, Ph.D.

Having Gallantry (creative courage) is about taking risks, traveling new paths. Having creative bravery is about building your inner strength and having the courage to face your fears confidently.

Day to day encounters; Souraya's Creative Courageous moment

I know of this amazingly talented girl — her family members talked about how beautiful her voice was. One day, while in a gathering at my son's house, (I brought my karaoke machine). I asked if she would want to have some fun singing Karaoke. She was very hesitant, shy, and tried to resist the request initially, however, I was very persistent until she did.

I truly wanted to hear her voice and evaluate it myself. I do have a few friends in influential positions in the entertainment industry, after all, I might be able to get her connected with someone who may discover her talent and help her pursue her passion for singing.

I cheered and clapped until she finally mustered courage and grabbed the mic. She started with a few giggles here and there, moved her body around feeling nervous, but gradually as she was tuned in with the words and music — now, I could truly see her talent.

Noticing the few people watching/listening, everyone tuned in, drawn to her mesmerizing, deep, and soul magnetizing voice. She started building her courage and her voice projected her inner strength with every minute that passed by, as she went from strength to strength.

It was such a great and joyful experience. I even took a video of her, and later with her permission, I asked her if I could share it on my social media platform. She agreed with a mile-wide smile.

Then I requested everyone on my social media page to give their feedback, I gave her a 10. In the next 24 hours, almost all of the comments had the same rating and response — a rising star, incredible, amazing, talented. All I can say that those were wonderful and very encouraging comments, which she was able to see and appreciate as well.

After having such great feedback, she got inspired and shared with me that she ordered a few things like the ring light and other equipment to start performing from her private space.

I believe, with enough practice and right social media exposure, presence, and connections, Sour (her nickname) will be a rising star. She will move the audience with her alluring voice, as she shares her beautiful gifts in this particular case, her voice, as she has plenty of other gifts to offer as well.

I share with you this story, so you may encourage someone you know that has talent but maybe is shy or needs a little encouragement to boost their creative courage. Or it may be that you have a talent (could be in writing, painting, designing, constructing, coding, etc...) and need to build your inner strength to take it to the next level. If so, then it is time for you to practice creative bravery.

Identify where your fear is coming from, knowing that it is always an ally that is trying to get your attention for what you need to work on, release, or heal. Fear was then more like a teacher, not an enemy. It was there to teach you a little more about yourself and a certain situation, perhaps to both protect you, as well to help you understand the situation and yourself better.

Realize that hiding, ignoring, or avoiding your fears, will not only suppress your emotions but will show up in your behaviors and dominate your decisions and actions. You must face your fears to understand it, to accept it, and then be able to release it with more ease, grace, and even gratitude. The opposite of fear is courage, trust, curiosity, and inner peace — all of which are important when it comes to having creative courage. The good news — like many character traits — courage can be taught, and if it is a trait you need to work on, then never delay your efforts.

START BY YOUR FIRST COURAGEOUS STEP AND THAT IS, TAKING ACTION.

What areas would you need to develop creative courage/gallantry more of in your life today?

For example; speaking up for yourself, trying new things, not being afraid to fall, not following the crowds, trying out different foods, mixing with different cultures, embracing challenges, not seeking validation, etc... Remember the more open you are to new experiences, the more you are aware of things you had no idea about and was not familiar with in the past.

Another way to be creative and grow in confidence is to explain things to yourself. Having a conversation with yourself can take place out loud, or in your head. That will boost your inner confidence and strengthen your gallantry.

Which of the different types of courage do you consider yourself to have more of?

Check the different types of courage and write down your evaluation, then start working on them to optimize your creative mindset and boost your innovation.

- Moral courage

- Intellectual courage

- Disciplined courage

- Empathetic courage

- Social courage

- Emotional courage

- Spiritual courage

Take a deep breath for a moment, clear your mind, and ask yourself again, what areas in your life would you need to add more gallantry, creative courage? (e.g. — self-esteem, business, spirituality, relationships, boundaries, and assertiveness).

"There is no soul liberation or inner peace without us

understanding and facing our fears with a courageous heart and

a willing soul." — Dr. Sofie Nubani

Yes, feeling safe is grounding and more soul-liberating when it comes to optimizing a creative mindset.

Safe, in knowing that it is perfectly fine to make mistakes, it's okay to be vulnerable, it's okay to have setbacks, it's okay not to be perfect, it's okay if you have to try several times before you reach your desired outcome. As Brenè Brown in one of her now-famous TED talks said once: 'Vulnerability is the birthplace of innovation, creativity, and change". You must be a row and real with self and when you are comfortable being the same with others, you will come to realize that being a little nervous is normal, responding to life from an uncomfortable space is having you at your growth zone, those moments and awkward feelings that you experience, are feelings that are giving you a signal making you aware, guiding you, creating a safe bridge between your concerns, doubts, fears, strength, courage, and confidence that you need to step into, so you can go after your dreams, vision and mission.

"A ship is safe in harbor, but that's not what ships are for." —

William Shedd

A Creative Genius is courageous in action and thought, challenges himself/herself, as well as others to step outside their comfort zone into their creative zone and so that they can truly make an impact.

A Creative Genius mutes the voice of self-doubt, and all the discomfort it brings about, they redirect their focus to their creative task at hand and protect the progress that self-doubt is trying to distract or attack.

Gallantry (Creative Courage) is not just an act, it is a feeling, a mindset, a soul set, a creative attitude that is dedicated, persistent, committed, and just continues to stand out.

Having the courage to make tough choices and take a step towards potential setbacks or rejection is key in moving forward and defeating self-doubt.

"Courage is the most important of all the virtues because

without courage you can never practice any other virtue

constantly. You can practice any virtue erratically, but nothing

consistently without courage." —*Maya Angelou*

Creative Leaders That Changed the World

Let's look at a few courageous creative leaders that changed the world, they made the impossible seem possible in their time. These leaders were always willing to try new things, break rules, challenge beliefs, and crossed boundaries that may have been limiting their best potential.

Right from the Middle East and respected for centuries by many around the globe:

1-Umm Kulthum: Queen of the Nile

Influenced by her father, a village imam who sang traditional religious songs at weddings and holidays to make ends meet, she learned to sing from him. When he noticed the strength of her voice, he began taking her with him, only he dressed her as a boy to avoid the opprobrium of displaying a young daughter onstage.

Egyptian society during Umm Kulthūm's youth held singing — even of the religious variety — to be a disreputable occupation, especially for a female. It took some bravery from her father and creative courage from the legendary Umm Kulthum — as a child to — dress like a boy and perform at her best despite how her appearance might have been mocked and criticized. Oum Kulthoum always wore dark glasses because she had a thyroid condition that caused her to develop exophthalmos — it involves bulging of the eyes. This condition is not uncommon for hyperthyroidism patients to suffer from, it also causes dryness of the cornea and sensitivity to light.

Source: Syrian research

She did not let her appearance bother her, her passion for singing and gallantry instead made her chignon look and dark glasses become iconic and still inspires pop artists and designers across the Middle East.

Through her courage, determination, and deep originality, Oum Kalthoum exemplified an unparalleled revolution in Arabic music.

"The Middle East's greatest ever singer was to her fans barely of this planet, her nickname "Kawkab Al Sharq", literally meaning, "Planet" or "Star of the East".

When Umm Kulthum sang, she was said to empty the streets of the most congested of Arab cities, even Cairo. Her voice, perhaps apocryphally, was said to be so powerful as to shatter glass. A strong woman, mysterious and bold, she sang of the love of God and men, women, and the homeland. Everyone loved listening to her. She sent mystics into a trance. Cloistered women dreamed of gallant love, illiterate people recited refined verses, nationalists glorified language and westerners discovered an imperial diva who, from Led Zeppelin, Bob Dylan, Maria Callas, U2 to Mick Jagger, would change the view of the world.

Often her shows would last for over five or six hours on end, a concert being composed of two or three epic songs.

The official recorded length of arguably her greatest song "Enta Omri" ("You Are My Life") is almost an hour but could go on for several more once Umm Kulthum got into her groove in front of an enchanted crowd."

Source: gqmiddleast.com

"Imagine a singer with the virtuosity of Joan Sutherland or

Ella Fitzgerald, the public persona of Eleanor Roosevelt and the

audience of Elvis and you have Oum Kalthoum, the most

accomplished singer of her century in the Arab world."

— Virginia Danielson, Harvard Magazine

Some Iconic lines from the ultimate Arab musical icon, by a contributor to step feed.com Ola Kseroof

1-"We ran and raced our shadows" from Al Atlal الأطلال

"And we walked in the moonlit path, joy skipping along ahead of us. And we laughed like two children together. And we ran and raced our shadows."

Lyrics by Ibrahim Naji

2- "And I chose to stay away, and I learned how to become stubborn, and even abandon you. See? See what cruelty does to you?" from Esa'al rouhak اسأل روحك

"And I've changed little by little. I've changed and I couldn't stop it. And I started forgetting my yearning to you, and hated my weakness and patience towards you. And I chose to stay away, and I learned how to become stubborn, and even abandon you. See? See what cruelty does to you?"

3-Has my tenderness hardened your heart?" from Esa'al rouhak اسأل روحك

Ask your heart. What changed it? What changed me is my suffering in your love. But you, what changed you? Has my tenderness hardened your heart even towards me? Has my acceptance made it easy for you to play with my heart?"

Lyrics by Muhamad Abdul Wahab

Egyptian singer Oum Kalthoum continues to inspire generations of people from the Arab World. She was one of the most famous Arab singers and public personalities of the 20th century and was listed as Top 25 most influential women in Egyptian History in an article in Rawi's Magazine.

How about the international icon Dynasty Di — a committed humanitarian!

2-Princess Diana

Diana, Princess of Wales (born Diana Frances Spencer; 1 July 1961 – 31 August 1997), was a member of the British royal family. She was the first wife of Charles, Prince of Wales, and the mother of Prince William and Prince Harry. During her years in the royal spotlight, she broke countless rules, especially when it came to raising her children, charity work, and fashion.

Princess Diana was very opinionated about raising her children, she put her children first. Traditionally, royal duty has often come before family life. However, Dynasty Di did not seem very accepting of it and created her own rules. Princess Diana marked "a real change" in the way royals approached fashion. She used it to promote the messages and causes she deeply cared about. She took advantage of her fame and public scrutiny and used it to deliver messages through her clothes. According to Anthony McGrath — celebrity stylist, and lecturer at the Fashion Retail Academy in London — shared on Express.co.uk: "Princess Diana often used her style to assist in promoting a message, whether that be in a flight jacket and baseball cap on downtime with her young sons or promoting causes close to her heart."

She helped draw the spotlight on certain fashion houses and designers, such as Catherine Walker, Versace, and Dior.

"Nobody in modern living memory has had more of an effect on the way fashion is viewed by the masses as Princess Diana. When it came to charitable work, Princess Diana worked tirelessly on behalf of charities around the world, using her fame to raise awareness of several key humanitarian issues. Princess Diana is noted for two major contributions to humanitarianism, — although during her lifetime — she was the President or Patron of over 100 charities. However, her work with landmines and her work on behalf of AIDS patients were forever noted in telling photographs and consequently, her efforts in these two areas of humanitarianism are most well-known."

Source: charity.lovetoknow.com

Some unknown facts about Lady Diana:

SHE WAS A BREAKTHROUGH ACTIVIST FOR HIV AWARENESS.

Diana made history in April 1987 when she was photographed shaking an HIV patient's hand without wearing gloves. The photo helped spread the message of HIV awareness and educate the public's perception of the illness. That day, the Princess opened the UK's first HIV/Aids unit at London Middlesex Hospital that specially treated patients infected with the virus.

SHE RECORDED MANY OF HER THOUGHTS ON TAPE.

"The Princess was talking about her unhappiness, her sense of betrayal, her suicide attempts — and two things I'd never previously heard of: an eating disorder called bulimia nervosa and a woman called Camilla," Morton said about the tapes. In 1992, Andrew Morton wrote Diana: Her True Story — In Her Own Words based on the tapes he had received from Diana. The book was a bestseller and forever changed the narrative about the princess."

SHE WANTED TO BE A BALLERINA BUT WAS TOO TALL.

Diana's ballet teacher Anne Allan opened up about her time with the princess in 2017, saying "she had dance in her soul. I realized the pure enjoyment that it gave her. She loved the freeness of being able to move and dance... I could see it helped to alleviate her emotional life."

Source: harpersbazaar.com

"I like to be a free spirit. Some don't like that, but that's the

way I am." — Lady Diana

This says a lot about her value to freedom, self and the bravery to stand up to conformity and confidence to change Royal family rules passed many years ago.

Her ability to think out of the box, to stand up for herself and question passed on traditions and beliefs that did not make sense to her, her intellectual openness to new experiences and risk tolerance, having the courage to speak up and lead in paths that were unfamiliar to support a cause and serve a mission in her unique style and originality demonstrates a creative soul expression, one that touched and influenced many lives.

Today, we see her son Harry taking after her footsteps, stepping away from his role from the Royal Family, though he will continue to hold his princely title but is losing his military titles and patronages, including Captain General Royal Marines, Honorary Air Commandant Royal Air Force Honington, Small Ships and Diving, Royal Naval Command: Commodore in Chief. Prince Harry spoke honestly about the grief he still felt over the death of his mother, Princess Diana, in a 1996 car crash in Paris, describing it as a "wound that festers" and one that motivates his actions today.

Today, Prince Harry and his wife Meghan are no longer 'working members' of the Royal Family. The couple was very honest at the end of 2019 about their struggles under the spotlight of the Royal Family.

Prince Harry on Diana

"My mother died when I was very young. I didn't want to be in the position I was in, but I eventually pulled my head out of the sand, started listening to people, and decided to use my role for good. I am now fired up and energized and love charity stuff, meeting people, and making them laugh."

"It's something my mother believed in — If you are in a position of privilege, if you can put your name to something that you genuinely believe in, you can smash any stigma you want, and you can encourage anybody to do anything."

"Every day, depending on what I am doing, I wonder what it would be like if she was here, and what she would say, and how she would be making everybody else laugh. Who knows what the situation would be, what the world would be like if she were still around?

Heartfelt feelings and not conforming — like a mother, like son.

How about the brilliant Ma Yun who for nine years, would ride 17 miles on his bicycle to give tourists tours of the area to practice his English. He became pen pals with one of those foreigners, who nicknamed him "Jack" because he found it hard to pronounce his Chinese name.

3-Jack Ma

Jack Ma – The Inspirational Story of the Alibaba Founder

There was a headline in the Shout Me Loud article on Jack Ma's back story. It stated:

"You wouldn't believe the number of times this man has been

rejected and failed."

In his early childhood, Jack Ma failed in his primary school examinations, not once, but twice! He failed thrice during his middle school exams. When applying to universities after high school. Not just that, he also failed the entrance exams thrice, before finally joining Hangzhou Normal University. Jack applied and wrote to Harvard University ten times about being admitted – and got rejected each time. This was only during his education!

During and after his Bachelor's degree, Jack tried and failed to get a job at a multitude of places. After spending three years to get into any university, he failed to land a job after applying to them 30 times! He recalls in his interview, "When KFC came to China, 24 people went for the job. Twenty-three people were accepted. I was the only guy who wasn't." He was also one of the 5 applicants to a job in the police force and was the only one getting rejected after being told, "No, you are no good." Also, on his entrepreneurial undertakings, Jack Ma went on to fail on two of his initial ventures. But that never stopped him in any way of dreaming bigger.

In one of his interviews, when asked about his rejections, this is what he had to say, "Well, I think we have to get used to it. We're not that good." Overcoming the pain of rejections and treating rejections as opportunities to learn and grow was what Jack Ma made of it.

After finally coming to terms with all of his rejections and failures, Jack Ma visited the US in 1995, for a Government undertaking project related to the building of highways. It was then that Jack Ma was first introduced to the Internet and Computers. Computers were pretty rare in China back then, given the high costs associated with them and Internet or e-mails were non-existent. The first word he searched on the Mosaic browser was 'Beer' and it popped out results from different countries, but there were no signs of China. He then searched 'China' and not a single result popped out! He decided it was time for China and its people to get on the Internet.

Finally, after persuading 18 of his other friends to invest and join him in his new e-commerce startup – Alibaba, the company began from his apartment.

"My dream was to set up my own e-commerce company. In 1999, I gathered 18 people in my apartment and spoke to them for two hours about my vision. Everyone put their money on the table, and that got us $60,000 to start Alibaba. I wanted to have a global company, so I chose a global name." -Jack Ma

"Never ever compete on prices, instead compete on services and innovation." -Jack Ma

Jack Ma / Ma Yun (Chinese) now runs one of the biggest E-commerce networks in the world he is the founder of the E-commerce giant Alibaba and is a stakeholder at Alipay its sister company which is an e-payment portal. Even without Jack Ma having any past experience in coding or selling to anyone, the company was growing rapidly. TODAY, Alibaba has a market value of $480 billion and is worth more than eBay, Visa and Johnson & Johnson currently.

Hard work, persistence, risk tolerance, and resilience all went to play when it came to finally reaching a sweet spot in this self-made billionaire's career.

"Jack Ma has a big heart, is extremely approachable, and he is not afraid of laughing at himself. Meanwhile he attracts huge attention by joking about himself which brings more attention to Alibaba as well." -Celine Fang

Making jokes about himself was very known to many, his sense of humor and outgoing personality made him approachable and easy to connect with. Ma's playful and creative side was shared in an article by Business Insider, which stated:

"He has always maintained a sense of fun at Alibaba. When the company first became profitable, Ma gave each employee a can of Silly String to go wild with. In the early 2000s, when the company decided to start Taobao, its eBay competitor, he had the team working on it do handstands during breaks to keep their energy levels up. The company also hosts annual talent shows, and Ma is a natural entertainer. At a company anniversary event, he dressed up as a punk rocker for a performance in front of 20,000 Alibaba employees."

It is very intriguing when we learn about the back stories of great successful leaders and businesses and very thought provoking when it comes to how creativity played a big role into their sustainable success. Jack Ma's openness to new experiences and willing to learn continues to be his soul signature.

"Many Chinese founders think of their companies as children, for them to raise as a parent would, but Ma has always seemed to prefer the teacher-student metaphor." - Guan Buyu, researcher

Ma is a former English teacher who is still nicknamed "Teacher Ma." He shared that he does not want to grow old and die working instead he would rather die on holiday. He mentioned in one of his interviews that he wants to retire younger than Bill Gates.

"There's a lot of things I can learn from Bill Gates. I can never be as rich, but one thing I can do better is to retire earlier. I think some day, and soon, I'll go back to teaching. This is something I think I can do much better than being CEO of Alibaba."

At the age of 54, Ma announced he plans to retire in a year and an interesting fact about the day Ma chose for his retirement as chairman is that it is "Teachers Day" in China.

His announcement about his plan to retire in a year at the age of 55 left many scratching their heads, including Russian President Putin.

Putin asks Jack Ma: 'You are still so young, why are you retiring?'

Ma answered: "I have been [running Alibaba] for 19 years and achieved something, but there are still many things I hope to accomplish, like education and philanthropy."

A month after he retired, Ma shared on CNBC news article he now plans to do philanthropic work in the education sector to better prepare the next generation for the shifting landscape by encouraging greater independent thinking.

"We (have to) teach our kids how to be innovative, constructive and creative so they can survive in the AI (artificial intelligence) period. I want to do more things about that."

Inspiring Quotes by Jack Ma:

"I don't think I'm a workaholic. Every weekend, I invite my colleagues and friends to my home to play cards. And people, my neighbors, are always surprised because I live on the second-floor apartment, and there are usually 40 pairs of shoes in front of my gate, and people play cards inside and play chess. We have a lot of fun." -Jack Ma

"I like to play cards. I'm not very good, because I don't want to calculate, I just play by instinct. But I've learned a lot of business philosophy by playing poker." -Jack Ma

"You should learn from your competitor but never copy. Copy and you die." -Jack Ma

"Your attitude is more important than your capabilities. Similarly, your decision is more important than your capabilities." -Jack Ma

"Opportunity lies in the place where the complaints are." – Jack Ma

"Help young people. Help small guys. Because small guys will be big. Young people will have the seeds you bury in their minds, and when they grow up, they will change the world." –

Jack Ma

Gallantry, Openness to new experiences, Risk Tolerance, Humor, Energy to shift state (handstands in breaks), Combinatory Play, Uniqueness are very dominant in Jack Ma's creative style.

"You may overcome many defeats, but you must not be defeated. Please remember that your difficulties do not define you. They simply strengthen your ability to overcome." —Maya

Angelou

Creativity and courage are very intimately connected. They feed on each other, having courage feeds your creativity and without courage your creative work will not come to life, both must coexist for any creative projects to exist.

Just like Courage and confidence are interlinked; you may need confidence to be courageous, just as how you would need to be courageous to build confidence.

Learn gallantry from these amazing legendries in areas of:

1. The Queen of The Nile- Umm Kulthum:

-Not to seek validation and feeling confident to stand out even when you look different from the crowds.

2. Dynasty Di- Princess Diana:

-Not to submit to conformity and having a bigger WHY to serve.

3. Teacher Ma- Jack Ma:

-Importance of collaboration, having creative fun team Spirit and treating failure only as feedback

"Failure is only FEEDBACK to the wise, learning from it will EQUIP you with a strong come back, and adding humor to it will DISSOLVE its impact." —Dr. Sofie Nubani

- Today, how can you start practicing creative courage?
- Is there an online product or service, very unique to you that you can sell/promote that resonates with you?
- At work, how can you be more creative?
- In your personal life how can you invite more humor, to charge your creativity?
- Are you a conformist?
- Do you seek validation from others?

Make time to self-regulate, reflect and gather your thoughts, in order to improve your creative courage and skills.

Gallantry is important when it comes to creativity, your mindset, soul set, attitude, curiosity, willingness to learn, vulnerability, risk tolerance, and even marketing your product.

Gallantry/Creative bravery are valuable attributes to creativity alongside authentic integrity, vulnerability and empathy.

On a personal level, I'm left with the conviction that as marketers, we only stay culturally relevant through creative bravery. Today, bravery isn't optional. It's the price of entry for brands as people's expectations rise and attention becomes harder to capture."-Rob Lenois, deputy chief creative officer at Grey New York.

Hope some of those stories inspired and challenged you to expand your creative vision and introduced you to some creative solutions. I also wish that they invite hope and faith to the endless possibilities and opportunities that are available for you to tap into and explore, practice curiosity, courage and creativity so you can manifest your innovation productively.

Courage – For best creativity leading to innovation, leaders, workers, employees or team members must experience psychological safety, have no fear speaking their thoughts and expressing their ideas. Courage is the key to great leadership. In areas of creativity, nothing will manifest to innovation without having creative courage, bravery and gallantry along with few other traits like ones shared in the acronym in C.O.U.R.A.G.E in addition to tenacity, empathy, humility, authenticity, which all need Courage in order to exist.

Courage is an important character in a leader and in this case precisely a Creative Leader.

"Courage is an inner resolution to go forward despite obstacles;

Cowardice is a submissive surrender to circumstances.

Courage breeds creativity; Cowardice represses fear and is mastered by it.

Cowardice asks the question, is it safe?

Expediency asks the question, is it politic?

Vanity asks the question, is it popular?"

-Dr. Martin Luther King, Jr

Originality, creativity and innovation extensively charge our soul. So why not Invite Strong Allies (such as gallantry, Intellectual openness, curiosity, consistency, constancy, smart risks tolerance and focused attention) in your life to foster more creativity and optimize YOUR creative mindset.

"Creativity is contagious, pass it on." -Albert Einstein

SO IS COURAGE, PASS IT ON!!!

"Let your courageous CREATIVITY be contagious, INSPIRING others to be bold and confident, easing them to step into their creative greatness." –Dr. Sofie Nubani

Chapter 8:
C.O.U.R.A.G.E. | Section 4

In This chapter, you'll discover...

- The 7th Trait of Creativity In C.O.U.R.A.G.E:

ENERGY:

PRACTICE ENERGETIC INTEGRITY

"Tapping into your CREATIVE ENERGY and connecting with your SUPER CONSCIOUS MIND, INFINITE INTELLIGENCE, your HIGHER SELF, your INNER SOUL WISDOM all is very THRILLING, ENERGIZING and OPTIMIZING to Your CREATIVE MINDSET." –

Dr. Sofie Nubani

Energy, which by definition, means the strength and vitality required for sustained physical or mental activity, is a property of matter and space, objects and fields. It can be transferred between objects and can also be converted in form.

Everything runs on energy, so does creativity, energy in all its forms is endless and abundant. However, it is our vibrational alignment influenced by our own thoughts/emotions and daily habits that may make us feel energy-depleted or charged at times.

Energy is all around us and it is constantly in motion, defining, and redefining itself when we are in alignment with our inner being. We have lots of energy to spend and share on things we love. Have you ever worked on a project professionally or personally that you had much passion for, only to notice how fast time passed by? It is exactly what happens when you focus your attention on something you love and feels so unified, pleasant and fulfilling to your soul that you lose track of time.

To expand your energy, engage in thoughts, activities, projects, hobbies and relationships that lift your spirit, charge your soul and make you happy. Understanding the relationship between our own energy and conscious awareness, body, mood, health, environment; will make it easier to understand our energy with ourselves and others. When what you want and who you are, both are congruent, the harmony you live from within will support the flow of your creative energetic field, and inspired ideas (through meditation, relaxation, association, contemplation, even confrontation) depending on one's personal experience and relationship to their conscious awareness of the present moment, they can further find threads of connections creating new possible realities.

Energetic Integrity:

Having Energetic Integrity is very important in developing a healthy environment of creative energy. Be true to yourself, know your core values, belief systems, explore your truth and notice how you may be hindering your own creative energy.

External factors can influence your creative flow, adapting, accepting, or resisting, if they are a result of fear, anxiety or stress (for example, you may be trying to protect yourself from the unknown, conforming or please people) Such emotions and actions will create a resistance in your creative flow. Your risk tolerance, intellectual openness to new experiences and gallantry all will be compromised and your creative energy will truly be challenged and tested big time.

Energetic Integrity requires you to Be AWARE, CONSCIOUS and INTENTIONAL on where and how you are directing, projecting and sharing your energy. Such awareness is vital for the progress of your creative endeavors. You must give yourself permission to discover and tap into your creative energy, or you will spend the rest of your life applauding those who dared to travel inwards, and boldly faced their insecurities then challenged themselves to be more creative and innovative.

Naturally, energy has to move in some direction, it either could move towards destruction or construction. The less conscious you are, the more your energy is used towards separation, distraction and stagnation. Direct and use your energy wisely.

"Fear holds a destructive energy field that is directed internally and projected externally, both are toxic to optimizing a creative mindset." –Dr. Sofie Nubani

If your creative projects are motivated by copying, competing, envy or jealousy rest assured the outcome will not be rewarding in the long term. On the flip side having PASSION towards your creative projects will increase the charge between you and your creative energy. Neglecting your true passion, originality and uniqueness of your own deep passions and interests, will often cause you to feel soul constrained, bored, living a predictable routine that you are habitually repeating and not enjoying; day in, day out. There is something exacerbating when we allow our curiosity to lead us to unknown and new paths that are yet to be discovered.

While on those paths practice Energetic Integrity, be energetically responsible with your thoughts and intentions, be self-aware and honest with yourself and others. Integrity (or adherence to moral and ethical principles; soundness of moral character; honesty) take place when the different aspects of life fit together coherently, in harmony and consistently.

Creativity (use of the imagination, original ideas or inventiveness) happens when individuals question traditional assumptions and are curious with how things are done, have gallantry and cognitive risk tolerance, are flexible in embracing and initiating change and apply positive discipline to cross over the bridge of innovation.

HOW ARE YOU COMMUNICATING YOUR CREATIVE ENERGY?

ARE YOU BEING ENERGETICALLY RESPONSIBLE?

On scale 1 to 10, with ten being the highest; how do you measure your energetic integrity and etiquette, then ask why?

Why are you a 3 how could you increase it to a 6? Or why are you a 10 and how can you continue to maintain a 10?

As a Reiki & Chios Master, I have adopted some energy clearing techniques that helped me clear, charge, cleanse and expand my energy, on a personal level that expands my energy as well allowed me to show up to life, places, spaces and people with much positive and vibrant vibe and energy. Such modalities are not based on any religious belief, as a creatrix I love to learn and explore, then use modalities that resonate with my soul. I invite you to think from a new box and develop habits that will support your Energetic Integrity, we are responsible for what type of energy we bring to others and to the spaces we share.

I intentionally clear my energy daily, just like I would brush my teeth. An empowering habit that leaves me feeling more energized, focused and intentional. I feel lighter and clearer.

Energy is such a wide topic and will be discussed in more depth in book two, there I share a step by step formula of how I clear my energy field and I also share some great modalities that will shift your strength and add more power and vitality to your energetic field. However, it is significant when it comes to creativity and innovation so make sure you are paying attention to your supply, demand, consumption, exchange and share of your energy, for now please be mindful of that and apply the few tips you have in this chapter.

Creativity is typically presented as a constructive activity if delivered with authentic integrity. Be fully present and enjoy creating from that space.

The 6 Segments that will ensure good energy while working on your creative projects,

1-Be intentional and have Intrinsic motivation towards your goals. (Create with passion, be vibrationally aligned with what you're creating).

2-Have a sense of what you're creating, gather information and be knowledgeable about what is involved or needed, generate ideas and select the ones that have the best potential. (That will boost your creative confidence and enthusiasm).

3-Practice different thinking styles based on what you're working with and on. Be open and allowing

4-Do what you are interested in, have intellectual curiosity, openness, and tenacity along with cognitive risk tolerance while pursuing your passion. (To achieve optimal results)

5-Be attentive to Connection Seeking and expanding your Association Cortex by learning and inviting more experience that will charge to your life. (Be Aware)

6-If you feel overwhelmed take a break (go for a short walk, rest, take a shower) even if it was not a scheduled one. Getting away will free your mind and help you come back more energized and fresher. (Stop, Recharge and Rejuvenate)

"Connect with your Intuitive Abilities, exchange Energetic

Integrity and practice Positive Discipline. Create from a place

of vibrant and grounded energy." — Dr. Sofie Nubani

YOU ARE NOT A MACHINE — it is good for your soul, at times, to get out of your daily routine.

Meet a good friend for a cup of tea, change your reading time, try a recipe from a different country, learn a new workout routine, or change your workout location!!!

Connect with activities such as cooking, gardening, solving math problems, taking a long shower, etc., and tap further into your creative energy.

Train yourself to be positively disciplined just as you would equally train yourself to be flexible and open for change and new experiences.

Body, Mind, and Spirit

The relationship between your healthy body and creative mind is surprisingly intimate. Though some people may create in pain even during tough conditions, which can be a good release, however, we also see a lot of great creators who suffered from mental illness, leading some to commit suicide due to those same conditions.

At a basic level, you will need to have enough healthy and vibrant energy to pursue your creative projects. Therefore, it is wise to start from your internal self (physical, mental, emotional, and spiritual bodies) and your overall health, as it is very vital to ensure creative success.

As I was contemplating on how I can spread more awareness for you to maximize your best creative energy, what became clear to me was, it all begins with a healthy body.

Although we have heard of a few amazing individuals who created groundbreaking work under very difficult conditions, despite their illness and even oppression, they came out stronger than ever, inspiring many with what they created; for example, Nelson Mandela, Viktor Frankl, Mohandas Gandhi, and to name a few. However, in this chapter, the focus is on the creative energy that most people access under normal circumstances (up to medium challenges) and can tap into their creative productivity and effectiveness.

Physical Health

To start, let's begin with our physical health, and what could be the root cause and disturbance in your creative growth and successful journey.

On a personal level, inflammation for me was a factor, (it is a major body indicator that may hinder your creative success and growth). Once you understand more in-depth about its influence on your body and overall health, you will realize how it can totally affect your creative talent and abilities. Let's take a look. Are you ready?

"Inflammation is the cornerstone of Alzheimer's disease and Parkinson's, multiple sclerosis — all of the neurodegenerative diseases are really predicated on inflammation." - David Perlmutter

Inflammation and influence on Creativity

I had worked on creative projects at different levels of energy — that includes both high, vibrant, and healthy to low, fatigued and weak, due to having severe pain and suffering from high inflammation in my neck due to a car accident years ago in 2009.

During that period of pain and discomfort, the level of my concentration and flow state noticeably decreased and affected me negatively when I had to use my creative productivity.

Though I believe (during those painful episodes of heat sensations from the increased inflammation in my neck), escaping and connecting with my creativity in between my flare-ups has helped me temporarily escape the pain, even for short periods. However, with all the transparency, the quality of my delivery was not optimal because, during that period, I was mainly escaping my pain. I later realized that I was simply releasing and expressing the feeling of my pain on paper through my writings.

This reality was clear to me, as I started reading my content, knowing the positive person that I am deep inside, reading the few things I wrote as I recovered months even years later, I noticed the drop of zest and vitality in my content, my luminous choice of words were dimmed, and not as vibrant in comparison to my prior writings.

My pain was painting the dull colors of my words. If it wasn't for; chiropractic adjustments, massages, salt baths, healthier food choices, therapeutic-grade essential oils, meditation, and prayers, which all played a big role in my recovery process, I would probably still be writing words that were dim and had no positive influence.

To this day, I don't even take any meds or over-the-counter pain relief pills, like Tylenol, Aleve, or Advil. For that, I am SO grateful!

I learned through a conversation with Dr. Bob Choat (who is also an expert in fitness) about the vagus nerve, and what I was doing that was contributing and helping me to stimulate it.

He suggested that I would CONSCIOUSLY tap into the power of my vagus nerve to create a state of inner-calm which would help reduce the inflammation in my body. In short, by stimulating my vagus nerve, I was lowering the inflammation in my body, which helped me tap into my creative energy and abilities in a much better way.

How interesting, I thought to myself! Before our conversation, I was not familiar with the vagus nerve and its functions. This includes its key role in our body and the different ways we can stimulate it so we can reduce inflammation.

The Vagus Nerve and Influence on Creativity

For those who are not familiar with the vagus nerve, here are some insights from Science News (for students and medical news) and how they define it:

The vagus nerve begins in the medulla oblongata (Meh-DU-lah (Ah-blon-GAH-tah). It's the lowest part of the brain and sits just above where the brain merges into the spinal cord.

The vagus consists of two large nerves — long fibers composed of many smaller sensory nerve cell bodies that send information around the body. One emerges on the right side of the medulla while the other one from the left. But most people refer to both the right and left at the same time when they talk about "the vagus."

The vagus nerve is the cranial nerve that connects the brainstem to the body. It allows the brain to monitor and receive information about several of the body's different functions.

The name "vagus" comes from the Latin term "wandering." This is because the vagus nerve wanders from the brain into organs in the neck, chest, and abdomen.

It is also known as the 10th cranial nerve or cranial nerve X.

I share this with you because I learned so much about how using the vagus nerve consciously, you can add tremendous value to the quality of your life.

I learned about how a higher tone index of the vagus nerve tone activity (which is measured by tracking your heart-rate alongside your breathing rate) is linked to physical and psychological well-being and ability to return to a state of calm and relaxation faster when under pressure and after stress.

On the flip side of the coin, I learned that a low vagal tone index is associated with inflammation, depression, negative moods, loneliness, heart attacks, and stroke.

I also later understood what Dr. Bob Choat meant by, I was doing a lot of the right things to help relax my vagus nerve, which was by applying remedies that supported a healthy, natural stimulation to my vagus nerve.

I also learned later about my chiropractic adjustments and how they assisted in my recovery, especially after understanding how chiropractic plays an important role in reducing chronic disease through adjustments that directly influence vagal nerve function.

As my intellectual curiosity was rising about the connection between our vagus nerve and spinal health, I started reading and wrote some questions so that I could get clear answers about them.

I remember not too long after my research one day, I came across an article by the "ChicagoLand Nucca" which piqued my interest and cleared some further connections regarding this topic. It explained the connection of our vagus nerve and spinal health and how chiropractic adjustments helped a lot to this end. The article was titled "What happens-in-the-vagus-does-not-remain-in-the-vagus" (I am sure, many of you will be able to remember this title which is a variation of the famous saying: "What happens in Vegas stays in Vegas") and shared:

Spinal health plays a significant role in directing the health of the vagus nerve. If the spine becomes altered in its positioning or ability to move freely, the information to and from the vagus becomes interrupted. Chiropractors play close attention to the alignment and movement of the spine to assure better vagus nerve activity.

New research from 2018 proves that a Chiropractic adjustment improves HRV (heart rate variability) by boosting the health function of the vagus nerve.

This bit was interesting to me, as I understood the role that my chiropractic adjustments played to maintain the wellbeing of my spine and vagus nerve as well, to my recovery.

Learning about the vagus nerve was fun and very educational for me. I started asking more questions and ran into additional, new information.

During my research and study about the vagus nerve, I understood how some scientists and researchers may take years to finalize one study or conclusion on a particular topic/study. Getting in-depth into a topic of interest can be very time consuming for those seeking answers to important questions. With that, I learned the more information I gathered, the more knowledge I gleaned, the more I found out I need to learn more. I truly came to believe that I am a lifelong learner who keeps discovering bits of information that are considered little drops in the ocean of knowledge. But those little drops splash my soul with such an energizing impact, that it keeps me going back wanting to learn more of what this ocean has to offer and share.

Yes, I further wanted to learn how I could increase the vagus nerve tone in my body. After all, it could help decrease the inflammation in my neck.

Stimulate your vagus nerve for better creativity

As I researched further, I learned that our vagus nerve is connected to our vocal cords and the muscles at the back of our throat. I also learned that we can increase our vagal tone by activating those muscles and stimulating our vagus nerves with simple activities like, laughing, singing, humming, chanting, and gargling.

In addition, I also learned that balancing the gut microbiome is very essential, as healthy bacteria increase the vagus nerve tone, creating a positive feedback loop.

The vagus nerve plays a central role in the rest-and-digest (parasympathetic) nervous system.

> *"Factors that may stimulate the vagus nerve naturally include yoga, meditation, prayer, cold exposure, singing, fasting, and massage. Nutrients and supplements that are being researched for boosting vagus nerve activity include probiotics, fiber, zinc, and omega-3 fatty acids. Research is still limited. Be sure to consult a doctor before taking supplements or making major lifestyle changes." - SelfHacked.Com*

The natural simulations of the vagus nerve had a positive influence and have shown to increase both heart-rate variability and vagal tone. In addition, I learned that gut instincts are literally emotional intuitions transferred to our brain via the vagus nerve. This got me curious to find out more about the extent to which the vagus nerve affects our stomach. Mayo Clinic's answer below was the one I liked the most:

The vagus nerve helps manage the complex processes in your digestive tract, including signaling the muscles in your stomach to contract and push food into the small intestine. A damaged vagus nerve can't send signals to your stomach muscles.

"Visceral feelings and gut instincts are literally emotional intuitions transferred up to your brain via the vagus nerve. In previous studies, signals from the vagus nerve traveling from the gut to the brain have been linked to modulating mood and distinctive types of fear and anxiety."- Christopher Bergland (a world-class endurance athlete, coach, author, and public health advocate).

It also made me think about how a damaged vagus nerve may negatively impact gut instinct (our second brain) and how that may disturb our intuitive abilities, concentration, and function. Connecting different studies including gut and brain health outside a vagus nerve context, I found out how they were so interconnected. From there, I was curious to see HOW adding a third factor to the equation — such as creativity — could be influenced by the vagus nerve. On my quest, I discovered a tool/technique that had few reliable search resources that actually assisted in how these tools can enhance divergent thinking, particularly in the creative process.

Transcutaneous vagus nerve stimulation (tVNS)

Transcutaneous vagus nerve stimulation (tVNS) is a non-invasive and safe technique that transiently enhances brain GABA and noradrenaline levels.

- Transcutaneous vagus nerve stimulation (tVNS) **enhances divergent thinking.**

- Transcutaneous vagus nerve stimulation (tVNS) **modulates flow experience.**

- Transcutaneous vagus nerve stimulation (tVNS) enhances response selection during action cascading processes.

The health of our vagus nerve is very important for creativity, starting at the core — that is its influence on our immune system and its effects on many parts in our body, all of which play a vital role when it comes to optimizing a creative mindset.

"When health is absent, wisdom cannot reveal itself, art cannot manifest, strength cannot fight, wealth becomes useless, and intelligence cannot be applied". – Herophilus

Help yourself by becoming more aware of choices that are available to you, help yourself by becoming more curious to explore. Give yourself permission to venture out of your comfort zone, be part of finding helpful solutions, and participate in the process of co-creating with all your available resources. Finding what may trigger the vagus nerve and cause it to dysfunction, were thoughts that often came to my mind while I was writing this chapter of my book — our book, to be exact. Educating yourself on what could be negative triggers disturbing the optimal function of your vagus nerve, will help create with more ease, less pain, and more joy.

WHAT IRRITATES THE VAGUS NERVE?

Answer by Sherry Walling, Ph.D.

Most people will experience a vasovagal response due to a stressor or overstimulation of the vagus nerve at some point. Some other problems linked with vagus nerve dysfunction include obesity, anxiety, mood disorders, bradycardia, gastrointestinal diseases, chronic inflammation, fainting, and seizures. Irritation to the vagus nerve will result in difficulty focusing and hinders your creativity.

"You cannot be in growth and protection at the same time." —

Bruce Lipton

"Consciously tap into the power of your vagus nerve and create a state of inner calm to help tame your inflammatory reflex." - Dr. Bob Choat, Ph.D.

HARNESS YOUR CREATIVE ENERGY THROUGH, FOOD, SLEEP, ELIMINATING TOXINS, MOVEMENT AND SOUND

Food

By eating intelligently, you can alter your mood, your body shape, and even your thinking processes. This is why it's so important to pay attention to what you put into your mouth. 'You are what you eat', as they say. Make sure your body is not deficient in any nutrients, vitamins, and hormones (OBJ). Get your yearly physical exams and blood work done to stay on top of your health matters. Notice any fluoride intake through water, toothpaste, and other sources as it will affect your brain's overall health, memory, and concentration — all of which are important for optimal creativity. Ensure that you have enough fiber in your body and are not constipated, check on your cholesterol levels and make sure that your arteries are healthy and not clogged. The health of your internal organs will support all your physical work, creative ideas, plans, and innovation.

When it comes to food you must pay attention to two areas:

1. The source and quality of your food
2. The quantities and portions

1-Regarding the source and quality of your food

Plant-based foods, whole foods, superfoods are all a good base to start from. Everybody is different, some may need more or fewer nutrients based on their DNA genetics, blood type, and overall health. Schedule a consultation with your MD or Homeopathic Dr, health coach or expert, from there they can recommend you the best diet that will assist in boosting your creative energy.

2-Regarding the quantity and portion of your food

Overeating or not eating enough — both — can have a negative impact on the energy you receive and exchange. If you don't eat enough you will feel weak and if you overeat, you will feel lethargic. The balance between both will make you feel more ENERGETIC.

It is wise to pay attention to the portions, not just the quality of the food that you are eating. Not having enough food in your body, will affect your blood sugar levels, and can make you feel dizzy and sluggish. The little amounts of food you do eat will be stored as fat. Furthermore, it has many other side effects such as feeling fatigue, weakness, and more, all won't help you tap into your creative energy. On the other hand, overeating is just as dangerous and shouldn't be overlooked either. Overeating will expand the stomach beyond its normal size, making you feel uncomfortable, tired, lazy, and definitely will keep your body in a digestion mode instead of a creative mode!

Sleep and Sleep Cycles

Sleep also follows the same principle. Being sleep-deprived or oversleeping will not promote the creative energy required to stimulate your creative mindset. After learning about sleep cycles and the importance of sleep for a healthy brain, I truly suggest paying close attention when it comes to understanding sleep cycles, how they work, what is their significance and consequence on the overall energy throughout the day, and why? I also suggest you learn, study, and read about the importance of sleep for the wellbeing of your brain, not just your body. Sleep deprivation affects performance and can damage brain cells. After reading an article on Dr. Bob Choat's page, I learned about the importance of sleep for brain health, memory, healing, and cleansing toxins from the brain. I learned that for a long-term brain longevity, sleeping a good 7.5 hours was ideal and ensures waking up on an up-sleep cycle. I learned that each sleep cycle is 90-minutes long and waking up on an interrupted sleep cycle or a down sleep cycle causes our body to feel tired and less energized throughout the day.

For example, waking up after 6.5 hours would be one less hour before a complete 90-minute sleep cycle. Waking up after 7 hours would mean 30 minutes less of a complete cycle. Even though you lost only 30 minutes of sleep, your body will feel more rested having wakened up after completing the REM sleep. Most dreams occur during REM sleep, and it is thought to play a role in learning, memory, and mood.

"During deep sleep, the human growth hormone is released and restores your body and muscles from the stresses of the day. Your immune system also restores itself." -*Much less is known about deep sleep than REM sleep. It may be during this stage*

that the brain also refreshes itself for new learning the following

day." —Jocelyn Zakri MPH

I am explaining this so that you can have better control over how to support your overall creative energy. As is the case, understanding your sleep cycles will make the difference between you feeling tired throughout the day or having more energy to create — that is when you wake up on an "up" sleep cycle. I noticed the difference after intentionally setting my alarm clock a few days to wake me on a down cycle, I noticed the difference compared to waking up on my up-sleep cycle in both my energy and creativity levels.

For example, if you wake up after 6 hours of sleep, you will feel more energized starting your day than if you woke up after 7 hours of sleep. According to the National Sleep Foundation:

Adults, in general, need 7-9 hours of sleep, in normal health conditions. So why not take up on the right sleep cycle now that you understand how it works. Sleeping 7.5 hours, in this case, would be most recommended, unless you're sick or an athlete with high-performance levels, your muscle will need to recover and heal. In such a case, 9 hours is recommended. Again, that is one extra sleep cycle, 90 min added to 7.5 hours.

NAPS & Sleep Cycle

Pay attention to your sleep cycle, even when it comes to taking a nap. For instance, 1.5 hours is better than one hour, otherwise, a 15minute or 30-minute nap may work just fine.

Set your alarm correctly

When setting your alarm make sure you give yourself 15 to 20 min to totally dose before you set your time, then calculate waking up on an up-sleep cycle. Remember 7.5 or 9.00 hours depending on your health condition. Understanding sleep cycles truly helped me personally. However, each body is different, if you have any particular health issues that may need different types of attention or instructions, please it is recommended that you consult with your health provider. According to a teaser book from "Harvard Medical School" research states: "Too little or too much sleep can increase your perception of fatigue. ... Research bears out the connection between too much sleep and too little energy. It appears that any significant deviation from normal sleep patterns can upset the body's rhythms and increase daytime fatigue." Which in essence will affect the strength and focus you have to tap into your creative energy.

Toxins

"With so much evidence of depleting natural resources, toxic waste, climate change, irreparable harm to our food chain, and rapidly increasing instances of natural disasters, why do we keep perpetuating the problem? Why do we continue marching at the same alarming beat?" -Yehuda Berg

Toxins do not promote the longevity of pure creative energy but to truly apply that, one must identify what does toxicity represents/mean to them. We know a few bacteria, maybe microbes may not kill you, it takes a certain amount of anything to get to before it is considered toxic, yet there are few things that with the least amount will cause immediate harm or possibly even a permanent damage to one's health on many levels. So, pay attention to what could be toxic and restrict our creative energy.

Toxic environments

On an environmental level, if you are working on your creative projects in closed space — which most of you properly are then — pay attention to:

- Taking enough outdoor breaks, breathe some fresh air, open windows in your living/working space (provided that the air quality outside is healthy).

- Change your air conditioner's filter as needed — Use an air purifier, if you live in areas with poor air quality or if you're exposed to cigarettes, hookah, candles, incense, or smoke from fires.

- Stay away from toxic chemicals, in food, cleaning products, or cosmetics. In addition, stay away from places that have hookah, cigarettes, or are high in air pollution.

- Protect your lungs from being a victim of second and third-hand smoke or living in areas that have low air quality.

- "Stay tuned with your body and aware of your environment. Your health is your FIRST wealth, BAD HEALTH choices, will cause REGRETS. Choose wisely to grow and prosper." – Dr. Sofie Nubani

Toxic Relationships

There may be a few people who can channel their abuse into creative projects — though the percentage of victims with such conditions, however, is low, (living on eggshells, having low self-esteem, not speaking up, compromising your self-worth, not being aligned with your values and having low self-concept, all will result in a lot more damage than repair). If you are in such a situation then, connect with your authentic power, seek help, and find a way to transition and transcend your situation wisely.

In some cases, a few individuals may build up their resilience and prove to themselves that they are bigger than their circumstances — they can achieve this by painting, singing, or writing. Their pain/sadness many times is often projected onto their creative works.

It is much healthier to create with a healthy soul and a healthy mental and physical space, charged by one's expanded imagination creating and not completion of work that is describing one's pain through their creative projects. Though that is still a better option than not tapping into one's creative mindset in such cases because with time it may be therapeutic and healing, assisting in their recovery and transformation of such individuals' creative levels.

In addition, at least those sad emotions being expressed through creative projects do not translate into future body syndromes, or trapped emotions suppressed in the body.

There is no better quality of relationships than ones that are built on bases of love, respect, trust, growth, and compassion. All are healthy ingredients when it comes to relationships, best recipes, and success.

Being in a toxic relationship is not recommended nor is it healthy for that matter. However, unfortunately, some individuals are dealing with such situations longer than others and longer than they need to (an example would be; a young child living with an abusive parent or a non-working, abused mother with younger kids and has no resources to be on her own to support herself or kids or the opposite, a father in that case).

Creativity requires minimal conflict and anxiety in most cases. Yes, we know of several known artists who suffered from anxiety and still did great work. In general, stress negatively impacts creative expression, especially when it comes to deadlines for creative assignments, choosing the best potential creative idea, problem-solving, and measuring creative work, and feedback. It is when our creative work is done with intrinsic motivation, a sense of deep desire that represents value and has a meaning to our life, then joy and a feeling of contentment fills our hearts and guides our creative path. In such cases, the same stress metastasizes differently in our body as the passion for what we are creating keeps us more centered and helps us manage our emotions a lot better.

A *CNN*'s published article stated that:

"They found that people working in creative fields, including

dancers, photographers, and authors, were 8% more likely to

live with bipolar disorder. Writers were a staggering 121% more

likely to suffer from the condition, and nearly 50% more likely

to commit suicide than the general population."

Emotional suffering is definitely not what we want to be linked to artistry and creativity for sure. That is why being aware of the purpose of your creative project is very important — it is a very good anchor as you go through the process and progress of your projects and creative growth. Always remember your 'WHY', as it is very grounding and shielding from negative forces that may try to distract you while pursuing your creative ventures.

It is best to stay away from toxic people, substances, thoughts, and the environment to connect with your best creative energy. Enjoy your magnificent work feeling whole within rather than feel a big void that your art is distracting but the pain is so deep and won't be healed unless you face it, understand it, and then solve it on a deeper level. Instead create projects that hold meaning and value to you, projects that will make you feel proud to offer to yourself and serve others with pride.

Toxicity drains, sucks, and saps your creativity. Creativity requires a clear passage, which means, less stress, least resistance, minimal irritation, panic, and anxiety, to function optimally. Toxic people cause these emotions to be triggered regularly and communicate with tension, resulting in the death of your creativity and very possibly even disease in your body. Eventually, they will disturb and affect all areas of your life. Toxic people can decrease your brain's performance tremendously, stay away from them at all costs, as it could cost you, your life.

If they're toxic and you know it, leave right away. If they are toxic and you don't know it, you will remain their prey. If you're lucky to escape, you can sigh in peace. If you are doomed and stuck, you might just have to pray, keep in mind that prayer alone without faith, and taking action is just false hope and leads to disappointment. It won't help you gain momentum; you WILL be stuck in inertia.

So, take action, have faith and compassion for yourself and the situation, challenge yourself to walk away, or seek professional help especially if you are abusing yourself or if you are verbally, emotionally, or physically abused by others.

Movement

Exercise is a great way to improve energy levels. Moving your body gets your heart beating and blood to flow. It boosts your energy, reduces stress, and uplifts your mood. Stretching, walking, jumping, dancing all are creative energy enhancers.

Oxygen is essential for brain function, and enhanced blood flow increases the amount of oxygen transported to the brain.

We have Stopped Moving

"In less than two generations, physical activity has dropped by 20% in the U.K. and 32% in the U.S. In China, the drop is 45% in less than one generation. Vehicles, machines, and technology now do our moving for us. What we do in our leisure time doesn't come close to making up for what we've lost."

(designedtomove.org)

We have become too creative that we have invested in many tools that decrease our need to move. It is vital to recognize the negative influence these tools have on our bodies in the long run. Therefore, it is wise for you to create good habits that will support your lifestyle, increase your movement, creative energy, and your health's longevity.

"Research shows that gestures facilitate new learning and evoke imagery, not only in the minds of the listener but in the mind of the speaker as well. Body movements not only help you in processing old ideas but also create new ones."

(blog.dropbox.com)

Movement is good for your body organs as it makes sure that you move more every day.

"Movement is a medicine for creating change in a person's physical, emotional, and mental states." - Carol Welch

"Let him that would move the world first move himself." -

Socrates

Other ways movement can support your creative energy is by:

Gesture — By using your hands when you speak, you stimulate your brain, especially if you involve your non-dominant hand. So, have a conversation with someone, and be sure to throw some hand movements in to get those creative juices flowing.

Move your eyes — By sitting still and having your eyes rove all around the room, you stimulate your brain to communicate back and forth across both hemispheres. So, dart your eyes back and forth for a minute or two and see what happens.

Headstand — You have to love the headstand. First of all, seeing the world from upside-down is definitely something that will help you gain a new way of looking at things. But more than that, the headstand encourages additional blood flow to the head – meaning you have more oxygen going straight to the brain. Oxygen is crucial for brain health as it helps your brain to heal and regenerate.

Dancing — Creative dancing is dancing freely, without any rules or acquired moves. It is dancing in the present — at this moment — it is dancing in the now expressing instantly everything that flows through you. Every dance can be new and unique. It will flow promptly from within and will become the representation of yourself, as well as all of your emotions, feelings, and experiences.

All emotions, sufferings, experiences, intuition, and visions can be expressed, communicated, and transmitted with a dance. So why not have more dance today, move more today and create more today!

"Life is like a bicycle. To keep your balance you must keep

moving." –*Albert Einstein*

Move to a shifting state, feel elevated rejuvenated, and to create from your best self and a healthier inner state.

Sound

Along with movement, sound can increase the vibration of your creative energy whether its soft, instrumental, natural, or even hip hop — whatever resonates most with you — have fun, enjoy, and use. A moderate level of background noise will help you have distracted focus, just enough to break your pattern of thinking and assist your imagination to wonder while working on your creative project. Research has shown that listening to music can reduce anxiety, blood pressure, and pain as well as improve sleep quality, mood, mental alertness, and memory. Be mindful of the importance of sound to your creative energy and mental health. A 'sound diet' is vital for brain health as Nina Kraus, an inventor, amateur musician, and director of the Auditory Neuroscience Laboratory at Northwestern University shared in a conference how; "Hearing loss will speed up cognitive aging," she showed how hearing loss impacts brain health greatly.

According to her, most people take sound for granted because it's invisible like gravity. But to keep our brains healthy as we age, Kraus stressed the need to keep a "healthy diet in sound." This means training our brains with music. Kraus investigated in their lab how brain processes sound and how it changes people's brains. Based on their findings from the study involving thousands of participants across different ages, playing music, learning a new language, aging, hearing loss, and language disorders can influence our brain's capability to process sound. To ensure a healthy "sound diet" for our brain, Kraus suggests long-term and short-term activities such as the following:

- Playing and performing music — Musicians can hear much better than those who don't play music. Older people who played music throughout their lives "have a brain that looks biologically younger." But you have to play and perform music, not just listen to one. "Simply listening to music does not seem to have an impact on listening, language, and cognitive skills," Kraus stressed. "You don't get physically fit watching spectator sports."

- Learning to speak a new language — Bilingual speakers, who frequently switch between two languages, exercise their attention skills better than those who know only one language. Switching mode is an exercise for our brain enabling us to focus better on a stream of speech when we are in a noisy place.

- Computer music training games — Kraus said that playing sound games on the computer may be effective in teaching older adults to hear better but it doesn't guarantee the motivation of a person in the long run. Training in music is still the best even if you started later in life because it is "inherently more emotionally and intellectually satisfying [in] nature... than a brain-training game."

The right amount of ambient background music as well as playing musical instruments or even listening to some music will help increase the amount and flow of your creative energy.

On that note, I would like to introduce to you Bill Protzmann, founder of *Music Care Inc*. Originally, I connected with The Talented Bill on LinkedIn after hearing a very interesting podcast interview he had with Dr. David Friedman on music-related sound healing. I decided to send him a LinkedIn connection request, I mentioned to Bill how I met him on Dr. David's "To Your Good Health Radio" podcast and enjoyed listening to the show and provided insights.

During that time, I was literally on sound, vibration, and frequency chapter, which will be discussed in more depth in Book Two of **Optimize Your Creative Mindset** three-book series. When I connected with the very talented Bill on LinkedIn Messenger, he ended our message communication with a question, what are you most passionate about currently? I responded by writing my first book, in which I am actually on sound, vibration, and frequency in this chapter.

I remember looking at his response the next day saying: 'Please let me know if I can help in any way.'

"Wow", I thought, "How amazing is that." It felt so grateful, especially coming from an expert in his field.

I thought about his question and how nice it would be to have his feedback and possibly his contribution on the sound, vibration, and frequency chapter in the area of music and creativity of his expertise. That would be great. So, I responded with just that. He kindly agreed and with such ease, I was overly stoked with his positive response.

You see, **Optimize Your Creative Mindset** has been such a beautiful journey, the vibes associated with it, the growth, the lessons, the positive discipline, all contributors who showed up, and were willing to share their stories expertise, the whole process was just both motivating and no less inspiring. In simple words, it was extremely exhilarating and very fulfilling. Talented Bill is the world's leading expert on music's power for physical, mental, emotional, and spiritual health. Bill's work was recognized by the National Council for Behavioral Healthcare with an "Oscar" for Artistic Expression in 2014 Talented Bill has been a witness to the power of music throughout his life and speaks openly about how he has used music as self-intervention in his behavioral health care, including confronting disturbing suicidal tendencies. His volunteer work in the field brings him into constant contact with people who are or have been homeless, abused substances, are combat-injured, or are caregivers. This led Bill to the idea that guides him every day: Between music-as-entertainment and music-therapy is a powerful opportunity to use music as a tool. Bill calls that opportunity "music care."

Bill's fascination with the near-medicinal effects of music has caused him to study the topic widely and stay constantly engaged with the latest research.

Music is the mediator between the life of the senses and the life

of the spirit. - Beethoven (1770-1827)

Bill Protzmann contribution to music and a creative mindset: In my musical life, I've found that the creative mindset I need is one of openness, especially to authentic feeling/emotion. This doesn't mean that I'm an emotional hairball 24/7! It does mean that I allow myself to experience emotions more deeply than I might otherwise want to. This practice of becoming deeply fluent with emotions is quite common for musicians since our job is to offer authentic emotion to audiences and we can't do that without practicing them first. Emotion has been the gateway for me for many things, ranging from musical creativity to choosing to keep breathing. When I was most suicidal and before attempting to take my own life, I took time to listen deeply to music that felt most aligned with my emotional state. As I sat there under the headphones with my personal suicide music* On repeat, I experienced a deeper emotional connection to sadness and grief than I'd ever felt before, and I wept for a long time before falling asleep with the music still playing. When I woke up, the positive power and energy that found me was overwhelming, and that has stayed with me to this day. I feel certain that whatever scientific knowledge I had at that time of sound, vibration, and frequency had very little to do with my transformative experience of deeply accepting emotion in a judgment-neutral, curious place.

Scientific or technical or theoretical knowledge of how music works wasn't important to the effect it had on me, and contemporary research seems to bear this out: it's not what one knows about music, it's what music can do when it is listened to or played with deep intention, honest curiosity, and judgment-free acceptance.

Bill Protzmann, founder of Music Care Inc * Rachmaninoff - Etude-tableau Op.39 No.2 in A minor (performed by Vladimir Ashkenazy)

If you learn music, you'll learn history. If you learn music,

you'll learn mathematics. If you learn music, you'll learn

almost all there is to learn. - Edgar Cayce

1. Learn from Bill to use music as a tool to connect you with deeper emotions, insights, and reflections.

2. Learn from Bill's Quote:

"It's not what one knows about music, it's what music can do

when it is listened to or played with deep intention, honest

curiosity, and judgment-free acceptance."

How to connect vibrationally to the words, sound, and meaning of what the music you're listening to.

1. Learn from Talented Bill about how being open and receptive, can make space for internal healing and better self-acceptance.

2. Learn from Talented Bill how a deeper connection and understanding to and with music, literally saved his life and helped him face his suicidal thoughts.

3. Learn from Talented Bill how he turned his wounds to wisdom, by being in service helping others and passing it forward.

4. Learn from Talented Bill how a growth mindset and continued research and learning can boost your creative abilities, adaptability, and relationships association.

"The music is not in the notes, but in the silence between." –
Wolfgang Amadeus Mozart

Sound, Vibration, and Frequencies

Sound, vibration, and frequency are very influential in the creative process and are an in-depth expanded topic in book two. In this book and this chapter, the goal is to remind you of the importance of incorporating sound, vibration, and frequency into your life, especially if you have an interest in raising your creative energy. Each sound natural or instrumental influences our thoughts, feelings, emotions, and mood. When it comes to creative energy, it is wise to understand how brain waves work and learn how you can actually manipulate them for better creative productivity.

Brainwaves and how they can influence your creative energy

"The brain produces brainwaves that govern your life, whether you are awake or fast asleep. The brain's ability to produce and transition between different waves plays a role in getting work done, managing stress, and achieving a state of relaxation. In each individual, the following brainwaves can be found – Alpha, Beta, Delta, Gamma, and Theta. Each brainwave affects a specific domain and can be stimulated by different activities." (MEDSENSE, 2018)

There are five different categories of frequency pattern, Gamma, Beta, Alpha, Theta, and Delta Waves arranged from fastest to slowest, let's start with the slowest:

1-Delta Pattern

Delta waves are the slowest brain waves, occurring primarily during our deepest state of dreamless sleep, suspense external awareness, present mostly in sleep stages 3 & 4.

Delta brainwaves, allows you to restore and rejuvenate your mind and body, as you reach a deep level of relaxation and regenerate needed chemicals that were used while you're awake.

You access information in your unconscious mind through Delta 0.1 to 3.5 Hz deep sleep.

2-Theta Patterns

Theta waves produce flashes of creative visualization through vivid imagery, feeling raw, deep emotions, heightened intuition, receiving information beyond normal conscious awareness just like being in a state of hypnosis.

Theta brain waves occur most often in sleep but are also dominant during deep meditation.

- Meditative state, intuition, and where memory is based.

- It helps us improve our intuition, creativity, and makes us feel more natural.

- Function in a very rhythmic manner, it's like wake dreaming.

Biofeedback world expert Dr. Budzynski notes that theta brain waves, if used appropriately, could "dramatically boost one's learning abilities" and "enhances the absorption of the material ... (as) a lot of work gets done very quickly". It invokes deep relaxation at 3.5 to 7 Hz, drowsiness (also the first stage of sleep) Twilight state.

3- Alpha Patterns

Alpha is the frequency of our conscious thinking and subconscious mind. We are awake but relaxed. Anytime you feel inspired or have an insight, your brain is producing more Alpha waves than usual. High amplitudes of Alpha waves have been linked to heightened creativity. This is the state where you can apply guided Imagery, visualization, and imagination. The unconscious mind is influenced by images and emotions which makes memory recall easier and faster. Alpha is like a door opening to lower brain waves that will make it easier to reprogram the subconscious mind and get you in a clear state and more focused. Alpha is accessed twice naturally throughout the day. As you go to sleep and when you wake up, Thus, are two best times to drop suggestions to the subconscious mind to influence your goals and play with your imagination and seal your creative ideas with the outcome you desire. The stage between Alpha and Theta is best for reactivating your goals through your imagination. The brain waves ending from Alpha and transitioning to Theta are very powerful and necessary to access to optimize your creative mindset. Though you can reach Alpha with your eyes open it is achieved faster with eyes closed as you eliminate the 85% stimulus immediately that comes from your outside environment.

Want to boost your Alpha waves?

Deep breathing & aerobic exercise along with going outdoors or having access to natural scenery as well as visual exposure to nature was all shown to boost your alpha waves. An article published in Psychology Today shared this:

Increasing alpha brain waves can stimulate creativity and minimize depression. Neuroscientists recently made a correlation between an increase of alpha brain waves — either through electrical stimulation or mindfulness and meditation —and the ability to reduce depressive symptoms and increase mental resourcefulness & creative thinking. It is triggered in a 7 to 14 Hz relaxed yet awake, aware, or meditative state,

Beta Patterns

Beta is the most common brain wave pattern. These waves are produced when we are wide awake, alert, active, and engaged in mental activity. Beta waves are responsible for thinking actions, anxiety, and the feeling of being stressed. For example, insomnia is the result of producing excessive beta waves. These waves are produced in the frequency range of 14 to 32 Hz when the person is highly alert and focused.

Gamma Patterns

Gamma brainwaves are the fastest of brain waves. With high frequency, they are associated with peak concentration, correspondence to high peak performance, and high levels of cognitive functioning. Gamma brain wave is the only frequency group found in every part of the brain. Gamma waves are present during REM sleep and visualization — both supports increased creativity. Gamma binaural beats are shown to positively affect our memory and can slow certain medical conditions, such as Alzheimer's disease. Did you know that you can increase your Gamma waves output by focusing on compassion and love? Neuroscientists believe that people can train themselves to produce more of the gamma frequency.

In a study on monks' brains and connection to Gamma state, something remarkable happened. In the study, Monks were asked to focus on feelings of compassion. Immediately, their brains moved into the gamma frequency in a rhythmic and coherent pattern. Increased focus — In the gamma state, your brain can process all sensory information faster and with greater sensitivity; thus, creating a highly memorable experience. People with high gamma activity have a higher memory recall for everything they experience – from general exposure to detailed information. For example, from the food, they ate to the music they heard, the conversations they had, even the names of people they met, and so forth. On a side note, don't get NBC confused between gamma rays and gamma brain waves, as they are not the same thing.

Optimize Your Creative Mindset

In short — "A gamma wave is considered to be the fastest brain activity. It is responsible for cognitive functioning, learning, memory, and information processing." (Abhang, Gawali, and Mehrotra 2016)

40Hz or higher: Zen mind mastery. Brain waves affect the quality of thought as we drop down in brain frequencies, the thoughts per minute change. When one is stressed, thoughts per minute are increased and are over 30 per minute. The average state is 30 per minute as we get more relaxed, the numbers drop to 0 thoughts. Advanced meditators are highly adept at it. Research has found that listening daily to CDs or audio files with binaural beats has positive effects on anxiety. When you are working on creative projects or need to trigger your creative mindset, then you need to be mindful of the environment you are surrounded with, as it will influence how you think and feel. Also, be aware that binaural beats should be listened to with ears or good quality headphones to ensure that the different frequencies enter your left and right ear (when played over a loudspeaker, the frequencies are mixed in the air. If your ears pick up the frequencies already mixed, it will not have the same effect in producing optimal results).

Listening to binaural beats is absolutely safe, and scientifically proven, but it is best to choose your beats wisely depending on what you are looking to achieve from listening to them.

The Sound Healing Network (founded in 2002 in the USA) says Western Medicine progressively recognizes sound healing as a therapeutic modality. That includes different instruments — crystal balls, tuning forks, singing balls, drums, flute, piano — to name a few.

Check what sounds relax, uplift, empower, or charge you, depending on the task and utilize the power of sound to fuel your creative juices and vitalize your creative energy.

According to an article by Karuna Meda of Thomas Jefferson University, there are things you can do from the comfort of your own home to strengthen desirable brain waves and help with stress, sleep, and productivity. Regular **meditation** has been shown to increase alpha waves – your relaxation brain waves – and reduce beta waves – the brain waves of active thought and learning.

Meditation can increase your creativity

Researchers have found that people who meditate 30 minutes a day for eight weeks have improved focus, memory, and cognitive flexibility. Meditation triggers high-frequency brain waves associated with attention and perception — it feeds the wellspring of human creativity.

What is meditation? Is it a technique that can be practiced? Is it an effort that you have to do? Is it something that the mind can achieve? It is not.

Thoughts of Spiritual leaders and Philosophers on meditation

"Meditation gives us peace of mind without a tranquilizer.
And unlike a tranquilizer, the peace of mind that we get from
meditation does not fade away. It lasts for good in some corner
of the inmost recesses of our aspiring heart." – Sri Chinmoy

Debra King on Meditation

Meditation involves turning your attention inward and focusing your mind to a place where you are connecting to the source and your universal self. While it is often considered a spiritual or religious practice, it has become much more mainstream practice in today's western cultures. It is a tool that many use for personal development and growth. You would be surprised to know that many successful and happy individuals swear by its benefits.

Meditation paves the way for emotional healing. It is also an excellent method to balance your chakras. On an energetic level, meditation will assist you in removing any blockages that come from holding onto anger and resentment. Meditation ushers in what may be the most important part of the energy healing process, forgiveness. Forgiveness opens up our connection to other people and paves the way for global peace. By raising your consciousness, you are helping everyone else on this planet do the same. We are all connected by one vast field of energy.

Osho on Meditation from (Ancient Music in the Pines, Talk #7)

"A state of meditation is an innocent, silent state. You are
blissfully unaware of your awareness. You are, but you are
utterly relaxed. You are not in a state of sleep; you are fully
alert, more alert than ever. Rather, you are alertness."-Osho

307

"All that the mind can do cannot be meditation – it is something beyond the mind, the mind is absolutely helpless there.

The mind cannot penetrate meditation; where the mind ends, meditation begins. This has to be remembered, because in our life, whatsoever we do, we do through the mind; whatsoever we achieve, we achieve through the mind.

And then, when we turn inwards, we again start thinking in terms of techniques, methods, doings, because the whole of life's experience shows us that everything can be done by the mind. Yes – except meditation, everything can be done by the mind.

Everything is done by the mind except meditation. Because meditation is not an achievement – it is already the case, it is in your nature. It has not to be achieved; it has not only to be recognized, but it also has to be remembered. It is there waiting for you – just a turning in, and it is available. You have been carrying it always and always.

Meditation is your intrinsic nature. It is you; it is your being; it has nothing to do with your doings. You cannot have it. You cannot have it. It cannot be possessed; it is not a thing.

It is you. It is your being."

Deepak Chopra's view about progress in Meditation

Deepak Chopra, one of the world's leading writers, teachers, and entrepreneurs in holistic health and healing, talks to Omega about meditation, transcendence, and the nature of consciousness.

Deepak Chopra's feedback about progress in meditation from an interview with the Omega Institute is given below.

Omega: If a student asks, "How do I know if I'm making progress"? "Meditation?" What do you tell them?

Deepak: You shouldn't be attached to progress, but yes, there are signs. On the level of cognition, you realize that your thoughts are not who you are. On the level of emotions, you are less drawn to melodrama, but you do have experiences of joy, love, compassion, empathy, and equanimity. On the level of memory, you're not victimized. Your memory is sharp, but it's there only when you need it, so your internal dialogue, which is mostly memory and desire, is very quiet. On the level of sensory perception, it's a much richer present moment, multisensory experience. On the level of identity, your sense of self is no longer confined to your body. Those are the earlier signs. Then later, there's more synchronicity, more flow, loss of fear of death, and less identity with the self. That takes a while, but it does happen.

In Book 2, there is a chapter dedicated to Meditation along with real stories of lifelong meditators, highly-creative achievers, experts, shamans who now are pursuing their dreams and creative passions. They share how meditation boosted their creativity in detail that will inspire you as well as open you more to learning different meditation techniques including a special meditation that was inspired and channeled exclusively for Optimize Your Creative Mindset readers — so stay tuned and continue tapping into your best creative energy vortexes.

As you incorporate habits that support your creative energy, your process of creativity becomes more fun.

Therapeutic Grade Essential Oils to charge your creative energy

Use the power of smell to charge your creative energy and projects. Just as hearing is considered as the fastest sense in the human body (our human body can hear faster than it can see, taste, smell, or feel). The sense of smell is considered to be the STRONGEST of all senses.

"Scents bypass the thalamus and go straight to the brain's smell center, known as the olfactory bulb. The olfactory bulb is directly connected to the amygdala and hippocampus, which might explain why the smell of something can so immediately trigger a detailed memory or even intense emotion." (discovery.com)

Knowing how strong the sense of smell is out of all our senses, then it will be wise to employ it to increase our creative energy. Studies have shown that certain smells can help stimulate your focus and creativity. According to environmental psychologist Sally Augustin, certain smells trigger psychological reactions. Lemon and jasmine, for example, can improve cognitive performance. Peppermint can improve focus/concentration and boost your energy. On the other hand, the citrus oils such as grapefruit, tangerine, orange, and lemon smell are very energizing and uplifting. While eucalyptus, rosemary, cinnamon, and vanilla smells can help enhance creativity, along with many other choices depending on the flavor you prefer, you can choose to use them accordingly.

Boost your creative energy with **Therapeutic Grade Essential Oils,** smell your way to a better brain function, and increased creative energy.

In addition, make sure your space and environment are supportive of your creative projects. Learn about the art of **Feng Shui** and how applying it to your space can increase your creative energy. Opt for an **Energy Healing** session such as Chios, reiki, crystal healing, sound healing, crystal bowl meditation. Use EFT/TFT to feel relaxed, rejuvenated, and more ready to start or continue with your creative projects. Additionally, learn more about **colors** and their influence on creativity, for example, from an answer to some questions like:

WHAT COLOR INCREASES CREATIVITY?

Ans: "Effect Of Colors: Blue Boosts Creativity, While Red Enhances Attention To Detail." ScienceDaily.

WHAT COLOR MEANS CREATIVITY?

Ans: Orange. Orange represents enthusiasm, fascination, happiness, creativity, determination, attraction, success, encouragement, and stimulation. To the human eye, orange is a very hot color, so it gives the sensation of heat." Color Wheel Pro

Boost Your Creativity in less than 10 min

1. Try looking at something bright and colorful — specifically green or blue. Again, studies have shown that looking at something in these colors will enhance your ability for tasks that involve deep thinking. Creative involves both divergent and convergent thinking. Maybe it's

time to invest in some new artwork for your office or paint some walls that will support your creative mood and energy.

2. Write the old-fashioned way — by hand. Not only do we remember things better when we write things out longhand, but we become more creative when we do. Try keeping a notebook nearby so you can doodle in or scribble random ideas as they occur and keep your creative energy flowing.

3. Travel in time — According to a study published in a social psychology journal, our problem-solving skills get a boost when we think about something that happened either a long time ago or something that will happen a long way in the future. So, it's time to walk down memory lane. Either that or imagine where you'll be in ten years. Then revisit the problem. Getting better at problem-solving and not feeling stuck or stagnant will boost your creative energy. Maybe it's time to book your next NLP (Neuro-linguistic Programming) session.

4. Ground Yourself — If you feel overwhelmed energetically, not centered or just out of your element. Ground yourself, step into your garden (or the park), without your shoes; the idea is to be close to the earth beneath your feet. You can choose to lay down on the ground or walk around in the dirt/grass barefooted. Another good way to do this also to visualize roots extending from your feet to the center of the earth.

5. Laughing — A positive mood makes for better creativity, so laughing, even when you don't feel like it, can create a mood more conducive toward creativity and shift your creative energetic state instantly.

To maintain that creative mood, take these items and build them into habits. By repeating these actions often you'll get your brain in line with creative thinking, meaning that you'll become a more creative person.

In Conclusion:

"When you're in a stagnant creative energetic rut, remain calm, open and curious to find ways out, TRUST that you have the ability to transform it." –Dr. Sofie Nubani

Tap consciously into the power of your vagus nerve, keep the levels of inflammation in your body low. Add massages, chiropractic adjustments, salt baths, laughter, the right foods to help calm your vagus nerve and reduce your inflammation.

Stay away from toxic environments, people, and relationships. Be mindful of what you're feeding your body and mind — a healthy diet will increase the levels of your creative energy.

Use the power of sound, music, dance, and movement to supercharge your creative energy.

Understand how brain waves affect the quality of thought and apply them to increase the power of your creative energy. Besides, practice meditation to help clear your mind, relax your body, and free your creative spirit.

"Alpha brainwaves are dominant during quietly flowing thoughts, and in some meditative states. Alpha is 'the power of now', being here, in the present. It is the resting state of the brain. These waves aid overall mental coordination, calmness,

alertness, mind/body integration and learning"

(brainworksneurotherapy.com)

Activate your senses with great anchors to support your creative energy such as Therapeutic Grade Essential Oils, art of Fung Shi, and colors that can charge your creative energy and stimulate your creative abilities.

Try different techniques and modalities such as the ones mentioned above to boost your creative energy.

"A lot of habitually creative people have preparation rituals

linked to the setting in which they choose to start their day. By

putting themselves into that environment, they start their

creative day." -Twyla Tharp

Set your day right by putting yourself in the right creative environment. A creative vision starts with the right creative attitude!

Chapter 9:
Spark Your Creativity

In This Chapter, You'll discover...

- Lessons from the lives of successful entrepreneurs, habits, and thinking styles that will inspire your creativity.

- Meet the Experts: Tim Ray, Dr. Lori Shemek, Chris Salem and Dr. Shahnaz Nensey

"Let your focus always be on the encouragement of innovation, experimentation, and creativity." -Germany Kent

"Experts were once amateurs who kept practicing." -Amit Kalantri, Wealth of Words

Meet the Experts:
Tim Ray | Dr. Lori Shemek | Dr. Shanaz Nensey | Chris Salem

Tim Ray

-Media Expert/Thought Leader and Founder-UI Media Network, Host of The Good Intentions Show, Awaken Atlanta & The Wake-Up Hour, Speaker, and known as "The Conscious Voice of the South."

Dr. Lori Shemek, Ph.D.

-3x Best Selling Author and a leading health and weight loss expert, known as "The Inflammation Terminator." A health contributor to Fox News; she is also a health expert for the ABC TV show and Good Morning Texas.

Dr. Shanaz Nensey

-Board Certified Doctor of Natural Medicine, Holistic Health Coach, Certified Natural Health Practitioner, Essential Oil Expert

Chris Salem

-Business leader Advisor– Keynote Speaker, Award-Winning Author, Life, and Business Strategist, Prosperity Coach, Wellness Advocate and Co-Founder of Empowered Fathers in Action (EFA). Change Agent/Expert

Being creative helps with your **self-awareness and self-confidence**. You get a better sense of who you are as a person and even think of ways to improve yourself.

Meditation and Creativity

Meditation and its influence on Creativity

By Tim Ray

Connecting to Source Energy

With the revival of conscious expansion, many people are aware of or have become aware of the power of meditation and its positive effects on the human body. I've been meditating for the better half of my adult life and meditation has been my connection to source and source energy. Meditation is an extremely effective way to ease an anxious mind or to help us relax, but it can also be used to tap into our superpowers — one of them is creativity. A novice meditation session may take your mind into the alpha state which is one level right below consciousness but with practice, one can go even deeper to the next level which is Theta and that is where the true genius starts to shine.

I was in such a busy industry, where shutting off my mind was difficult at best; I was craving stillness and ease and was able to achieve it via meditation. It took me a while to learn how to quiet my mind but when I did it, it was like I had discovered a spiritual drug, I wanted more and more. So many people are lost in the everyday shuffle and when we are this busy, we lose track of self and in creeps "stinking thinking". On average, we have over 90,000 thoughts a day and most of these thoughts are negative and repetitive.

My definition of living life intentionally is living in the present moment with your thoughts. Once you are conscious of what your thoughts are, you can be conscious of what you are creating.

Many people think of meditation as sitting in a dark room with your eyes closed and shutting off your mind. While this is one form of a surface level meditation, I like to go as deep as possible.

There are four main types of brainwaves that we associate with different states of consciousness — Beta, Alpha, Theta, and Gamma of these types of brainwaves oscillate at a different frequency and are associated with a particular state of consciousness.

Many years ago, I met a doctor by the name of Dr. Vern Morgan, he introduced me to his invention that would allow me to go even deeper into theta, delta, and deep delta. Dr. Vern's programs are amazing, they tackle the subconscious mind by taking you into theta or delta and implanting strategies directly into your subconscious mind. The program that I use mostly is the FastTrack Millionaire program which is designed to deliver over 70,000 success strategies into the subconscious mind every 30 minutes. I also use the FastTrack to sleep program which takes you into a deep delta state while sleeping which is where the body repairs itself and you awaken fully restored and recharged.

These programs changed my life and taught me that meditation comes in many forms.

When I founded the United Intentions Foundation, my goal was to help people understand themselves and see that we are all connected to Source, God, Universal energy, and that we are co-creators in this reality.

One of the many ways I connect to source energy as mentioned before is, via meditation, it is in the deep states of subconscious connection that we "plug-in" to source and are closer to God. It is in that closeness that our true self begins to shine through and for me, that is when my creativity comes out.

Creativity plays a significant role in my job as a media host. Media is all about capturing the viewer or listeners' attention by giving them valuable information which is what UI Media Network does — it allows them to speak their authentic truth and grow personally.

I founded the network after seeing that the world needs this type of information, an alternative form of media that gives people the tools and resources to make authentic choices from a place of love and compassion.

My dream is to take conscious media mainstream and help people connect to their higher power, not to toxicity, misconceptions, myths, and lies.

I urge you to find and join us!

Subconscious Mind Power Lessons

From Expert and Thought Leader Tim Ray:

Tim addressed how meditation is important for a better mindset. He gave insights that he discovered and applied when he used Dr. Vern Morgan's program that enabled him to go into a Theta state quickly and remain there longer. From there, Tim went into deep Delta state for better sleep and brain repair. Overall, his brain started functioning much better. He founded the United Intentions Foundation to help others discover the power of connecting to the "higher consciousness."

Inflammation and Creativity

Optimizing your health and Creative Mindset by lowering Inflammation

By, Dr. Lori Shemek

Optimizing health is key to a happier life and a more creative, abundant life. The good news is that we have within us, the power to create the life that we truly desire. However, many of us do not realize this fact.

From my own experience, my mother was a prime example of making unhealthy choices. Most of the memories I have of my dear mother are of her being ill with a constant stream of different health conditions. But my mother's 'choices' led her down an unhealthy path. She had a very inflammatory diet of which sugar and other refined foods were the main components. Due to this reason, she was verging on obesity. She smoked heavily, a robust 1.5 packs of cigarettes a day and she was under enormous stress. You can imagine the kind of stress one would be under trying to raise three young children all on her own. She had no support. An absent father complicated our lives, she had no family support and she had very little income. When you combine all of these factors, you can see what an inflammatory, poor quality of life she led.

I remember often, walking into her darkroom and seeing her lying there, in the dark, suffering and it broke my heart. However, I knew intuitively, even as a young girl, that she could make different choices. Unfortunately, she never did and she passed away at the young age of thirty-six leaving behind three young children with literally nowhere to go.

We all have choices to make every single day with our diet and our lifestyle to optimize our whole body and mind. Choosing a lifestyle that is protective and helps reverse inflammation such as an anti-inflammatory diet, which is an excellent place to start.

There are two types of inflammation — acute and silent. Chronic or silent inflammation that has a powerful effect on our ability to create in any area of life. When our health is not optimal such as with silent inflammation, it can wreak havoc in every area of our lives – including brain health.

Acute Inflammation is a necessary part of our immune system – it helps us heal. For example, let's say you cut your finger. When that happens, 'soldiers', if you will, rush to the site of the wound to repair the wound. The wound heals, the soldiers go away, the inflammation goes away and all is well. Without acute inflammation, we would not be alive.

Silent inflammation, on the other hand, never goes away. It is with us 24/7. It is like having a sore on the inside of your body that never heals – unless intervention occurs with diet and other lifestyle choices.

One of my clients, I'll call her Lana, suffered from low motivation. She was highly inflamed, overweight, and had Type 2 Diabetes. Lana was working as a high school drama teacher at the time. She hated her work and wanted to quit. Lana felt that she wasn't respected and found comfort in junk foods.

She came to me seeking help and after evaluating her, I was able to put her on my special protocol which helped her reduce her inflammation. This led to her losing 50 pounds and increasing her energy levels.

Lana found renewed motivation in her life. So much so that she started to write. She became a prolific writer and submitted her work to several publications that agreed to publish them. Later, Lana applied for several scholarships in Europe and was granted admission easily.

Lana is an example of how the right diet can reduce one's chronic inflammation and lead to unleashing a creative mindset. Each of us has a choice and if you want to know how you can reduce chronic inflammation, I've laid out a simple protocol.

Choose healthy, anti-inflammatory foods at every meal to optimize your health and creative expression. Without a healthy mind and body, our ability to create diminishes.

Examples, of foods that enhance and are protective of health, brain health, gut health, and more are:

- Leafy Greens such as Spinach or Arugula

- Berries such as Raspberries or Blueberries

- Teas such as Green Tea or Black Tea

- Spices such as Turmeric and Ginger

- Fatty Fish such as Salmon or Cod

- Healthy Fats such as Avocados or Olive Oil

- Cruciferous Vegetables such as Broccoli or Cauliflower

- Nuts such as Macadamia or Cashews

Additionally, address other lifestyle causes of chronic inflammation, such as lack of sleep, lack of exercise, lack of exposure to nature/clean air, processed foods, eating out, and stress. These choices will then become a fuel source for the energy of expansion, openness, receptivity, and ultimately, creativity.

INFLAMMATION AND ITS INFLUENCE ON CREATIVITY

The main lesson from "THE INFLAMMATION TERMINATOR" Dr. Lori is the importance of reducing your body's inflammation so you can have expanded energy, be more open to new experiences, be receptive to new ideas, and ultimately be able to optimize your creative mindset. It's important to realize how much nutrition and lifestyle play a big part regarding how much chronic inflammation affects us, including our mental state.

By shifting your diet and lifestyle, you'll be able to better digest your way to eliminating inflammation and raise your creativity.

Cooking and Creativity

Cooking and eating can be so much deeper than a chore and necessity.

By, Dr. Shahnaz Nensey

Cooking and eating can be so much deeper than a chore and necessity. All through my career as a health and wellness coach I have found that food is the biggest struggle people encounter. They feel the need to fit in a box, a box created by the latest fad, the newest discovery, or someone's dollar generating gimmick. But, because we are all vulnerable when it comes to our health and body, we feel the need to plug our belief system to the greatest new ad/fad out there, allowing ourselves to bypass our best gauge — our intuition.

I don't blame you.

It's all very convincing and very confusing. But what if we all learned to quiet our insecurities, be fully present to the experience that food actually is, and listen — our inner wisdom will tell us exactly with WHAT and HOW we should nourish our bodies. Think about all the times you had cravings. That was your body telling you what is missing.

So, in this chapter, I invite you to drop all your confusion around food just for a bit and get playful with me. We will see how much fun it can be to look at food from a different angle. Let's plug-in thinking styles and the play of food. There is an answer to every thinking style.

Welcome abstract thinkers! — You always see the bigger picture and can relate random things to each other. You don't like routine and get bored easily. TRUE? In that case, a recipe can be used as a guideline. Use your playfulness in adding ingredients or subtracting some. Every meal will be an adventure! The big picture – you need food to nourish your body. Giving a little attention to the table setting with flowers or perhaps candles make the meal even more pleasurable. No more boring meal times.

The analytics – sometimes overthinkers but great problem-solvers. You are the best at fixing what isn't at par in your recipe. Too salty? You add a raw potato to balance it out. Too spicy? You know that a little lime can drop the heat. You're an amazing fixer-upper!

For the creative's what can I say? The sky's the limit! You always come up with ingenious ways to solve the dilemma. Curry or sushi? You can find a way to incorporate both by making a new creation perhaps a "Sushi Curry" because you can flow and the artist in you is not afraid. You can blend cilantro from Mexico, cumin from India, and Tahini from the Middle East to create a whole new, fearless recipe. That's the way to do it!

Blending ingredients to create a new dance in your palate keeps eating interesting.

Concrete thinkers — You have the potential to be a better baker than a cook. Your ability to follow the recipe to the T is unsurpassable. If you're looking for a consistent taste experience, this is your chef. Always on point!

Critical thinkers – Your careful evaluation keeps chefs like me in line from being carried away. But you are an amazing cook when it comes to blending the right ingredients, spices, and seasonings for the desired result. You understand the value of combining ginger with garlic. As garlic is believed to be a natural blood thinner and ginger is applauded for its ability in enhancing circulation. You are always looking for synergy.

CRITICAL THINKERS — "FOOD ART" NEEDS YOU!

Convergent thinkers — Just as you can process combining multiple perspectives to find a single solution. In the kitchen, you apply that most amazingly. In Ayurveda, which is a 5,000-year-old philosophy, it is recommended to use all six flavors to create balance at each meal. The 6 flavors are sweet, sour, salty, bitter, astringent, and pungent. Who better to create a dish using this philosophy than convergent thinkers?

Divergent thinkers — You're not afraid of going far and wide in search of solutions. Your desire to explore allows you to incorporate cuisines of the world to find one that best suits your fueling needs. The quest for "food as an adventure" always prevails.

I hope you can see that there aren't excuses if you're ready to embark on this journey of healthy eating.

We all fit. There is always the perfect plug for every switch. Open your mind, make space in your palate for new flavors, experiences and take in the joy of eating with a conscious spirit. Let's change that "I can't" to "I could".

In my case, as a creative, I found the energetics of food as the most applicable thing for me. We all know that food is mostly described by how much protein, fat, or calories they contain. However, traditional Chinese medicine focuses on the distinct energy and characteristic properties of food. Just like Hippocrates said, "You are what you eat".

Depending on what my emotional and physical state needs that day, I can cater to my body in a very customized fashion. Here are some examples — if I am looking to feel a little more grounded and relaxed, I would incorporate root vegetables, fish, or beans.

If my creative spark needs to shine brighter and I am looking to feel lighter and more flexible, my food choice would be leafy greens, wheat, quinoa, fruits, and even chocolate. Raw foods are great for boosting energy and creativity, too.

Things that make us really tense and create anxiousness are sugar, caffeine, or alcohol.

And for the ultimate feeling of harmony and connectedness, I try picking fruits and vegetables that are grown in a garden or at a local farm. I use organic food as much as possible. Taking the time to indulge all my senses in the picking and preparing allows me to have that experience of total harmony.

I hope this gives you a glimpse of how food can be used to fit your particular style. Eating is a sacred experience and I wish for each of you reading this book, to find a loving connection with food. May every morsel you take in with intention and mindfulness fill your spirit and nourish your body.

Creative Cooking Lessons from Dr. Shanaz:

Wellness Coach Dr. Shanaz explained the importance of connecting to different food choices and experiencing a plethora of flavors with a creative mindset. When you dive into the art of cooking, you are opening up more of the divergent thinking needed for creativity. She explained that bringing in convergent thinking allows you to be more focused as the minute flavors are involved and more.

Furthermore, Dr. Shanaz mentioned the power of analytical thinking, whether concrete or critical, helps with understanding the process of cooking and from there, expanding to getting creative. That part builds the foundation before opening up to something more creative.

Risk Tolerance and Creativity

Why Taking Calculated Risks Can Make Your Life Extraordinary?

By Chris Salem

Calculated risks make the difference between an ordinary life and an extraordinary life. A calculated risk means that for every opportunity in life and business, we have gone from a risk unprepared to one that has some element of control with known intelligence. This does not mean that we know everything but what we do know and through our intuition in the present moment free from limiting beliefs.

Its self-limiting beliefs established from childhood that leads us to avoid or find reasons not to take calculated risks triggered by fear from a current situation where the opportunity exists. Fear resides in the past and the future when operating from a fixed mindset. This fear when offered an opportunity immediately aligns in the past to self-limiting beliefs and gets projected simultaneously in the future which leads us to struggle to make a calculated risk. We are not operating from clarity but fear that clouds our confidence and the ability to take action.

I know how I struggled in the first thirty years of my life in making decisions and taking risks. It was easier at the time to avoid decisions and take risks only later to regret and struggle with feeling stuck and not living up to my full potential. The reason was my self-limiting beliefs tied to issues with my father which later led to the constant need for validation in my life. Making a decision seemed impossible, always overanalyzing opportunities and allowing fear from lack of confidence to push them away. It was living in fear from the past and the future not being present that kept me stuck in my head for not trusting my intuition, capabilities, and core values — which I had not even realized at the time. Finally, one day after so many years, I decided to challenge the fear. It came to me that nothing would change until I changed.

I had to get creative and adopt a different way of thinking of learning versus knowing. This shift over time to optimize a creative mindset created new opportunities that I never saw with my old style of thinking. Life is always going to be a risk. You risk everything and still like to be as risk-averse as possible. Simply, it was the ability to face the fear and just do it when it felt unnatural at the time but knowing logically it would be right.

So, how can you grow your risk tolerance to change over time to achieve more? It comes from resolving the root cause of self-limiting beliefs from childhood and adopting a daily process to shift from a fixed to a growth mindset — freeing yourself from those self-limiting beliefs. A daily routine of meditation and journaling over time along with other key disciplines to truly forgive the source (in this case my father) and most importantly myself.

Once resolved, the pattern or routine continues daily for the rest of your life to develop your level of confidence and risk tolerance. You have to overcome these self-limiting beliefs to raise your level of confidence while learning to be present for clarity. It is through clarity rather than fear which leads to being more decisive and taking action with calculated risks. Making decisions in the present moment where the feeling of fear is reduced allows one to trust their intuition, core values, strengths, and intelligence they have to take a calculated risk.

A growth mindset knows that we must come out of our comfort zones to grow. Mistakes including failures are part of the process to grow into your success as part of taking risks. It is shifting your thinking from embracing the process of success and letting the results be a byproduct of it. Apart from that, it's having a daily plan for life and business strategy to follow so the process can flow no matter the circumstance or challenges that come your way. It is not coming from expectations that are tied to the outcome.

Expectations tied to outcomes often do not have a specific or structured plan and operate from a fixed versus growth mindset. Life is going to present many difficulties. This isn't something to fear but something to embrace —called the process.

Focus on what you can control and let go of the rest — do not tax your mind with it. Trust the process of doing your part and watch how taking calculated risks will get better along with your creative skills.

Mindset and Belief

Lessons from Prosperity Coach and Expert Chris Salem

Chris Salem shared his insights on how self-limiting beliefs can stop us from moving forward in life, as it did to him for the first thirty years. He learned that adopting a daily practice of meditation and journaling, helped him deal with the deep-seated issues he faced and led him to the path of confidence and risk tolerance. He was able to develop a creative mindset from his learning. Today, he uses and teaches the same methodology of shifting beliefs so that it can open up the mindset for growth.

In this chapter, you have met very diversified personalities and experts that shed light on topics that will help optimize your creative mindset. Maybe not everything resonates with you on a core level, however, if you can pick one or few habits you will improve your creative abilities.

"One learns from books and example only that certain things

can be done. Actual learning requires that you do those things."

--Frank Herbert

Once I learned about brain waves back in 2009, I was fascinated by the information I had received, especially when I found out how crucial they were to all aspects of brain functioning — thoughts, emotions, and behaviors. As I got more curious, I learned how accessing Alpha waves — for example, generates unusual associations —results in finding more novel ideas and less expected answers. I started getting myself more into an alpha state. Then I learned the power of Theta state and how in both Alpha and Theta states, we are more open to suggestions. This was very intriguing and interesting to me, I was excited and started experimenting with the different brain waves using different methods and the results were just exhilarating.

How cool is it that all of us can adopt and use brain waves to elicit a receptive state — this, in turn, can be very useful to examine and explore new and more favorable ways of working with bad habits/behavior or self-limiting and disempowering beliefs. Manipulating brainwaves for better mental health is something accessible to each one of us so why not employ them for the best of your highest good.

An example, by using a program, such as the FastTrack for sleep (like what expert Tim Ray shared above), one can access different brainwave states, oscillating at different frequencies (associated with a particular state of consciousness, like in sleeping as you access a deeper delta state), can change your level of conscious awareness. This is why it is a good idea for you to check out and try.

"My definition of living life intentionally is living in the present moment with your thoughts. Once you are conscious of what your thoughts are, you are able to be conscious of what you are creating." – TIM RAY

How about lowering inflammation and making better food choices and habits as health expert Dr. Lori Shemek shared? You cannot be your best creative self while you have high levels of inflammation coursing through your body. It's time to be, think, and feel well. People pay a lot of money for good advice. It's a blessing when experts share their advice because they want to pass it forward. Take the blessing and continue to move onward in life. According to Dr. Lori,

"One small change at a time will help you to get on that exciting road to optimal health all the while feeling younger, healthier, creative, and more vibrant."

OR JUST IMAGINE

Imagine, a group of 6 chefs gathered and each with a different thinking style, all trying to come up with an exclusive new menu for an upscale restaurant. It would be pretty cool to see the results of their menu creation, wouldn't it?

Now, on the other hand, how about if you created a new food recipe and after the idea is charged up in your mind, you explore by pretending to have a conversation with friends that have different personalities and thinking styles. For example — analytical, expressive, amiable, driver personalities; or convergent, divergent, obstructive thinking styles.

Imagine your friend, Vishal, who has a driver/analytical personality, is an analytical/convergent thinker, what could he be adding to this "your" recipe? What other spices or ingredients may he be thinking of?

Then imagine and start thinking about your friend, Tera, who has an amiable/expressive personality and is a divergent/creative thinker, what could she be combing, deducting and creating to "your" recipe?

Or what would your friend, Mo, who has an expressive/driver personality and is a blue-sky/abstract thinker be possibly selecting for the ingredients or how would he be designing his plates?

Or what would Chef Ramzy or Chef Shanaz be adding! Would it not make your cooking experience more fun?

"Your desire to explore allows you to incorporate cuisines of the world to find one that best suits your fueling needs. The quest for "food as an adventure" always prevails." - Dr. Shanaz Nencey

How about a breakthrough in shifting your beliefs, forgiving your past, and moving forward with confidence by adopting better habits, having clarity, and embracing the process of self-transcendence that a growth mindset offers, as Business, Life Strategist and Prosperity Coach Chris Salem shared.

And as Chris states, "Success is a process of being consistent to daily habits, discipline, and smaller attainable goals that serve you."

Because our habits dictate all the small details that make up our everyday lives, they also are directly related to the bigger issues in our lives, such as how much money we earn, the kind of person we marry or live with, lack of creativity, our physical condition and health, and every other area of our lives.

Our habits determine our character, the type of person we project to the rest of the world, and, ultimately, our destiny. So, if we embrace bad habits – those habits which have a negative impact on who we are – then those same habits will prevent us from achieving excellence in our lives, holding us back from reaching our full potential.

It's only by breaking bad habits and replacing them with good ones that we can ultimately succeed in life and be the people we were truly meant to be. The purpose of these insights and stories is to show you how to break bad habits – any sort of bad habit, from those that are damaging to your health, like smoking or not tapping into your best creative potential, to those that affect your self-esteem, such as negative thinking, self-doubt, fear-based decisions or overeating – and replace them with positive behaviors that can become part of your daily life and finally cause you to see the results you truly want.

Albert Einstein once said that the definition of insanity was performing the same task over and over again and expecting a different result. When you keep repeating the same bad habits, you would have to be insane to think that anything will ever change in your life. To start living your life to its fullest, you need to abandon bad habits and replace them with positive ones.

This book is all about expanding your consciousness, exploring and practicing different thinking styles, employing strategies, embracing processes and discovering new parts of yourself that are waiting to assist you in your co-creating process, breaking bad habits and replacing them with better ones. This will help you not only in developing your creative skills but your life skills in general as well.

"Never become so much of an expert that you stop gaining expertise. View life as a continuous learning experience." -

Denis Waitley

Chapter 10:
Creativity and the Concept of Yin and Yang

In this chapter, you'll discover...

- The power of the Yin and Yang

- Understanding the concept of different Boards.

- How to vibrationally align with your vision/action and dream boards

Yin and Yang Concept

"When people see things as beautiful,

ugliness is created.

When people see things as good,

evil is created.

Being and non-being produce each other.

Difficult and easy to complement each other.

Long and short define each other.

High and low oppose each other.

Fore and aft follow each other."

-Lao Tzu, Tao Te Ching

So, what do the Yin and Yang mean?

The following poem by Shih-tou will open up your understanding:

"Within light there is darkness,

but do not try to understand that darkness.

Within darkness there is light,

but do not look for that light.

Creativity and the Concept of Yin and Yang

Light and darkness are a pair,

like the foot before and the foot behind in walking.

Each thing has its own intrinsic value

and is related to everything else in function and position.

Ordinary life fits the absolute as a box and its lid.

The absolute works together with the relative,

like two arrows meeting in mid-air."

Yin-yang refers to a concept originating in ancient Chinese philosophy where opposite forces are seen as interconnected and counterbalancing. The principle of Yin and Yang is that all things exist as inseparable and contradictory opposites. There's light and dark, day and night, good and evil, yin and yang.

"True observers of nature, although they may think differently,

will still agree that everything that is, everything that is

observable as a phenomenon, can only exhibit itself in one of two

ways. It is either a primal polarity that is able to unify, or it is

a primal unity that is able to divide. The operation of nature

consists of splitting the united or uniting the divided; this is the

eternal movement of systole and diastole of the heartbeat, the

inhalation and exhalation of the world in which we live, act,

and exist."

—Johann Wolfgang von Goethe

Now that you are a little bit more familiar with what Yin and Yang mean, let's have a better understanding of "What does the Yin and Yang symbol represent?"

Delineating the Symbol

The universal yin-yang symbol holds its roots in Taoism/Daoism, an ancient Chinese spiritual philosophy centered on energy and the way of living. The circle that represents the whole is divided into Yin (black) the dark swirl associated with shadows, femininity, and Yang (white) the light swirl, represents brightness, growth, and passion. Both halves — the two polar are in harmonious balance.

The two smaller circles in the centers (the eyes), shaded in the opposite color, illustrate that within Yin, there is Yang, and within Yang, there is Yin. Yin and Yang contain within themselves, at their very centers, the concept of dualities and polarities, change, and transformation.

The curve dividing them — the S-Line is a manifestation of dynamic change — it is an important reminder because the universe is always in flux. That indicates the change is dynamic and continuous, the line between was not straight but in a shape of s-curve as it is longer than a straight line, which creates a more intimate relationship between Yin and Yang symbolically.

Each half is in the other half and establishes itself in the center of its opposite. It is commonly represented by the yin-yang symbol, a circle made up of black and white swirls, each containing a spot of the other. This means that there is always Yin in Yang, and Yang in Yin and that is the basis of transformation.

"How else could it have occurred to man to divide the cosmos,

on the analogy of day and night, summer and winter, into a

bright day-world and a dark night-world peopled with fabulous

monsters, unless he had the prototype of such a division in

himself, in the polarity between the conscious and the invisible

and unknowable unconscious?" -Carl Jung

In the creation of Yin and Yang, it also demonstrates the expansive and constrained creative techniques.

CREATIVITY REQUIRES BOTH EXPANSION AND CONTRACTION, CONCENTRATION, AND LETTING GO!

Expansive creativity techniques are intended to "open your mind" and encourage "free-thinking", such as idea generation, mastermind sessions, and imagination. For example, you can begin a creativity session by increasing your curiosity and expanding your awareness, releasing all of the preconceived ideas you have about a topic and start questioning all of your assumptions, In addition, you can tell yourself that you have to gather information and find at least 50 other possibilities and ways to solve a problem.

On the other hand, constraining creativity techniques force your mind to focus. Constraints can seem like the last thing you would want for a creative project, but they are actually beneficial when it comes to doing good work. For example:
SUMMING UP YOUR LIFE IN A SENTENCE: SIX-WORD MEMOIRS

Speaking of six-word writing restrictions, the book Not Quite What I Was Planning is a collection of memoirs written by famous and not-so-famous writers in exactly six words.

Here are some examples from the book:

BORN IN THE DESERT, STILL THIRSTY.

- GEORGENE NUNN

I ASKED. THEY ANSWERED. I WROTE.

- SEBASTIAN JUNGER

PAINFUL NERD KID, HAPPY NERD ADULT.

- LINDA WILLIAMSON

Summing up your life in just six words sounds hard, but then imagine writing a whole book about your life, then six words seem a lot easier to describe, does it not?

Constrained creativity can be a very helpful tool for many, from setting deadlines to having specific goals, delivery style to the target market — all of which work towards better creative discipline and outcome.

The Yin of constriction which is also aligned with the energy of divergent thinking uses more right brain-directed cognitive activities such as empathizing, ideating, and imagining. On the other hand, Yang of expansion which is aligned with the energy of convergent thinking, employs more left brain-directed cognitive processes like analysis, critical evaluation, and rational decision-making.

Expansion and divergent thinking, alternating with constraints and convergent thinking, all of which are very contradictory yet inseparable in creating harmony during the creative process.

While each part of the brain has its function, creativity involves the whole brain. Understanding how our brain works help us understand its functions better and allows us to employ them a lot wisely during our creative process. An article shared on the Healthline website explains the theory of the left and right side of our brain:

The theory is that people are either left-brained or right-brained, meaning that one side of their brain is dominant. If you are mostly analytical and methodical in your thinking, you are said to be left-brained. If you tend to be more creative or artistic, you are thought to be right-brained.

The two hemispheres are tied together by bundles of nerve fibers, creating an information highway. Although the two sides function differently, they work together and complement each other. You never use only one side of your brain at a time.

Still, it's a fact that the two sides of your brain are different, and certain areas of your brain do have specialties. The exact areas of some functions can vary a bit from person to person.

REGARDING THE YIN AND YANG CONCEPT, YIN DREAMS UP IDEAS, AND THEN YANG BUILDS A FRAME AROUND THEM.

By now, you understand the gist of the Yin and Yang concept and its relationship with creativity.

Yin and Yang's concept is a very supportive tool to apply for both business and personal life, especially when utilizing the Yin and Yang vision and dream boards — these have been created exclusively to aid and help you gain more clarity, have more structure, ideas, and order to Optimize your Creative Mindset.

Vision, Action, and a Dream Board

So, what are vision, action, and a dream board and how do they work? Since your mind responds strongly to visual stimulation, representing your goals with pictures and images, you will strengthen and stimulate your emotions, which are the vibrational energy that activates the Law of Attraction, Law of Vibration and the Law of Action!

A Vision Board

A vision board is a tool used to help clarify, maintain focus, and concentrate on specific intentions and goals. It is any sort of a board that displays focused intention images, personal or career goals, subliminal messages, affirmations, incantations, even statements and quotations that represent whatever you want to be, do, or have in your life. They are simply effective ways to invite more success into your life provided you are also prioritizing and putting in the effort and actionable steps towards what you would like to accomplish.

"I have been impressed with the urgency of doing. Knowing is

not enough; we must apply. Being willing is not enough; we

must do." — Leonardo da Vinci

The law of attraction alone without your vibrational alignment will not help you manifest your dreams. Positive thinking alone does not work — you must combine it with positive action.

Any of your board's creations will not work with outputting the effort required for you to succeed. This has been scientifically proven, so use all the tools to help yourself to succeed while you continue taking action towards your desired outcomes. For example, instead of just visualizing you succeeding, as a result, visualize yourself doing the necessary work that will ensure success.

Practice makes progress even in visualization; incorporate the practice of visualization in your work and daily effort, which will result in the success you wish to achieve. So, instead of visualizing a $50,000 in your account, you may want to visualize you negotiating a deal and closing on a contract that will earn you that same amount.

Many successful people swear by the enormous impact vision boards had on the lives — Oprah, Steve Harvey, Reese Witherspoon, Katy Perry, even Beyonce, to name a few. You may have to try it to experience firsthand. Additionally, if you tried it in the past and did not get the result you wanted, I encourage you to follow the recommendations and steps of how to set your Yin and Yang Board.

For the most part, a vision board works best with short-term and high-priority specific goals. The best duration to work with is about 6 to 12 months. Your vision board sets grounds for the success and realization of your dream board.

A Dream Board

A dream board consists of your biggest long-term, dream bucket list of goals — these could be personal and professional goals. It represents what you want your life to eventually look like. Usually, it is used for longterm goals that could range anywhere from 5 up to 10 years.

An Action Board

Action board is an evidence-based system founded on ground-breaking research studies in social psychology, positive psychology, mind-brain science, and goal achievement.

It is putting your vision board goals into actionable goals, by giving them an extra focus by setting time, date, and action needed to accomplish those goals, you are simply slicing them and providing the framework on how to achieve them.

"When a dream is given a date, it becomes a concrete goal." -

Alder Koten

The dream/vision/action boards are a collage of images, pictures, and affirmations that can be of different sizes, shapes, designs, and colors based on individuals' personal preferences of one's dreams and desires.

They are designed to serve as a source of inspiration and motivation, using both the law of attraction, vibration, and action to attain goals.

Most common is paperback, however, there are a few digital apps today that provide access to them as well.

Ingredients of an effective and empowering Vision/Action/Dream Board

Focused Intention

Vibrational, intentional, and conscious preparation...

Every action starts with a thought. The realm of ideas is on a different and higher plane than our living world. Our thoughts create our reality. Whatever we think, we experience or become! Intention counts for more than 90% of your success. The remaining 10% is the work it takes to bring your intended result into reality. Voicing intentions will take your mind off of your problems and perceived limitations. We all possess the power to manifest our intentions into the world of form, with the 'Power of Focused Intent'!

Consider how setting the right intentions can make you more productive and effective in addition to positively Influence and transform your intentions into a living reality. Setting and living your intentions allows you to focus on who you are and what you want at the moment as well as recognize, and live your values. It empowers and raises your emotional vibration.

Focused intentions give action better clarity, direction, more zing, flare, essence, and integrity. Intentions give actionable purpose as well as the inspiration and motivation to achieve your purpose. Having a sense of purpose will keep you focused, charged with determination, and filled with hope. Most importantly, it adds meaning to your life.

"Action is the what and intention is how that informs the what." - Jeffery Davis

- Focused intentions can magnetize support that is — both visible or invisible — to you, helping you achieve your goals.

- Focused intentions are fundamental ingredients when it comes to creating your Yin and Yang vision/dream board.

- Focused intentions are placed on the yin side of your board!

Visualization

Visualization is more than just seeing an image in your mind that excites or motivates you. It is activating your senses with the vibrational alignment of what you're visualizing, it's a combination of bringing up images, smells, sound, and colors that match those images for instance.

The power of visualization/imagination has long been known to Olympic athletes, have been using it for decades to improve performance. Psychology Today reported that brain patterns activated when a weightlifter lifted heavyweight which are also similarly activated when the lifter just imagined (visualized) lifting weights. The same goes for the champion boxer, Mike Lee, who has famously stated that before he steps into the ring for a fight, he has already fought that person 200 to 300 times and the outcome is always the same — his hand is raised. Mike states that when visualizing the boxing ring, he can smell things associated with it, like the leather gloves, sweat and if one assumes that smells are important, perhaps what the people at ringside are eating and drinking, are part of his visualization. He hears the crowds, the referee, his opponent, and other associated sounds. The belief he holds is that the brain can be tricked by doing this and that by repeating his visualization several times, his brain believes his victory has already taken place. Visualization is one of the most popular and effective mind workouts that you can do. Vision boards provide you with a daily visual reminder of your dreams and goals. The reason that vision boards work so well is that you visually see them every day.

Affirmations

Positive affirmations are simple sentences that people use to describe how they want to be, or how they want their circumstances to be, in a way that affirms that it's already true, or on its way to becoming true. Realize that every complaint is an affirmation of something you think you do not want in your life.

Affirmations can be positive or negative, choose wisely what you want to feed your thoughts and influence your mind. It eventually will manifest in your life.

"Every thought you think and every word you speak is an affirmation. All of our self-talk, our internal dialogue, is a stream of affirmations. You're using affirmations every moment whether you know it or not. You're affirming and creating your life experiences with every word and thought." - Louise Hay

Positive affirmations help overcome sabotaging, negative or disempowering thoughts, and increase one's sense of self-worth which in essence will improve one's overall well being. Writing positive affirmations that you truly believe and connect with, is a great way to use your imagination to help change your life. You need something concrete on which to focus your thoughts in order to re-educate your cognitive processes. This is where positive affirmations come in.

"Your brain will work tirelessly to achieve the statements you give your subconscious mind. And when those statements are the affirmations and images of your goals, you are destined to achieve them!" – Jack Canfield

Incantations

Incantations referred to here are defined as a written or recited formula of words designed to produce a particular effect. With incantations, you are changing your physiology and changing your state, leading to a different and more positive outlook and approach to each day. Incantations are meant to reverberate throughout the body and mind and alter one's sense of self.

One of the greatest scientific discoveries has been that you can alter your emotional mood by a radical shift in your physiology, and we can start to achieve that through incantations." -Tony

Robbins

Therefore, using both affirmations and incantations is one of the most powerful ways you can boost your confidence, connect to your goals, and change your life. You can think of affirmations as brain thoughts and incantations as the feelings of what you're thinking.

"Incantations are the manifestation and embodiment of

affirmations" -Dr. Bob Choat

Utilize Your Three Brains for Better Manifestation

Understanding the Three Brains that Control Our Intellect and Intuition on a deeper level will help us integrate all three brains to serve our desired outcome at best. The heart's electrical field is about 60 times greater in amplitude than the electrical activity generated by the brain.

So, we should access its vibration and energetic powerful field of influence. The human heart is the most powerful generator of electromagnetic energy in the body, and that should be a good reason why you would want to utilize its power. It will assist you in arriving at your distended distinction of manifested action plan and goals by connecting to your affirmations and intentions with your charged heart vibration.

WORKING WITH YOUR 3 BRAINS MAKES A LOT OF SENSE THEN!

Thinking of something with the brain without the same thought being felt in the heart and the intuition of the gut (2nd Brain) will throw off the vibrational alignment between the three brains. This alignment is very much needed in order to fulfil your goals, dreams and focused intentions.

The same principle applies when it comes to your heart's intelligence and its effect and influence on brain memory — an area you can dive deep into when it comes to the power of manifestation in your vision and dream board creation.

"The heart is a state of intelligent consciousness." – The Stanford and Oxford University

André Malraux said, "What the mind sees the heart feels."

Take some time to truly, visualize, feel, and align with your affirmations and learn how to apply incantations for optimal results using your Yin & Yang vision board.

Subliminal Messages

The term subliminal message was popularized in a 1957 book titled The Hidden Persuaders by Vance Packard. This book detailed a study of movie theaters that supposedly used subliminal commands to increase the sales of popcorn and Coca-Cola at their concession stands. However, the study was fabricated, as the author of the study, James Vicary later admitted.

A subliminal message is a signal or message designed to pass below (sub) the normal limits of perception. For example, it might be inaudible to the conscious mind (but audible to the unconscious or deeper mind) or might be an image transmitted briefly and unperceived consciously and yet perceived unconsciously.

There are two means of subliminal stimuli:

- Audio – low volume sound that we are unable to hear.

- Visual – quickly flashed messages or pictures that we are unable to see.

Even though we do not hear or see subliminal messages, our minds can still register it.

Subliminal messages have been used successfully in many self-help areas. In the early '90s, a groundbreaking book by Tony Robbins titled "Unlimited Power" was immensely popular. It was later turned into a cassette tape program. Included in the tape program, were two subliminal tapes with hidden personal power messages layered below the music. The idea of using subliminal messaging in self-development became wide-ranging and many sports champions used programs to boost their potential.

"Subliminal perception or cognition is a subset of unconscious cognition where the forms of unconscious cognition also include attending to one signal in a noisy environment while unconsciously keeping track of other signals, They work through a process in which external sensory stimuli work to trigger reactions without us noticing the signals (e.g. one voice out of many in a crowded room) and tasks done automatically (e.g. driving a car)." (Psychologist world.com)

So, as long as you do not have a subconscious resistance or self-limiting beliefs, the subliminal messages generally take 26 to 30 days to make permanent lasting changes to your subconscious. You can reprogram your subconscious mind with positive subliminal messages using your vision/dream board. This will help you stay on course and committed to achieving your goals. The subliminal messages will help you make better choices in your life and help you remove negative habits.

"The subliminal threshold between your conscious and unconscious mind, between what you are aware of and what you aren't, is different for different people. Pushing against the subliminal edge expands your awareness. Subsequently, you recognize more, have more choices and more opportunities to create the kind of reality that you really want." — Shunyata

SUBLIMINAL MESSAGES ARE POWERFUL AND THEY CAN EVEN ALTER YOUR DNA.

"DNA comes and goes every six weeks and subliminals can affect the DNA, because it is encoded in our cellular memory. There has been a new study that meditation and words can change DNA, and thousands claim on the internet that they morphed their physical traits by watching subliminals." – *James Ferguson Town*

It's a great opportunity to use subliminal messaging and encourage yourself to make better choices in life. Interestingly, subliminal messages can be a useful tool in your Yin and Yan Board as it raises the chance and rate of your success in achieving your goals.

Clear Goal Setting

Having a positive vision when it comes to achieving your goals is not optimistic but realistic. Being clear about your goals and writing them down has proven to be an essential part of success. So, it is integral to celebrate it once you achieve them. In fact, studies show that when you write down your goals, they are highly likely to come true. Your vision and dream board are the visualization of your goals.

Defining goals that you want to achieve is essential in ensuring that you are always growing and becoming the best version of yourself. Creating a vision and dream board helps you visualize your goals and reminds you of what you are working so hard toward when challenges come in the way.

It is important to have your personal or career/professional goals on your vision and dream boards to manifest your desired future. Having different boards that represent each one separately is strongly recommended. For example, your career/professional vision and dream board may be in your office or career section of your house as per the Feng Shui Bagua map (The Feng Shui Bagua map also called Pa Kua is a symbol of abundance. It serves as a powerful tool for manifesting your goals by influencing the natural energy flow, chi. It specifically shows which areas of your home or office to connect to the specific areas of your life that you want to change or improve).

Your goals, vision/dream boards should be in your room, or a place you can spot them easily as you spend time going over them as much as you need to stay inspired and motivated. However, no matter how many times you wish to use them, make sure that you look at it in the morning and before bedtime as a foundation and base.

Instant Relaxation

Instant relaxation is a trick that many high-performers use. They work extremely hard, using all the physical and mental abilities they have. When they recognize a certain level of overexerting and a drop in performance, they take a very short break. They have learned to take that short time and go into instant relaxation. It may be the ability to mentally transport themselves to a secluded beach or see themselves in a hot tub with every muscle at ease. They have a mental or physical trigger which they use to relax instantly. Once this short period is over, they can return completely refreshed and work at a high-performance rate.

One example of a person who was able to use this technique to the fullest was basketball legend Michael Jordan. The directors who filmed Michael Jordan's basketball games, frequently put the camera on him during any break time he had from the game — there was a very good reason for this. In comparison to other players that were either talking or drinking water, moving around on the bench, Jordan preferred to stay still. He would be on the bench, with a towel hanging around his neck, leaning forward slightly with a very neutral expression on his face. It is highly likely that the towel was in fact, a trigger. Once he sat down and placed his towel, he immediately went into a state of relaxation. It didn't matter what was going on the basketball court. Jordan remained super calm and relaxed, withdrawn from the world. When it was time to come off the bench, he would go back into the game as if he had just started to play.

Hypnosis and self-hypnosis are used by athletes and power performers in business to assist them in reaching their full potential. Although hypnosis has been around for a long time, it is still shrouded with doubt in regard to sports and business applications. This is due to the carnival atmosphere that is used in stage performances to make the audience laugh. Champion athletes have turned to NLP experts, skilled in both NLP and hypnosis, to get the best results for their clients. NLP is neuro-linguistic programming. It was developed by two men, who called it the language of the brain.

Imagine that you want to be the number one salesperson in your organization or win tennis championships consecutively. Using NLP and hypnosis, you model everything a champion salesman or tennis player does and thinks. You would discover your disempowering beliefs about your abilities and replace them with the beliefs you need. Then you would set anchors/triggers by doing something like pressing your thumb and index finger together while remembering a time when you were unstoppable. By repeating this over and over, you set the anchor, so that when you need total self-confidence, you fire the anchor off by pressing those fingers together. Your brain then ignites the self-confidence that you need. As mentioned, your vocabulary would be changed by practicing the words that empower you and eliminating the words that have a negative influence on you.

Many sports teams use NLP to improve their games and personal lives, too. The Los Angeles Kings brought in Tony Robbins back during the early nineties to work with their players. There is also a branch of hypnosis called "sports hypnosis," that was created to help players in all aspects of their performance. There are a wide number of players, former and current that use it. Wayne Gretzky was noted for it and his ability to visualize where the puck will be. He stated that he didn't follow the puck, he visualized where it would be and would go to that spot and wait for it, then take his shot. Today Sidney Crosby, Captain of the Pittsburgh Penguins uses sports hypnosis as do many NBA and UFC players/fighters.

Instant Relaxation is a practice that is great to adopt. In the next chapter, you will see the two best areas, to add this positive habit to your Yin and Yang Board.

Habits

Habits are formed by repetitive actions, thoughts, or feelings that are reinforced over time until they become subconscious, or automatic — they can make or break us. Any habit you have, good or bad, is built up from repeating the same process over and over. Habits can form physically in the brain. Much research has been done by neuroscientists, on how the brain forms habits. They discovered that all habits, good or bad are formed in a portion of our brain, called the basal ganglia.

The forming of a habit is a 3-part series of events. First, something occurs that causes your brain to go into automatic mode and then a behavior good or bad starts up. The second part is indulging in the actual behavior for some time. Last part is the reward aspect.

The brain finds something it likes and approves of, about the habit, even if it is a bad habit. Repeating the habit makes a physical connection in the brain between neurons and the habit continues without any conscious knowledge of it. That is why bad habits are so hard to break.

Champions take advantage of this by hardwiring good habits into their brains — this is done by repeating a positive action. That could be getting up at 5:00 a.m. no matter how they feel. Once the clock chimes, they are up and perhaps running for an hour on a cold, rainy day. Developing championship habits and combining visualization is very powerful.

Forming positive habits creates champions in all walks of life. You can be a champion earner, creating a lifestyle that makes a deep and loving connection with your family. An Olympic champion like Michael Phelps has created habits that have served him even in very unusual ways. Michael was involved in another one of his fantastic pool events. After entering the water at a high speed, he realized that his goggles were loose and water had seeped inside. This became problematic because he could not see in the pool properly. Michael Phelps used visualization and habits to become the most successful swimmer ever.

Many people would have lost total focus at that moment. Yet Michael remained calm and thought about how to continue and win. He instantly realized that his habit of counting strokes was now his key to success. After many years of counting exactly how many strokes from one end to the other end of an Olympic size swimming pool, all he needed to do was put his focus on his count. Although he could not see properly, Michael went into deep focus, counting his strokes and won his event with flying colors.

HABITS AND GETTING "INTO THE ZONE" GO HAND IN HAND.

Pro-performers understand building great habits. They also know that when a coach or fellow athlete gives them criticism, it means that they already have strengths and that they need to correct the flaws. By correctly the flaws and turning them into strengths, they can achieve powerful dreams. Some habits of professional athletes could be termed as anchors. You see a pro baseball player tapping their baseball ball over and over in a set way — which means they are "getting in the zone and powering up for action." The basketball players may dribble the ball in one type of movement only, to achieve the same feeling and visualize what they want to occur.

Musical performers, like Mick Jagger, continue to astound audiences with excessive energy and movements that most people in their seventies would not be able to perform. He has set routines of exercise for his body and his vocal cords. Before heading off to a concert, one thing Mick will do to not only stretch his vocal cords but also get in the zone is to perform sets of intense vocalizations. These vocalizations pump him up mentally to go out every night to put on an amazing show.

Habits can last a lifetime and make sure you are developing positive habits that are supportive of a healthier lifestyle. During your vision/action/dream Yin and Yan Journey, it is recommended to have a complete view and identify any negative or toxic habits that will hinder your success and distract your motivation.

Work on eliminating your bad habits, commit to your health, and have a fresh start. Replace your bad habits with healthier habits because they are definitely a much better ally to celebrate your success journey with.

In the next chapter, you will be able to design your Yin and Yang board and will be able to anchor your positive new habits into the action section of your board.

Now that you have a better understanding on how to align vibrationally with your vision/action/dream board, (for example; images, focused intention, affirmations, incantations, instant relaxation, mediation/NLP / hypnosis, goals, positive habits) make sure to utilize them during your co-creation process to help you reach your desired outcome.

Never delay doing your part and taking action, your success is waiting to celebrate you!

"The Universe likes speed. Don't delay, don't second guess &

don't doubt. When the opportunity is there, when the impulse is

there, when the intuitive nudge from within is there, act. That's

your job. And that's all you have to do." – Joe Vitale

Chapter 11:
The Yin And Yang Vision-Action-Dream Board

In this Chapter, You'll discover...

- How to design your Yin and Yang Board

- How to anchor your positive new habits into the action section of your board.

HOW DOES THE YIN AND YANG VISION BOARD WORK TO HELP OPTIMIZE YOUR CREATIVE MINDSET?

First, let me be clear while you are in your creative journey, developing creative skills will progress and your creative individuality will be strengthened leading you to be able to provide more creative contribution.

Realize as you continue to grow and create more ideas, you may see it fit to do some adjustments to the action steps towards your vision and dream board. Remaining open to new possibilities and flexibility is very important during the process. You are not changing the goal but maybe the direction for better results. If you planned to develop a subdivision on an acre of land and you know about the action steps that you need to undertake, but as you are getting ready and going through the process, you are informed that the land is susceptible to sinkholes. It will not be wise to proceed and spend your hard-earned money on that land but looking for a new location to invest and build on will be comparatively more favorable.

Changing direction and the ability to adjust and continue with the same enthusiasm and focus will lead you to continued success in your creative endeavors.

While being mindful about how staying focused, dedicated, and committed to your goals is important, it is just as important on the other hand to remain open and flexible if/when facing unexpected challenges along the way.

View your challenges as an opportunity to advance your creative skills and problem-solving further and not a reason to give up on your goals and dreams just because you simply feel exhausted.

"Winners never quit, and quitters never win." – Vince

Lombardi

The purpose of the Yin and Yang Board is to connect you inwards and outwards with your personal and individual desired goals and future vision of success and then bring them to life.

Having the necessary tools, the right mindset, and the best vibration alignment will help you accomplish your goals through a harmonious process.

The Mission of the Yin and Yang Board

The Yin and Yang Board is to help every individual gain more clarity about their prioritized goals, practice setting-focused intentions, and following simple action steps to help them achieve their desired outcomes.

This will result in celebrating more wins in their lives, as they will strengthen their relationship with their goals and expand their awareness allowing them to be more fully present in the moment.

As you continue developing your creative skills, expanding your imagination, and having clarity of what you would like to accomplish in your life, it will assist you in realizing your dreams and accomplishing your goals.

The Vision of the Yin and Yang Board

When the Yin and Yang Vision/Action Dream Board is placed at any professional or personal space, it will anchor, reactivate and charge one's subconscious mind with their original set intention, purpose, and mission.

It will provide them enough animation to keep moving forward towards their dreams, reminding them of their 'why' while fueling their 'how' with courage knowing that their goals/dreams are attainable and within reach!

"When you infuse your intentions with high-frequency emotions (like enthusiasm, joy, gratitude, determination, confidence, generosity and love), they will anchor more powerfully and are realized more effectively." – Dr. Sofie Nubani

The Concept of your Yin and Yang Vision Board

With all the concepts of polarity that Yin and Yang expresses, I chose to have the S-curved line as a third and vital component in the Yin and Yang vision/dream board project.

Following the Gurdjieff teachings — the key to freedom of positionality introduced by the triangle as the building block of the third dimension (think of this as a concept rather than a triangle. The line in the middle of your board represents the middle of the triangle).

The entire issue of duality pales when we become aware that this three-dimensional reality is built on triads, not pairs. So even with both the light and dark sections representing dualities, the S-Curve line is the third component that transitions from the beginning stage to the completion stage.

Here is the Law of Three formulated by Gurdjieff: "The higher blends with the lower to actualize the middle, which becomes lower for the next higher or higher for the previous lower."

This is the fundamental formula for all energy transformation in the three-dimensional universe.

It is also the basis for all spiritual transformation which seeks to develop the higher energies required for self-realization and resonant contact with the source of all energy.

Your Yin and Yan board will be divided into 3 sections.

Below are the description and role of all 3 sections of the YIN and YANG Vision /Action Dream Board.

- The first section — Yin Input

- The second section — S-Curve Action Steps

- The third section — Yang Input

Each has a different role and function. When applied and utilized, you will have the best outcome.

Yin section

Details, ingredients, and input go in the Yin (dark section): Ideas

Imagination

Generation

Intuition

Clarity

Desire

Intentions

Receptive

Flow

Vision

Purpose

Clear Goals settings

Affirmations

Evidence

Data

Tools

Coach / Mentor

Support Circle

Tactics

Preparation

Discovery

Plan

Yang section

Details, ingredients, and inputs in the Yang (white section): Images

Goals

Mission

Strategy

Visualization

Incantations

Quotations

Symbols

Subliminal Messages

Accountability

Products

Market

Aggressive

Growth

Action

Achieved outcome

S-curved line

Suggested ACTION steps for this section: Healthy diet

Exercise

7 1/2 hours sleep

Deep breaths

Stretching

Declutter Mind/Space

Personal commitment

Vibrational alignment

Meditation/Prayer

Motivation

More laughter

Self-Care ME TIME (salts baths, massages, breaks, energy healing, engage in hobbies)

Eliminate distractions

Set boundaries

Be Assertive. Say No when You have to!

Focus/Concentration

Confidence

Believe

Engage with all your sense

The Yin And Yang Vision-Action-Dream Board

Repeating affirmations & incantations

Learning

Reading

Journaling

Consulting coach/ mentor

Connecting with support circle

Stay open

Be flexible

Measurement

Feedback

Be fully present

Utilize sound

Therapeutic oils

Feng Shui

Positive habits

Consistency

Repetition

Good air circulation and quality (Air purifier/plants)

Relax

Stay positive

Celebrate little and big wins along the way!

"Don't let your dreams be dreams." - Jack Johnson

Be clear about your goals and then decide a way forward that you would like to that in conjunction with your vision/action/dream Yin and Yang Board.

Remember that what you focus on, is what expands!

Where should your focus be for you to achieve your goals?

- Love & Romance,

- Wealth & Prosperity,

- Career & Life Path,

- Health & Wellness,

- Mind & Soul

- Family & Community,

- Travel & Adventure,

- Creativity & hobbies,

- Reputation & Authority etc.

Do you want to make more than one Vision/Dream Yin and Yang Board to be more specific to each goal or do you want to combine your top few priority goals in one board?

When you are clear and aligned with your core self, purpose, and mission, your truth, your vision, your purpose, your authentic integrity... not others, only then your vision and dream board will work to its best potential.

If you are working with a team on a professional level, the team's purpose, mission, and vision must be aligned with your core self to achieve the best results.

You always have to be true to yourself and clear in your vision when starting any project. As a matter of fact, having a vision/action/dream board will help you feel more organized, clear, and engaged.

There are 6 phases of Vision/Action/Dream Board process:

The Yin And Yang Vision-Action-Dream Board

• Preparation Phase

• Action Phase

• Progress Phase

• Creation Phase

• Manifestation Phase

• Celebration Phase

Each phase plays an important role while going through the process, so be patient and allow everything to unfold in its divine timing. The more relaxed, you are the better you will attract the results that you desire.

Your energy will create your reality, what you focus on is what you will experience!

First and foremost, you must set an intention and you have to believe in your vision/action/dream board — as is the case, intention creates meaning.

Second, make sure that you put the start date, the universe likes speed and it also makes the process of manifestation more fun and focus-driven.

"I fear not the man who has practiced 10,000 kicks once, but I

fear the man who has practiced one kick 10,000 times." —

Bruce Lee

The more you practice the Yin and Yang Vision/Action/Dream Board principals and connect with your goals, the more you will maximize your visualization practice. You will start to get better at manifesting your dreams into a living reality.

Your subconscious mind will continue rehearsing all the commands, suggestions, and inputs that you deposit in it. When those statements are goals being registered in the form of images, repeated affirmations, incantations, and are charged with practices such as meditation, hypnosis, or instant relaxation — rest assured, you are destined to achieve them.

Now depending on the type of Yin and Yan Board that you are creating, (for personal or professional goals), the supplies and materials may vary.

Creating your Yin and Yang Vision/Action/Dream Board

Preparation phase

To start, think about what goals you want to reach in the next 6 months to a year or for seem boards think of the goals you want to achieve in possibly the next 5 to 10 years. These could be areas concerning your health, career, relationships, and finances.

"Where are the people who don't have goals headed? Those 97 percent end up working for the three percent." – Shiv Khera

Think big goals but make them specific. Write your goals down, get them out of your head, and put them on paper. Make sure they are SMART goals (Specific, Measurable, Achievable, Relevant, and Time-bound).

1-Gather Your SUPPLIES

Images, quotes, positive affirmations, symbols, holy phrases...etc... anything that motivates and inspires you.

Get something to attach images to, such as:

- Blank art book with mixed media paper, a poster board, corkboard, or small canvas.

- A stack of old magazines, books, images that inspire action towards your goals/dreams that can be cut up

- Scissors

- Markers, pens, or paint

- Glue, tape, thumbtacks, clips, or pins to put your board together

- Colorful or plain paper for adding personal flair

- A happy or inspiring photo of yourself

2-Create your Sacred Space

Now that you have your supplies, it is time for you to 'create a sacred space' and make your process and preparation for getting started enjoyable and meaningful.

You can choose to work on a large table or floor if you're working on a personal project or from home — either can work.

If you are working on a personal project, you may also want to light candles. In that case, look for a candle that will burn safely and does not affect the quality of your air.

Candles that are 100% made of soy, beeswax, or vegetable-wax based candles which do not blend with paraffin are your best options as they burn with less toxic effects.

Also, you can have a salt lamp — it will bring a nice, decorative touch and a warming glow to your space. It all depends on the type of project and mood you need to be in.

If not that, then maybe you can have a fabulous view and can enjoy the outdoors energy to prepare your board in, provided that the weather and environment are conducive for that.

3-Use Sound

Play some music — Anything that is inspiring to you can work, however, now that you have learned about the different brain waves and hertz, maybe you can start creating new habits that will support reaching desired states and help increase your focus levels as well as regulate your mood.

There are many for you to choose from. Here are some I recommend music to listen while preparing your Yin and Yang Board.

1-Serotonin releases music with Alpha waves stimulation to boost your creativity and resilience to stress.

2- Nikola Tesla 369 code healing music with 432 Hz tuning and sub-bass pulsation

3-432 Hz Cognition enhancer deep Alpha binaural-beats

4- Activate olfactory sensory (Smell)

You can diffuse therapeutic grade essential oils, any uplifting ones can work. Some of these are great — orange, lemon, or peppermint to keep you alert and support your creative mood.

5-WEAR COMFORTABLE CLOTHING

Be relaxed and feel comfy while preparing and working on your Yin and Yang board. Create a harmonious atmosphere so you can anchor your project with positive, energetic cord attachments to your experience.

6-FEEL GOOD

If you feel tired, have a headache, or just finished arguing with your partner, then wait until you feel better, calm, and collected before you start.

There are no rules on how to create your board, but there is one important reminder and that is to focus on your feelings.

You want to feel relaxed, positive, and excited as you connect to your Yin and Yang vision/dream boards energy.

"I am an extension of Source Energy, who has practiced my

vibrational frequency into such alignment with my true nature

that anything less than that feels off to me. And because I care

about the way I feel, I guide myself easily now toward the things that feel good. And therefore, I am always on my path." -

Wayne W. Dyer,

7- Set a TIME BLOCK

Time blocking is a time management technique/method that schedules your day into the set, controlled units.

Having time blocks will help you become more organized, focused, less distracted, and uninterrupted. You will have more control over your time and liable to manage it a lot better.

Set a time you want to block for working on your board. You will need anywhere from one hour to three hours depending on the tools you have and the speed you work at.

In addition, set the time you want to visit your vision/action/dream board daily to connect with your goals.

8-Feel CONNECTED

Connect with your thoughts, feelings, goals as you apply your materials.

The more emotion you put in what you want to create, the faster you will create, and the more you will celebrate.

Visualize yourself working on your goals, putting the effort, and believe your efforts have manifested your goals already.

Trust with no doubt or with any resistance.

Keep your vision board VISIBLE to you and make sure you connect with it at least twice a day, preferably first thing in the morning and just before you go to bed.

Create an environment that will allow you to manifest your desires by feeling vibrationally aligned with what you want to create.

Action phase

In the action phase of your S curve section, you want to put everything that will inspire your action towards goals.

You can set an action plan weekly or monthly. You can ask yourself; What can I do this week that will help me reach a specific goal or a group of my goals?"

After you have completed this section of your Yin and Yang Board, then you need to activate those goals by;

- With intention, view your board at least two times a day.

- Apply everything in the S curve section that supports your daily habits. For example: Instant relaxation is a practice that you should adopt in different stages of your Yin and Yang Vision and Dream Board process and progress especially in these two phases:

1- At the S-Line Curve, the action and charging section in between both your Yin and Yang inputs.

2- After achieving your goals — After accomplishing the goals on your board, you can apply any of the positive practices you adopted (instant relaxation, walking meditation, mini getaways, NLP, hypnosis, massages, etc.) during your goal setting, action, and manifestation process and adopt this positive new habit in other areas of your life.

3-At this stage, you are putting the effort via practicing through visualization as well in real life. Buy practicing visually that you are putting the effort daily, it becomes easier to put in the effort and accomplish your goal in reality. You will improve and progress, and start to enjoy your process more.

An action board is (an important section in creating your Yin and Yang board). Not just that, it is an evidence-based system founded on ground-breaking research studies in social psychology, positive psychology, mind-brain science, and goal achievement.

What Actions Can You Take to Work Toward your Yin and Yang Board Goals?

Progress phase

At this stage, I like to recommend a very supportive tool, and that is having a manifestation journal.

KEEP A YIN and YANG MANIFESTATION JOURNAL

1-Document your goals

2-Write the date on which you have set the intentions of your goals.

3-For every goal and set intentions you accomplish, go back and highlight it in your journal. This time on the bottom of your highlighted goal, write the date you accomplished/manifested it.

This is such a cool tool that will keep you charged and motivated, especially as you start mastering the process.

As you practice using a Yin and Yang Board and writing in your manifestation journal, having a lot of highlighted pages will be a normal experience for you.

Second, if your Yin and Yang Board is for professional use, then I would recommend that you connect with your team for support and accountability during your process progress.

Lastly, trust the process and enjoy the journey.

"PRACTICE makes PROGRESS, be PATIENT, and

embrace the process." –Dr. Sofie Nubani

Creation Phase

In this stage, you have got what you need to complete your project through the steps and action plan from prior focused intentions and goal setting that you applied on your Yin and Yang Board.

For example, one of your goals could have been:

- Create a course within 6 months

- Buy a house in one year

- Travel to Norway this summer

You have put your daily effort and visual and vibrational connection with the goals on your board.

In the first goal with the example of creating a course within six months, at this stage, you have finished your content creation, curriculum, and all the files and materials — now you are ready to launch your newly completed course.

For the next example of buying a new house in one year, in this phase, you have the cash to pay it in full or the deposit needed for your down payment within the year or possibly before — you know what area you want to live in, and working with a realtor or straight with the developer. You have good credit and are ready to decide what house you favor most that meet your standards for you to move in.

In the third example of traveling to Norway during the summer, in this creation phase, you have the funds to buy your ticket/tickets. You know what you want to do and places you would like to visit. You have your trip itinerary ready and feel confident about your trip and plan. Summer is a few weeks away and your excitement is off the charts.

You may be experiencing high feelings of synchronicity, serendipity, and expansive joy, things just feel extraordinary, real, alive, and thrilling.

You have participated and dedicated your time and effort in the process of co-creating to accomplish your goals. You feel fulfilled, satisfied, and content.

During this phase, life simply feels magical, (the anticipation of your success launching that new course, or living in that new beautiful home, or how amazing your experience visiting Norway will be and all the great memories you will be creating) delightful, and exciting.

At this stage, you are one step away from fully realizing your dreams and manifesting your goal/goals. Anything could happen just at the last minute and interrupt the flow and completion of your result.

To ensure better flow and completed tasks and goals you must be very open, relaxed, and continue to be in a blissful state of mind.

"If you will take the time to line up your energy, to attune your vibration with the vibration of your desire — nothing can keep it from coming to you." -Abraham Hicks

Manifestation phase

This is the last phase of your vision/action/dream board.

At this point, you will feel empowered, confident, and more secure. Remember to have an attitude of gratitude. It will attract more of such blissful experiences into your life. In addition, always nourish creativity that will lead to innovation by having the right creative attitude and mindset in all phases of your Yin and Yang Board creation.

This phase is also a good base to set new goals and continue to create. You will be experiencing peak experiences and feel elevated with a high sense of self with a deep sense of gratitude.

"Attitude is the little thing that can make a huge impact in every single area in your life. When your attitude is right, you will thrive and flourish. The universe feels your attitude and you will manifest whatever your attitude reflects. So, let your attitude be electric!" - Law of Attraction

The Vision-Action-Dream Board Process

When looking at a vision board and a dream board, one is more medium-term while the other is long-term. Medium-term meaning, 6 months to one year, and long-term is beyond one year.

Regarding the vision board, look at that as medium-term. Your focus should be on creating your project with goals that you can envision (using your "vision board") for what you want to create within 6 months to one year. Let's break it down further and add the "S" curve from Yin and Yang.

Following the steps on creation above, make sure to first imagine what you really want to achieve or to happen within that year. This is important. You will need it to make it emotional. The more your body can feel it, the more likely you're going to make it happen. Think back on something you really wanted and imagined that you had it along with the added emotions, you found a way of making it happen, right?

That is why a vision board cannot be just putting images up and believe it's going to happen. You have to feel it, too. Earlier, I talked about incantations back in Chapter 10. Use that so that what you have on your board becomes part of your physical feelings. "Think it, See it, Smell it, Feel it."

By the way, this same process is what you are going to use when creating your dream board, too.

One of the foundations that you should understand is your current reality. When creating your vision and dream boards, understanding where you are currently at is also important. You have to be honest with the resources you currently have and what you will need to make your visions and dreams become a reality in the future.

If you put on your vision board that you wish to be a billionaire in one and you have never started anything to build wealth, then that reality is not something that can happen based on your current reality. It's not impossible (as there is always a possibility that you may inherit it or win the lottery), just highly improbable that you can become a billionaire.

Now, if you want to reach a high 6-figure income and your current income is low — 6-figures or even high 5-figures — then that is something based in reality towards the first year.

Now, you can look at the dream board going out over a longer period as a system to realize bigger dreams. I would suggest that you start with the vision board and then add a series of vision boards that will help you build your dream board.

Think of these vision boards as milestones for the dream board. Each vision board, from one year to the next, leads towards the dream board. It does not matter if a vision board is 6-months or one year. It's about the steps for now.

The Yin And Yang Vision-Action-Dream Board

Each day, you are going to take from what you had in the "S" curve of Yin and Yang to help make what you wish to happen. Without action, nothing is created. In the business world, there are strategies and tactics. Strategies look at the long-term and factors in tactics which are the action steps to make the strategy happen.

Use the journal to help you keep track of your action steps and milestones. This will let you know if you are on track and the adjustments you have to make. Make sure to have the things from the Yin and Yang sides, as well as the "S" curve action steps, too.

Keep moving forward and soon you will realize the fruition of your vision and dreams.

Vision/Action/Dream boards are used by many of the most powerful people. Even though they may be extremely busy, have multiple meetings to attend, and hundreds of things on their to-do list, these go-getters still find time to make a vision/action or dream boards.

Meet some Successful Vision/Action or Dream Board manifesters:

John Assaraf

John Assaraf is a successful entrepreneur and brain researcher. He established a multi-million-dollar empire in the fields of Internet software, real estate, life, and business coaching, and brain research. Assaraf was featured in the movie 'The Secret' where he credited a lot of his success to making vision boards. The most interesting story was that John had been making vision boards for years and made one with his dream home on it. Five years later, he realized that he had moved into the exact home on his vision board without even knowing.

Ellen DeGeneres

There's an episode of the Ellen show where she shows the audience her vision board about her dreams of being on the cover of Oprah's magazine. For nearly every issue Oprah had been the cover girl, and then Ellen got her dream.

Katy Perry

In an interview with MTV in 2009, Katy Perry describes making a vision board when she was only nine years old.

She explains that "Her teacher asked the class to make a "vision board" — a collage of images cut out from magazines that represents the dreams and aspirations you hope to manifest in life. The year was 1993 and Selena had just won a Grammy Award, so the nine-year-old Katy chose a photo of the young Latin pop singer holding her golden statuette."

Fifteen years later, Perry was nominated for her first Grammy Award.

Celebration phase

You are on track, with steady progress as you take daily action towards your vision, make sure you celebrate every win, big or small along the way. Celebrating is appreciating the blessings big or small and it's a habit that reminds you to stay in a state of gratitude. Besides, you are sending a message to the universe that you are worthy of receiving. A state of joy and gratitude boosts your frequency and supercharges your vibrational alignment to realizing your goals. Celebrating also anchors your emotions to positive memories relating to the feeling of accomplishment. Such positive anchors will motivate and energize you to keep moving forward.

Keep in mind that there are no rules on how to work out your vision board, the main goal is to get started to be clearer and more connected to your goals, creating a healthy environment, positive habits, and strong commands to your subconscious mind during the process.

According to Forbes Magazine:

1. Almost two-thirds of small business owners believe that visualizing goals helps them map and develop their business plans.

2. One in five small business owners used a vision board or other visual representation when starting

their business — 76% of those business owners said that today, their business is where they envisioned it would be when they started it.

3. Eighty-two percent of small business owners that used a vision board from the get-go reported that they have accomplished more than half the goals they included on that board.

Whether you are using a vision/action/ dream board for business or personal growth, using them will increase the success rate of achieving each goal. So, give your goals and dreams the unity and individuality of The Yin and Yang Vision/Action/Dream Board experience. Life is full of beautiful places and things to explore and experience in addition to enjoy and discover. Stay committed to your dreams and goals manifesting each of them with one vision/action/dream board at a time.

Happy manifestations!

You are now powerfully on your path and you will just be beginning the best part of your life's journey.

I would love to hear your feedback on your **YIN** and **YANG VISION/DREAM BOARD** Experience. **ENJOY!** Keep in mind while you are on this beautiful journey that,

"What you get by achieving your goals is not as important as

what you become by achieving your goals." - Zig Ziglar

#BePresentNCreate

Chapter 12:
The Circle of Creative Masters (COCM)

In This Chapter, you'll discover...

- What is the circle of creative masters

- How do you create a circle of creative masters

My Inspiration for the COCM

I was inspired by the concept of Masterminds, which was initially coined by Dr. Napoleon Hill. In his book Think and Grow Rich, Dr. Hill described the Master-Mind principle as:

"The coordination of knowledge and effort of two or more people, who work toward a definite purpose, in the spirit of harmony." He continues. "No two minds ever come together without thereby creating a third, invisible intangible force, which may be likened to a third mind [the master mind]."

I always admired the Master Mind concept and truly believed in its possible effectiveness, benefits, and positive impact, especially when the vision and mission are clear and united in purpose to its members.

While optimizing my creative mindset, I further thought "what if I can create a similar concept", however, in this case, the main focus would be on CREATIVITY. I invite like-minded creatrix and creatives to increase their creative levels and unleash the power of their metacognition. Originally, I thought of different names and the one that resonated most was inspired by a vision that I had of creating a unique physical or virtual space and a specific time where (and when) the creatrix and creatives can identify with, grow from, and collaborate on novel/innovative ideas.

Then I thought WHO could this circle benefit most then I asked WHY and HOW. Upon contemplation, what I envisioned had the answer to all my 3 questions:

Who is the COCM for

A circle that consists of seriously interested and committed creative individuals, from an intersection of fields, disciplines, or cultures, that have a collective like-minded intelligence. They are curious people committed to growth — in their creative skills and levels —, have good core and moral values and are interested in innovation. They are not afraid to make a mistake. These are transparent individuals who hold a positive creative attitude. They evaluate and make decisions using a holistic approach of giving effective support to guide and lead each other by their good example.

Why Create the COCM

We, as a global community, witness how change could be so sudden in today's highly competitive business environment, life challenges, and personal struggles. As a result, this realization could affect how we work, where we work, and who we work with.

The Circle of Creative Masters offers space for leaders, entrepreneurs, executives, mentors, luminaries and genuine influencers to share their experiences, challenges, and creative solutions. Working together as they face challenges, by uniting their collective creative intelligence towards projects, tasks they are assigned/committed to or challenges they are facing.

COCM offers creative, manageable, and flexible solutions that will lead its members to new paths and mindsets that will support their transitions and growth to maintain a competitive advantage over other businesses, organizations, companies, governments, and communities.

How to Create the COCM

The Circle of Creative Masters achieves its WHY by creating a culture of inclusion, respect, trust and understanding between all members from the top down. COCM establishes a sense of psychological safety, effective trust and the ability to express and communicate directly with ease, and more openness.

Having clear principles, processes, and agreements will increase the chance of a Circle of Creative Masters being successful.

A COCM members should have a clear understanding and acceptance of their:

1. Creative vision and mission individually and collectively.

2. Location and beginning date/time and completion deadline.

3. Rules and Agreements.

374

4. How to start and run a Circle of Creative Masters

Foundation:

1.   Create an intention then have a clear purpose, mission/vision and a goal.

2.   Set a start date and time.

3.   Commit to a regular, recurring frequency.

4.   Have a Clear Agenda for each meeting.

5.   Decide on the technology and structure in advance.

6.   Create an attendance Policy.

7.   Invite a culture that fosters multiculturalism, diversity and growth.

8.   Have Clear, Respectful, Open communication, shared values and dedicated missions.

9.   Member accountability/support

10.   Magical Seat (similar to hot/help seat)

Location

1-On/Off-Line depending on Convenience and accessibility.

2-Indoors or outdoors

3-On Land or Cruise

Number of Participants

A COCM is best conducted with the participation of nine members. It could be twice or thrice of it, but not restricted to just that.

Creative Masters Ratio and distribution are as follows:

Facilitator:

Is Certified as a Creative/Creative Master-C.CM

Male or/and Female

4 x Males

4 x Females

For example, in addition to one facilitator/host, it could total anywhere from 9, 18, or 27, etc. or one more if there are two CCM.

The group reaches maximum capacity at 38, including facilitators.

2 Certified Creative/Creative Master-C.CM is a mandatory number when facilitating a group of over 16 participants.

Diversified Culture and Religion

A COCM welcomes all walks of life for its optimal success.

"People with different tribes, races, religions, and nationalities

can come together and accomplish something extraordinary. The

key is the culture of unity and teamwork." ~Farshad Asl

The COCM consists of various religious/spiritual backgrounds and nationalities. There is no discrimination or racism. ALL Creative humans Masters are welcome without any discrimination, and that also includes service animals.

Examples of what a COCM consists of:

- Religious/Spiritual backgrounds

- Judaism

- Christianity

- Islam

- Sufism

- Buddhism

- Hinduism

- Confucianism

- Taoism

- Atheism

All & any Nationalities/Ethnic groups and backgrounds like:

- Middle Eastern

- American

- European

- Australian

- Canadian

- Brazilian

- Russian

- African

- Jewish

- Indian

- Asian

A minimum of three different religious backgrounds and at least three different nationalities are required to qualify a proper and adequate COCM arrangement and set up.

The principle of such a setup is to be connected with Creative Masters from different ethnic, religious groups, and nationalities from all around the globe. It will be conducted with love and acceptance and will draw from each other's creative strengths and innovative talents.

Cultural diversity (diversity includes age, ethnicity and culture, gender, race, religion, class, sexual orientation, and capabilities) can also serve as a boost to creativity as well as innovation. Diversity and cross-cultural intelligence/multiculturalism are becoming more significant, relevant, and crucial than any other time in history.

They are promising elements for civilization, society, and people, which makes them very favorable and positive. We need to reinforce such integrations and cultivate them in our lives. That is necessary if we want to rise and thrive in our creativity/innovation skills.

Clear and effective leadership of a COCM requires intentional facilitation of ethical values, holistic thinking with new box thinking. It also requires expanded awareness when it comes to maximizing the creative potential of its members.

Encouraging diversified insights, philosophies, beliefs, and viewpoints, allows a COCM collaboration to tap into a cross-culture collective intelligence and wisdom. That will help tap each individual into their innate creative ability and collectively also tap into their peers/partners. This will be done by providing help and support to one another through inputs/outputs of shared ideas, challenges, and solutions.

Openness to new ideas, insights, experiences, and perspectives can help increase integrative complexity. It is the capacity to recognize new patterns, improve metacognition, and sharpen our association cortex. That can be accomplished by finding links among seemingly unrelated pieces of information.

Today, we live in a highly competitive business and personal environment. Therefore, it's more important than ever before to invest in yourself and the workforce.

Facilitate diversity to increase your COCM's global social/cultural awareness, affective trust, and the ability to combine existing concepts into a large number of extraordinary new ideas, creative problem-solving skills, as well as innovation abilities.

Start with a diverse team

This can be done by building a team of contributors from different backgrounds, experience levels, and expertise. Avoid falling to cognitive traps of the Einstellung Effect. The Einstellung effect is the negative effect of previous experience when solving new problems. That in itself will lead to innovative solutions by diminishing cognitive bias.

A 2011 study conducted by Daniel Frings of London South Bank University set out to research on how fatigue (more on that in #2, below) impacts the Einstellung Effect. The study concluded that while people who are fatigued experienced an increased Einstellung Effect, those working in groups did not, and the quality of the solutions developed by the groups was often better than those developed by individuals.

Having a team of Creative Masters invites new box thinking and better relationship understanding. At the same time, that connects the dots of new possible solutions. These solutions assist other members to feel safer and not fall into the Einstellung Effect.

Diverse team members can challenge one another's ideas and assumptions, fostering growth, expansion, and development to their creative skills. It doesn't take one person to come up with new ideas; it takes a small group of people that can work together effectively.

The Qualifications of a Circle of Creative Masters Facilitation

1-Facilitator of the group is Certified Creative/Creatrix Master "C.CM" by The Circle of Creative Masters Institute (CCOMI).

2-Members will be qualified through a survey they fill and complete to COCM standards and qualifications. It is to ensure quality, high standards, and provide value to all members during the collaboration process.

3-The ratio of male and female participants has to be balanced apart from the Certified Creative Master (C.CM) if only one person is hosting meetings. If two Creative/Creatrix Masters C.CM's are facilitating meetings, then it would be a Male/Female.

4-Minimum attendees should be five, including the facilitator. Max of 30

Groups over 20 require two magical Creative Masters C.CM to host the meetings.

5-Meetings are conducted as often as once a week and at a minimum just once a month.

A COCM group encourages peer-to-peer accountability & mentoring. That will help everyone to stay focused, learn, share, and grow while they take consistent action steps towards their creative goals.

COCM Goals setting

The COCM divides its goals into three;

1-Outcome Goals

2-Process Goals

3-Performance Goals

Each of the three types of goals sets paste to words COCM's particular mission and vision, at the same time remaining flexible and adaptable to the possible change in direction, and goals are measured to ensure progress, effectiveness, and productivity.

It is about staying focused without attachment to outcome is key for the best flow while working on your creative projects. Realize the goals you have the most influence and leverage over are your PROCESS goals, whilst the goals you have the least control over are your OUTCOME goals.

You set your long-term, medium- and short-term goals clearly after purpose/mission and vision. Then the COCM is established. Next, the interaction, exploration, and feedback of the team start maneuvering towards achieving those goals.

Six Essential ingredients for a COCM's success

Six main ingredients/values that are important to have when organizing a COCM that will invite creativity leading to innovation:

Authentic Integrity – It is about being honest, genuine, and adhering to ethical values and principles that you won't compromise even when no one is watching. Authentic Integrity is having good intentions that match your actions and living by them. Practicing authentic Integrity will foster effective trust and confidence between all groups/teams of the COCM. As the southern Bell mom from your mama's kitchen by Johnny Tan shares,

"Your authentic charm may open door. However, it is your Authentic Integrity that keeps the door open."

Curiosity-The key to creativity and innovation, having an interest in something with intellectual curiosity, can lead the COCM group/team to discover better ways to go about solving problems. Curious Creative Masters are often attracted to novelty. They ask lots of questions and consciously like to learn. They are interested in new ways of doing things, unusual approaches, or things that are outside of their area of expertise.

A Creative Master consciously does not know the answer and always is seeking to find new ones instead. He/ she is always consciously learning.

Courage – For best creativity leading to innovation, COCM members/team must feel safe, have no fear in speaking their thoughts and expressing their ideas.

Courage is the key to great leadership and in areas of achieving creative goals. Nothing will manifest to innovation without having creative Courage, bravery, and gallantry. Courage is an important character in a leader, and this case here is precisely a Creative Leader/Master. It is about getting out of the comfort zone and collectively stepping into the **CREATIVE ZONE**.

"Courage is an inner resolution to go forward despite obstacles;

Cowardice is submissive surrender to circumstances.

The Circle of Creative Masters (COCM)

Courage breeds creativity; Cowardice represses fear and is mastered by it.

Cowardice asks the question, is it safe?

Expediency asks the question, is it politic?

Vanity asks the question, is it popular?"

-Dr. Martin Luther King Junior

Tenacity- It is the key to creativity, it is an important skill to develop and have when it comes to creativity, and that will lead to innovation. Having tenacity in a COCM/organization/business means you are persistent, determined, and you don't give up as you continue to find solutions for unsolved problems to reach your resurrection goals.

I like a speech that Thomas Leighton, a Princeton alumnus and founder of the web infrastructure company Akamai that delivered the event's keynote address, shared at the Keller Center's 10th Anniversary Symposium. That is celebrating the center's decade-long mission of fostering innovation in education and entrepreneurship regarding tenacity:

"You can start a successful company, but you are expected to work really hard, the key to a successful business is not just working with great people to come up with a great product; it is to be "tenacious as hell. You have to operate with a sense of urgency. Once you have an idea, you have to do something about it fast because if you don't, someone else will."

Besides, in my opinion, it is good to practice, intellectual tenacity in particular. A person with intellectual tenacity in a COCM group/meeting or an organization engages in facing challenges seeks to confront them and not avoid them. They do it first by looking at the bigger picture when working towards reaching a goal. Secondly, they do it by finding the best solution that is serving for the betterment of all.

"Fostering growth in intellectual tenacity requires fostering intellectual humility as well."-Dr. John Kelly

Humility – By definition, it means: freedom from pride or arrogance, that is, the quality or state of being humble.

A creative leader/Master must be able to take responsibility, admit to his/her mistakes. They are open to accepting the fact they may not be right as well as willing to learn from their mistakes and others. They internationally continually seek to add value to others.

Stay connected to your creative goals

Take your creative thinking and abilities to higher levels, and connect with CREATIVE MASTERS that will introduce you to new worlds you have not visited before. Illuminate your creativity skills with positive feedback and construction from your peers. These are who are seeking in you to do the same.

Let the joy and production of the C.CM of your COCM group facilitate the right creative environment for you and others. This is so your creative talent can continuc to flourish and prosper.

Contact the *Circle of Creative Masters Institute*, if you are interested in hosting a COCM meeting. Do it as well as if you are interested in getting Certified as a Creatrix/Creative Master (C.CM) and facilitate your meetings and organized groups. You will find in more detail at the Institute about the program.

"Make a conscious effort to surround yourself with positive, nourishing, and uplifting people — people who believe in you, encourage you to go after your dreams, and applaud your victories. Surround yourself with possibility thinkers and idealists." ~Jack Canfield

I wish you blessings of fulfilled creative dreams and innovations. Best wishes to you in your creative growth and journey.

The Circle of Creative Masters (COCM)

Stay connected and reach out to me if you need any assistance. Till next time with love and gratitude,

#BePresentNCreate

Bonus Chapter: Top Creativity Techniques to Optimize Your Creative Mindset

- Creativity can be something you lost, but it does not have to stay lost forever. You can certainly learn to be creative again, as well as improve upon the creative spark that you already have. The only requirement is you taking massive action and fine-tuning of your Power of Creativity.

- Engage in creative projects, read books on creativity, travel more, paint, dance, sing, and move. Energize your body, learn to shift your thoughts, and clear your mind so you can better create.

Creativity Techniques

Creativity techniques refer to certain methods that encourage the development of a creative mind, which would help you in many areas, such as the arts, your business, and your personal life.

They focus on a variety of different aspects of creativity, including techniques for generating ideas, thinking different, problem-solving, mindset, methods of reframing problems, and more.

Here are a few of the most popular Creativity techniques.

Assess to determine which is best suited for you or your business.

You should make some notes of this section if you haven't already been doing that.

Rearrange the order of techniques according to the ones you are choosing to work with. Have the one's best suited for you at the top of the list.

Give each technique your full attention and focus and apply the ones that feel exciting, productive, and inviting to your soul. Maximize the power of your creative skills.

1- Mind Mapping

This technique is creative in its very nature. Mind mapping could be done with pencil and paper or by using mind mapping applications. In mind mapping, you can use words, images, and colors, which will spark your creativity. By placing the idea, by mind mapping at the center, you can then add branches of subjects and its sub-subjects. Another benefit of mind mapping for creativity is how you will learn to retain your ideas. The words and images would be at your fingertips for easy reference, and due to the combination, it will stay at the forefront of your thoughts.

A mind map helps you create more ideas of creativity than sitting down and making a written list. A branch on a mind map could have a sub-branch added, with a new idea of exploring. People who use mind maps for everything from business to creativity find that it in time allows them to delve deeper into their minds for ideas that may be hidden deep in the subconscious.

For creative writers, a block often comes up in between. They stare at a blank page and cannot get started. Writers who use mind maps find that it overcomes was called "writers' block" as they start at the center with just one central idea and work outwards, word by word. It's best to use an image for the center of the mind map because images spark a paragraph of words in your mind, rather than one single word. The mind map allows writers to see what they want to say and then further expand upon it. As they build a branch, they make sure it is curved and not straight.

The reasoning behind this is to keep your brain engaged and wanting to give your ideas. Straight lines put your brain into neutral while curving lines are like gear shifting to your brain.

Start exploring mind maps for creativity today as I assure you of generating some great ideas.

2-The SCAMPER Technique

The SCAMPER technique stands for Substitute-Combine-Adapt-Modify-Put to Another Use-Eliminate-Reverse. The theory behind this technique is that there is nothing new, but we modify the old to create something new and useful. The concept came from a business person wanting to spark creativity in brainstorming sessions with a group.

When using SCAMPER for creativity, you don't have to follow it in a straight line, you can go from S to A if that's what works. Let's break down each letter, as they are individual techniques.

S - Stands for substitute. So you ask a variety of creative questions about what would work better and how you could change mix it up. Depending on the project, you may be re-assigning someone to take over a certain task that they are more suited for or removing a part of your project and after brainstorming, putting in something that works better.

C - Stands for combine, where you look at taking two ideas and putting them together to create a whole different product. The idea of putting a calculator on a watch is how combining works. In creativity, nothing is unreasonable when looking for ideas. For example, putting a flotation device that can be activated on a wheelchair, so that people can enjoy the water just like anyone else, may seem outlandish, but it works.

A - Stands for adapt, and in this, you are looking at methods to improve the process or tweak the product to make it more appealing and to a wider range of people.

M - Stands for modify or even magnify. In this case, you are seeking creative ways to make the project larger, to produce more sales, or to modify it to improve the process of creating it.

P - Stands for put to another use. Here you are brainstorming different ideas, such as taking an existing product that is used in the accounting department and looking to see if there's a way to use it in the receiving department. Another creative idea is looking at the volume of recycling that you produce and find ways to use that material. In an individual idea, for example, there's a person who creates boats out of used flip flops that wash up on the island he lives on. This is creativity at its finest.

E - Stands for eliminate. When you're working on a project, having too many pieces can stifle up the creative process. Look for areas to trim, which will, in turn, lead towards creative growth.

R - Stands for reverse and working backward through in a project to come up with creative solutions. If you're looking at it from a writing point, many people come up with the ending first and then work backward to manage and create the plot.

This idea of SCAMPER is considered to be one of the easier and direct ways to be creative in any type of project. Explore it and play with it, to see some great results.

3-Thinking in New Boxes

This creative process can be compared to the "what if."

When Bic pens decide what to buy, they created a new box.

Instead of selling their yellow plastic pens with the blue tops, they decided to create light and easy disposable lighters along with some razors.

This simple creative shift brought in several hundred million dollars in profits!

Their idea had the theme of light products that were easy to use and carry around.

When thinking in new boxes for creative ideas, you brainstorm different product ideas, and nothing is impossible. You will then eliminate what would not work and build up what will. Another theme in this would be to doubt everything to really challenge how you perceive things.

Do not believe the world is black and white, see it as many colors, with some blended together.

4-Reframing the question

This is something we should do in all areas of our lives. Too often, we ask ourselves, "how bad could this get?" Instead, we need to ask, "What can we learn, and how will this help us to grow?"

Reframing questions sparks creative answers and ideas that would propel you forward with joy. Reframing can prompt you to come up with some creative new ideas.

Ask questions like, "how could we?" Or what actions could we take now to make us best in our industry?"

5-Storyboarding

While storyboarding is fantastic for any person's creative endeavor, in this section, we shall talk about it as it applies to groups. Storyboarding is part of brainstorming creative ideas.

To use storyboarding, you need basic drawing skills to get the point across, while sparking the creative juice in a given team. The figures in some storyboards may be simple stick figures or simple rounded figures with round heads and basic features for nose and eyes.

A sample storyboard might have 8-10 rectangular boxes, and each box has a theme in the upper left-hand corner of it. The first three boxes might be "what we will accomplish-who does the training-what software is required?"

Each box will contain figures which represent the people on the team, along with sub-topics relating to the main theme. Storyboarding can be used for deciding a new marketing strategy to gain new customers or new product creations for starters.

The user's experience and how to improve it is something that successful companies work on a daily basis. In using storyboards, a group can use a customer experience from start to finish.

The storyboard reflects what a customer goes through when making a purchase from start to finish. It highlights the good as well as the bad of the buying experience and lays it out on a storyboard, groups can discover where the customer is not being served 100% and take steps to fix that.

6-Brain Shifter

This concept is sure to make you feel alive and wonderful while doing it. It is a sort of mind mapping where you don't use your frame of mind but someone else's.

Doing this as an individual who needs to mind map for creativity, you would pick a role to play. You may pretend you are Robert De Niro, a favorite cartoon character or a superhero like Wonder Woman or perhaps an action character like Thor. Start by taking the time to get into that character's brain.

Think about how Thor would think or Lion King would. Once you have transformed yourself, start by drawing out the character that you are playing. If it is Thor, you need a thick stick figure with long hair and a big hammer.

Then starting writing down all the ideas that came into Thor's brain. Get as much down as you can, and it will help if you have large drawing paper. Once you finish your session, be yourself and edit the mind map, keeping the ideas that inspire you.

For groups, you work in the same way but to make it more fun, have someone decide for everyone else, what role they are to play. This makes people more creative because they are not coming at this with preconceived ideas.

Use as many colors as you are able to. Once ideas get put up on the drawing board, individuals should feel free to add a piece to someone else's idea for maximum creativity.

It's recommended to have a break and a fun exercise like jumping jacks to keep everyone pumped up. Do not forget to hydrate the group with enough water or better, maybe some lemon water.

The recommended time frame for this fun exercise is about one hour.

Conclusion: A New Beginning

By now, you are aware that you are able to soar your creativity by learning new ideas and apply them to your personal and business life. Like any new skill, you need to train your brain to practice, patience, present, and persistence.

There will be challenges in life to whatever you may attempt to apply. Your job is to get excited and curious as you think of ways how you're going to face those challenges. That will be with the right creative attitude, mind/skill/Soul set, thinking styles, and effective tools, habits that will help you overcome those challenges.

Connect to your creative mindset and people, hobbies, and groups that will inspire your creativity.

Don't let ANYONE dull your CREATIVE SPARKLE, including you.

Create Your Destiny by the thoughts you choose and the actions you take

Creating your destiny may be hard, but not if you truly want to live life on your own terms. When you have the motivation and the drive deep within you, anything is possible.

If you really put your mind and heart into it, no one could stop you. Your destiny is yours and yours alone. It is ready for you to take it. You just need to figure out how to. So, here are 4 secret ways you can use to create your own destiny!

1. Figure out who you really want to be

You cannot create your own destiny if you don't know where you want to go. The first thing you ought to do is to figure out who you really want to be in life. You are free to be anything you want; however, you've got to choose something realistic and sensible. Otherwise, you're setting yourself up for big-time failure!

2. Change your attitude

You do not have to be on the receiving end of things all the time. Creating your destiny entails taking over the reins. This means being in charge of your life.

Tell the world you are going down the road less traveled if need be. But you are not going to be wasting your time waiting for the rest of the world to join you. You will simply take matters into your own hands and live life the way you want to live it!

3. It's all in the details

If you want your vision for yourself to come to reality, then you need to plan out how you are going to get from where you are now to what you want to be in the future.

You cannot just say, "Oh, I'm sure all the pieces will fall into place someday." Remember, you have to change your attitude and take life by the horns instead of letting it take you where you don't actually want to go!

4. Don't be afraid to take chances

Take every opportunity to learn whether it is from your failures or successes. Applied knowledge can't ever be underestimated. It is what will help you grow as a person. It is what's going to arm you in the future and make you future-proof, so to speak. When the opportunity to get you closer to your destiny presents itself, don't be afraid to dive headfirst!

Final Words...

Right now, you hold in your hand a roadmap to a new and creative journey. It is up to you in the direction you want to go. As a creative soul, you're taking each step with a focus on bringing out your best work. I do applaud you for coming this far and look forward to where it is you are going. You should, too.

In my case, this book is the foundation of the series... It's been a wonderful journey so far in my creative venture. I wanted you to take from this book and make what you learn your own. That's being a wise and creative being that makes a difference in your work, life and in the world. Now, I invite you to go forward and upward into the next phase...

"The way must be in you; the destination also must be in you and not somewhere else in space or time. If that kind of self-transformation is being realized in you, you will arrive." ~Nhat Hanh

References

6 Ways to Instantly Stimulate Your Vagus Nerve to Relieve Inflammation, Depression, Migraines and more. https://www.iahe.com/docs/articles/6_Ways_to_Instantly_Stimulate_Your_Vagus_Nerve_to_Relieve_Inflammation.pdf

Albert Einstein, Sailor. Sea History for Kids. https://seahistory.org/sea-history-for-kids/albert-einstein-sailor/

Ali Khaled.Led Zeppelin, Bob Dylan And U2, How Umm Kulthum's Influence Transcended The Middle East. GQ Magazine. November 14, 2018. https://www.gqmiddleeast.com/a-voice-that-could-shatter-glass

Andy Ash, **The Rise and Fall of Blockbuster.** *Business Insider*, (January 16, 2020). https://www.businessinsider.com/the-rise-and-fall-of-blockbuster-video-streaming-2020-1?amp

Angela S. McLean. Cultivating Marital Intimacy: Types of Intimacy. https://resilientfamilies.com/tag/types-of-intimacy/

Anna Powers (August 30, 2018). Creativity Is The Skill Of The Future. *Forbes.com*. https://www.forbes.com/sites/annapowers/2018/04/30/creativity-is-the-skill-of-the-future/#4acd917f4fd4

Baryniene, J. and Dauknyte, B. (2015). Creativity as the Main Factor for Organizations' Success: Theoretical Approach. *European Integration Studies*. No. 9, (pages 235-243). http://dx.doi.org/10.5755/j01.eis.0.9.12810

Basal Ganglia, Wikipedia, https://en.m.wikipedia.org/wiki/Basal_ganglia

Bazaar Magazine (July 1, 2019), 30 Things You Never Knew About Princess Diana. https://www.harpersbazaar.com/celebrity/latest/gmp22549179/princess-diana-life-facts/

Bethany Brookshire. Explainer: What is the Vagus? Science News for Students. June 7, 2018. https://www.sciencenewsforstudents.org/article/explainer-what-vagus/amp

Bob Burg and John Mann (2008), The Go-Giver, Portfolio

Bri Stauffer. What Are the 4 C's of 21st Century Skills? *Applied Educational Systems.* May 7, 2020. https://www.aeseducation.com/blog/four-cs-21st-century-skills

Catherine Shen. Creativity, tenacity, critical thinking urged at Keller Center symposium. Princeton. October 15, 2015. https://engineering.princeton.edu/news/2015/10/15/creativity-tenacity-critical-thinking-urged-keller-center-symposium

Cavdarbasha D and Kurczek J (2017) Connecting the Dots: Your Brain and Creativity. Front. Young Minds. 5:19. doi: 10.3389/frym.2017.00019

Charyton, C., Jagacinski, R. J., & Merrill, J. A. (2008). CEDA: A research instrument for creative engineering design assessment. *Psychology of Aesthetics, Creativity, and the Arts, 2*(3), 147–154. https://doi.org/10.1037/1931-3896.2.3.147

Cotterill RM. Cooperation of the basal ganglia, cerebellum, sensory cerebrum and hippocampus: possible implications for cognition, consciousness, intelligence and creativity. *Prog Neurobiol.* 2001; 64(1):1-33. Doi: 10.1016/s0301-0082(00)00058-7

Creative Play. https://creativeplayuk.com

Dana Mitroff Silvers. Minimizing the Einstellung Effect in Design Thinking: How to Arrive at Innovative Solutions by Diminishing Cognitive Bias. Medium.com. August 1, 2018. https://medium.com/@dmitroff/minimizing-the-einstellung-effect-in-design-thinking-how-to-arrive-at-innovative-solutions-by-21f6311ec850

Daskal, Lolly, 7 Mindsets That Will Radically Improve Your Life Right Now, Blog Post, https://www.lollydaskal.com/leadership/7-mindsets-that-will-radically-improve-your-life-right-now/

David. Innovation Space 4P's. *Innovation Management – Group 4.* October 2016. https://pla55106group4.wordpress.com/im-innovation-space-4ps/innovation-space-4ps/

Difference Between Inquisitive and Curious. http://www.differencebetween.info/Difference-between-inquisitive-and-curious

References and Biographies of Contributors

Dobos, Julius (July 11, 2017). The Importance of Collaboration and Teamwork in the Creative Industry. Retrieved from https://cogswell.edu/blog/importance-collaboration-teamwork-creative-industry/

Elback, K. and Hargadon, A.B. (2006). Enhancing Creativity Through "Mindless" Work: A Framework of Workday Design. *Organization Science.* 17(4):470-483. Retrieved from https://www.researchgate.net/publication/247824420_Enhancing_Creativity_Through_Mindless_Work_A_Framework_of_Workday_Design

Explaining the Four Ps Model. *National Chiao Tung University.* https://www.futurelearn.com/courses/creative-problem-solving/0/steps/43750

Francis, Erik M. (June 4, 2016), The Return of Synthesis: Connecting Critical and Creative Thinking, LinkedIn Pulse, https://www.linkedin.com/pulse/return-synthesis-connecting-critical-creative-thinking-francis/

Gastroparesis. Mayo Clinic. https://www.mayoclinic.org/diseases-conditions/gastroparesis/symptoms-causes/syc-20355787

George Land and Beth Jarman, Breaking Point and Beyond. San Francisco: HarperBusiness, 1993

Glăveanu, Vlad Petre (2011). *How are we creative together? Comparing sociocognitive and sociocultural answers.* Theory and Psychology, 21 (4). pp. 473-492. ISSN 0959-3543. https://core.ac.uk/download/pdf/221026.pdf

Hill, Napoleon. Think and Grow Rich. Ralston Society: Meriden, Conn. 1937

HOW CAN WE SOLVE AMERICA'S "CREATIVITY CRISIS?" *The Genius of Play.* https://www.prnewswire.com/news-releases/how-can-we-solve-americas-creativity-crisis-300685600.html

Intellectual Tenacity. Intellectual Virtues Academy. April 4, 2013. http://www.ivalongbeach.org/community/blog/posts-on-master-virtues/105-intellectual-tenacity

James J. Kerley (1994). Creative Inventive Design and Research. NASA Goddard Space Flight Center, Greenbelt, Maryland. https://ntrs.nasa.gov/archive/nasa/casi.ntrs.nasa.gov/19940029213.pdf

Jayme Cormie. Your Creative Brain. https://www.alchemyassistant.com/topics/TppT7eNEZ2pYPWqF.html

Katie Kindelan, Prince Harry and Meghan no longer 'working members' of royal family: All your burning questions answered. Good Morning America. January 18, 2020. https://www.goodmorningamerica.com/amp/culture/story/prince-harry-meghan-step-back-royal-duties-burning-68153907

Kenneth Acha. Three Types of Goals. KennethMD. (nd) https://www.kennethmd.com/three-types-of-goals/

Kylah Goodfellow Klinge. Mapping Creativity in the Brain. The Atlantic. March 21, 2016. https://amp.theatlantic.com/amp/article/474621/

Kyung Hee Kim (2011): The Creativity Crisis: The Decrease in Creative Thinking Scores on the Torrance Tests of Creative Thinking, *Creativity Research Journal*, 23:4, 285-295 http://dx.doi.org/10.1080/10400419.2011.627805

MacKay, Donald G, and Rutherford Goldstein. "Creativity, Comprehension, Conversation and the Hippocampal Region: New Data and Theory." *AIMS neuroscience* vol. 3, 1 (2016): 105-140. doi:10.3934/Neuroscience.2016.1.105

Mat Helme. The Four P's to Problem Solving. *Medium.com*. December 5, 2014. https://medium.com/@MatHelme/the-four-ps-of-problem-solving-6e15a39a0712

Meredith Patterson, Following My Bliss – All About Anandamide. GBSciences (October 10, 2019). https://gbsciences.com/2019/10/16/following-my-bliss-all-about-anandamide-and-how-to-make-it-yourself/

Michael Michalko. Thomas Edison's Creative Thinking Habits. Think Jar Collective. 2014. https://thinkjarcollective.com/tools/thomas-edisons-creative-thinking-habits/

References and Biographies of Contributors

Mind-Sets site, https://mind-sets.com/

Morgan Shortle. Your Brain on Cognitive Creativity – With
Illustrations. Grio. September, 2016. https://blog.grio.com/2016/09/your-brain-on-cognitive-creativity-with-illustrations.html

Mumford, M.D. (2000). Managing Creative People: Strategies and Tactics
for Innovation. Human Resource Management Review. Vol. 10, Issue 3 (pages
313-351). https://doi.org/10.1016/S1053-4822 (99)00043-1

Nick Skillicorn (August 5, 2016). Evidence that children become less
creative over time (and how to fix
it) https://www.ideatovalue.com/crea/nickskillicorn/2016/08/evidence-children-become-less-creative-time-fix/

Puya Yazdi. 19 Factors That May Stimulate Your Vagus Nerve Naturally.
Selfhacked.com. January 6, 2020. https://selfhacked.com/blog/32-ways-to-stimulate-your-vagus-nerve-and-all-you-need-to-know-about-it/

Rebecca Hoyle. Interdisciplinary Creativity. *Durham University.*
2014. https://www.dur.ac.uk/ias/2014conference/callforpanels/interdisciplinarycr/

Reio T.G. (2012) Curiosity and Exploration. In: Seel N.M. (eds)
Encyclopedia of the Sciences of Learning. Springer, Boston, MA

Richard Florida (October 2004), America's Looming Creativity Crisis.
Harvard Business Review, https://hbr.org/2004/10/americas-looming-creativity-crisis

Rick Ackerly Blog (October 10, 2012). If You Come out of School Thinking
You Are Not Creative, School Failed. http://rickackerly.com/2012/10/10/creativity/

Saul McLeod. Social Identity Theory. SimplyPsychology.
2019. https://www.simplypsychology.org/social-identity-theory.html

Schank, Roger (1988). *The Creative Attitude.* Macmillan Publishing
Company

SparcIt. 4Ps of Creativity: What Are They?. Medium.com. August 19,
2016. https://medium.com/sparcit-blog/4ps-of-creativity-what-are-they-8e639423f5a1

Spontaneous
Creative. http://scienceandentertainmentexchange.org/blog/creative-science/

Steven Kotler, Flow States and Creativity. Psychology Today. February 25, 2014. https://www.psychologytoday.com/us/blog/the-playing-field/201402/flow-states-and-creativity

Tan, C-S, Lau, X-S, Kung, Y-T and Kailsan, R A/L (2016). Openness to Experience Enhances Creativity: The Mediating Role of Intrinsic Motivation and the Creative Process Engagement. Journal of Creative Behavior. Volume 51, Issue 1 (Pages 109-119). https://doi.org/10.1002/jocb.170

Tanner Christensen, Where Exactly Does Creativity Exist Within the Brain? September 20, 2016. https://creativesomething.net/post/150681325800/where-exactly-does-creativity-exist-within-the

Types of Creativity: Descriptions and Examples. https://study.com/academy/lesson/types-of-creativity-descriptions-examples.html

Valorie Delp. Charity Work of Princess Diana. LoveToKnow. https://charity.lovetoknow.com/Charity_Work_of_Princess_Diana

Walden University, Institutional Accreditation, https://www.waldenu.edu/about/who-we-are/accreditation

Wallis' Model of the Creative Process. http://members.optusnet.com.au/charles57/Creative/Brain/wallis.htm

Wesley Carpenter (November 27th 2019). The Aha! Moment: The Science Behind Creative Insights, Toward Super-Creativity - Improving Creativity in Humans, Machines, and Human - Machine Collaborations, Sílvio Manuel Brito, *IntechOpen*, DOI: 10.5772/intechopen.84973. Available from: https://www.intechopen.com/books/toward-super-creativity-improving-creativity-in-humans-machines-and-human-machine-collaborations/the-aha-moment-the-science-behind-creative-insights

Western, Dan. 15 Different Types of Mindsets People Have. Wealthy Gorilla. https://wealthygorilla.com/15-different-types-mindsets-people/

What Happens in the Vagus. Does Not Remain in
the Vagus. https://chicagolandnucca.com/what-happens-in-the-vagus-does-not-
remain-in-the-vagus/

Yasmine El Dorghamy. The 25 Most Influential Women in Egyptian
History. RAWI, Egypt's Heritage Review. Issue 3. https://rawi-
magazine.com/articles/25women/

Zabelina, D. L. (2018). *Attention and creativity*. In R. E. Jung &
O. Vartanian (Eds.), *The Cambridge handbook of the neuroscience of creativity* (p.
161–179). Cambridge University Press. https://doi.org/10.1017/9781316556238.010

Biographies of Contributors

Bill Protzmann

Bill Protzmann is an award-winning advocate and teacher of music as self-care. He lives in San Diego California with his wife and three step-daughters and is very involved as a volunteer teacher of self-care tools with homeless and at-risk populations, including military Veterans.

http://www.billprotzmann.com/

Bob Burg

"The King Of Referrals" Bob Burg, author and coauthor of a number of books including the 'Go-Giver" series which has sold well over a million copies.

He speaks for corporations and associations internationally, including Fortune 500 companies, franchises, and numerous direct sales organizations.

Bob has shared the platform with top thought leaders, broadcast personalities, Olympic athletes and political leaders including former United States President.

Learn more about him: http://www.burg.com

Bob Choat

Dr. Bob Choat is known as "The Transformational Grandmaster" and has a multifaceted background. This includes in psychology, hypnosis, martial arts, fitness, Marine Veteran, Los Angeles Police Officer, entrepreneur and more. He is a published author and has appeared on radio, TV and numerous podcasts. You can find out more about him at bobchoat.com

Chitra Lele

Is a young software engineer, solution architect, record-setting author, peace poet and research scholar. Apart from progressing in the Software field, Chitra wants to contribute to the greater good of the world through education, culture and peace. Her publications include scholarly articles, research papers, poetry anthologies, and academic and reference books. Her professional, academic and creative blog: http://chitrathesavvysynergist.blogspot.com/p/about-me_20.html

Chris Salem

Christopher Salem is an Executive Coach for entrepreneurs, business leaders, sales professionals, and companies to build and protect their brands by raising their level of influence as trusted advisors to maximize their results. His book Master Your Inner Critic / Resolve the Root Cause – Create Prosperity addresses this and went international best seller in 2016. His weekly radio show Sustainable Success is part of the Voice America Influencers Channel.

https://christophersalem.com/

Davey Williams

Davey Williams is a Speaker & Coach, who specializes in Lifestyle Empowerment, as well as Golf Psychology. He's the creator of The CSure Lifestyle & CSure Golf. He teaches alignment in mentality and methodology to attract results, all through simplicity!

https://idealgolfshop.com/

David Friedman

Dr. David Friedman is the International award-winning, #1 national best-selling author of Food Sanity, how to eat in a world of fads and fiction. He's a Doctor of Naturopathy, Clinical Nutritionist, Chiropractic Neurologist, Board Certified Alternative Medical Practitioner, and Board Certified in Integrative Medicine. He's a former teacher of neurology and author of the college textbook, "Understanding the Nervous System."

Website: DrDavidFriedman.com.

Jo Anne White

Dr. Jo Anne White is an International #1 bestselling, award winning author and speaker recognized as a Goodwill Global Ambassador for civil and humanitarian work in education, entrepreneurship, coaching and women's issues.

A certified life, spiritual and business coach, and energy master teacher, she empowers and inspires men, women, families and businesses to achieve greater health, wellness, success, thrive and triumph.

www.drjoannewhite.com

Johnny Tan

Johnny Tan is the founder of From My Mama's Kitchen® and Joyful Living 360. As an Experiential Life Coach and Mentor, he helps executives, entrepreneurs, and individuals "Design Their Life" using "Strategic Thinking and Planning" to live in their "Genius Zone." Johnny is a multi-award winning & bestselling author, talk show host, and a Reiki Master Teacher & Healer. Discover more at his website: www.JoyfulLiving360.com

LaChelle Adkins

LaChelle Adkins "America's SuperMom" is a lifestyle designer who juggles marriage, ministry, coaching, podcast and 10 of her 15 children with a smile. SMILE is her movement to empower women to check in with their mental health. She believes these key markers are key to depression free living: Sleep, mood, Inner voice, laughter and energy. Find out more about her at: lachelleadkins.com

Lori Shemek

Dr. Lori Shemek is a leading fat cell researcher and recognized authority on inflammation and its role in weight loss, preventing disease and optimizing health.

She is the bestselling author of 'How To Fight FATflammation!' with HarperCollins and the bestselling author of "Fire-Up Your Fat Burn!' She has been featured on CNN and Fox News, and in Dr. Oz's Best Life Magazine, Health, Shape, Woman's Day, Redbook, Ladies Home Journal, and numerous others. Learn more at drlorishemek.com

Marilyn Scott

Dr. Marilyn D. Scott lives in the holistic world as a Motivational Speaker and Author. She has a flair for the Amazement in Life. Her Book, "Be Amazing! Powerful Results Are Just a Leap Away!" has been a powerhouse for those seeking a happier, stress free life. She resides in Richmond, Virginia with her husband, Xen. Website is healthylivingwithmarilyn.com

Patricia Rogers

Retired Correctional Lieutenant, Patricia Rogers completed 29 years in law enforcement for Miami-Dade County where she trained thousands of employees to excel in their careers.

Retiring in 2016, Pat invested in herself. International Public Speaker|Best-Selling Author|Event Coordinator On & Offline Events|Legal Service Provider|

Her zone of genius is spotlighting public speakers and entrepreneurs.

Website: PatriciaRogers.com

Dr. Shahnaz Nensey

Is a Board certified Doctor of Natural Medicine & a Holistic Health Coach.

She brings clarity to clients regarding their life, health and wellness, by guiding them through the process of healing themselves as they continue their search for a healthy happy, full of energy life.

She does this by guiding them to achieve balance with their emotions, nutrition, and spirituality. Find more about her:

www.shahnazlife.com/meet-shahnaz

Tim Ray

Tim Ray known as the "Conscious Voice of the South" is an award-winning international, paradigm-shifting, no "BS", truth-seeker. After spending many years working tireless hours and going about the everyday shuffle Tim eventually hit a crossroad, he was either going to bury his head in the sand or shift the mindset of people across the globe. So, in 2009 he founded the United Intentions Foundation & the UI Media Network a nonprofit foundation whose mission is to assist others in learning how to transform worrisome thoughts into positive intentions. Website: TimRaySpeaks.com

Acknowledgments

First and foremost, I want to thank my creator for assisting me in Co-Creating Optimize Your Creative Mindset-OYCM book series and allowing me to manifest the right support and helping hands. This book is what started as a thought, vision, a feeling became a shared dream, and now a living reality.

THANK YOU for all the wonderful mentors, fantastic supporters, loving family members, loyal friends, and naysayers in my life who piqued my curiosity, challenged my creativity and stimulated my higher thinking. All of this resulted in pushing me to go further and higher in reaching my goals. For that, I am utterly grateful.

We are indeed one big human family, and what we give, we inevitably receive back in multiple folds.

THANK YOU to the school of life that kept me hungry, excited, and imaginative. I learned a lot from the valuable lessons it gave; similarly, it gave me a lot of reasons to celebrate and cherish.

The lessons and celebrations were necessary for my resilience, growth, and the development of my creative skills. This gave more meaning to my life and a feeling of a more profound sense of gratitude. SPECIAL Thanks to the supporters/contributors, who worked overtime to make O.Y.C.M. mission/vision possible.

1. **THANK YOU, Dr. Bob Choat, "The Creative Transformational Grandmaster"**

A significant contributor to the O.Y.C.M. writing journey. I honor him for bestowing my work with his valuable time, effort, insightful suggestions, recommendations, technical support, proofreading the whole manuscript, and constant feedback. Your assistance and patience made this book possible.

2. **THANK YOU, "Creative-luminary" Johnny Tan**

For feedback and inspiration on book title tweak and cover. Also, the review and suggestions of the main chapter titles. Your feedback was constructive, valuable, and useful.

3. THANK YOU, Rawy Rayan, "The Champion"

Talented Creative-son/photographer for making our outdoor photoshoots fun and indoor studio experience with mini-me" Sour" such a great, excellent, and memorable experience.

4. THANK YOU, Suhair Noubani!

My awesome creatrix-sister for being such an excellent supporter through my writing journey and for proofreading a few chapters. Also, for brainstorming with me anytime, I had questions and was looking for constructive feedback.

5. THANK YOU, Valentino

"Tino The Divo," my precious angel cat. His affectionate soul made my writing journey more joyous, pleasant, and peaceful. Thank You, Tino, you da best!

A HUGE Thank You to all of the O.Y.C.M. story contributors, who were precisely selected to share their personal stories and expertise. They bestowed the book with the insight of their authentic integrity, servant leadership, global influence/contributions, and inclusive human service. I would need another whole book in writing space to give their worth and value in the O.Y.C.M. journey.

You are ALL powerful Creative/Creatrix Masters, making a positive impact, changing lives around the globe. This book would have NOT been the same without you. Much love, appreciation, and gratitude to all of you.

Thanks to the following:

- Dr. Lori Shemek, the "Creatrix-Inflammation Terminator"

- Dr. Jo Anne White, the " Creatrix-Empress of Encouragement"

- Ms. Patricia Rogers, the "Tenacious-Creatrix Queen of Networking"

- Dr. Marilyn Scott, "The AMAZING-Creatrix Doc"

- Dr. Shahnaz Nencey, the " Creatrix-Wellness Coach"

- Lachelle Adkins, "America's Super-Creatrix Mom"

- Chitra Lele, the "Creatrix-Success Magnet"

- Bob Burg, "Creative-Exceptional Influencer"

- Dr. David Friedman, "Creative Genius"

- Tim Ray, "Creative-Thought leader."

- Chris Salem, "Creative-Change Agent"

- Davey E Williams, "Golf Psychology Creative Coach/Expert"

- Thank You, F.C.W. Publishing team: Lisa Taylor, Daniel Garcia, Blake Edwards for your pleasantness and professionalism."

Teamwork makes the dream work. Grateful for all of you.

Thank You, to all fans of O.Y.C.M. on social media, and to all of the readers that pre-ordered their copies before the book launch, your love and support is much valued and highly appreciated.

About The Author

Dr. Sofie Nubani, DSD, DD is a Creatrix Interpersonal Executive Coach who is dedicated to enlighten executives, entrepreneurs and the world about the power of a creative mindset. In addition to creativity, she brings in mind enhancing training and coaching using Neurolinguistic Programming (NLP) and Emotional Intelligence (EQ) to help her clients and students positively transform the way they think, work and live. Additionally, her unique coaching style helps people release emotional pain and reach a higher mental state.

Her journey began in Jordan where she started her learning that eventually led her to where she is now. Each step, while living in different regions in the world from the Middle East, Mediterranean and North Africa allowed her to experience many areas of the culture there, before moving to the United States.

Dr. Nubani is a Certified NLP Master Practitioner, Coach and Trainer; Emotional and Social Intelligence Coach; EFT and TFT Practitioner; Master Life Coach; Chios Master; Reiki III Master; Laughter Yoga Instructor and working towards her PhD in Transpersonal Counseling.

Follow Author on Her Social Media Channels

LinkedIn: https://www.linkedin.com/in/sofie-nubani-44710373/

Twitter: @NubaniSofie

Instagram: @Sofie.Nubani

Facebook: https://www.facebook.com/sofie.nubani.5

Facebook Groups:

Optimize Your Creative Mindset:

https://www.facebook.com/groups/225003035458764

Wisdom Café: https://www.facebook.com/groups/547874505579659

Facebook Page: https://www.facebook.com/NubaniSofie/

Connect More with Her at…

Websites:

SofieNubani.com

CircleofCreativeMastersInstitute.com

LaughterMindset.com

Transcendence.care

Email: NubaniSofie@gmail.com

To book Dr. Sofie Nubani for speaking, coaching or training for your business or organization, send her an email or call (407) 754-5811

Lightning Source UK Ltd.
Milton Keynes UK
UKHW032039300720
367452UK00011B/416